HANDBOOK OF SOCIAL WORK

Edited by

Dr. S.C. Joshi

AKANSHA PUBLISHING HOUSE
NEW DELHI - 110 002 (INDIA)

AKANSHA PUBLISHING HOUSE
R-37B, Vani Vihar, Uttam Nagar
New Delhi - 110 059
E-mail: ektabooks@yahoo.com

Handbook of Social Work

First Published, 2004
Reprint 2008
Reprint : 2012
ISBN 81-87606-59-2

PRINTED IN INDIA

Published by M.P. Misra for Akansha Publishing House, New Delhi - 110 059 and Printed at Tarun Offset Press, Delhi.

To

The Autochthons

of Lovely North East India

Contents

Preface

Any of various social services, designed to alleviate the conditions of the poor and aged and to increase the welfare of children, are known as social work in conventional sense.

The poor, downtrodden, sick, mentally charged, physically handicapped, tribals located in rough and isolated geographical terrain need special attention and protection from the society and state for their survival and development. In yore days volunteers and religious missionaries used to offer their services for such social work.

Now the meaning, concept, scope and arena of 'social work' has undergone sea change. Earlier Social work was taught under sociology with minor inferences. Later 'Social Work' emerged as a fullfledged academic discipline. Persons pursuing a career in social work began to be trained professionally. Now, almost all prominent universities run a separate department of Social Work. Tremendous job opportunities are there for social workers in unorganized, organised and government sectors.

'Handbook of Social Work', is designed to meet the need of students, teachers, and professionals in field. Basic concepts, practices, modalities, nature and scope, management, and environment pertaining to Social Work are given a thorough review and explanation.

The material is based on the findings of empirical research of various scholars in the field. Hence no claim for originality. And is based on secondary sources.

We owe a deep sense of gratitude to all men of letters whose works are cited or substantially made use of. Finally we express our thankfulness to our well-wishers, friends, family members, colleagues and superiors for their constant moral support and inspiration. Last but not the least, Mr. M.P. Misra deserves my appreciation for publishing this book in nice getup and that too within a short span of time.

—SCJ

1

Introduction to Social Work

In the yore days the poor, the handicapped and the weak were looked after by joint families, castes, communities and religious institutions. But with the process of development and expansion of urbanisation and the growth of industrialisation, ancient social security and welfare system started changing its role in relation to these needy individuals. Industrial revolution created problems that were different in types and were threatening to society having social and political significance. Malfunctioning appeared in the area of interaction between the individuals, families, group, and their environment. These problems compelled the society to create social welfare agencies. Later on when it was observed that these problems required scientific outlook for proper and permanent solution, a new system of scientific assistance came into existence, i.e. social work. Social work, unlike an early charity practice, attempts to help the individuals, groups and communities to get a clear insight into the problems that strengthens their ego to face conditions as reality and then try to improve them. At the same time social work attempts to mobilise social forces to resolve those social and economic situations that lead to ill health, mental suffering frustration and social behaviour. To make the concept of social work more clear, some of the important definitions given by various authors are quoted here.

Social Work Defined

Social Work includes all voluntary attempts to extend benefits in response to needs which are concerned with social relationships and which avail themselves of scientific knowledge and methods. [*Cheyney*, Alice (1526)]

The prime function of social work is to give assistance to individuals in regard to the difficulties they encounter in their use of an organised groups service or in their performance as a member of an organised group. [*Witmer* (1942)]

Social work is the provision of services designed to aid individuals, singly or in groups in coping with present or future social and psychological obstacles that prevent or are likely to prevent, full or effective participation in society. [*Fink* (1942)]

Social work is a professional service rendered to people for the purpose of assisting them, as individuals or in groups, to attain satisfying relationships and standards of life in accordance with their particular wishes and capacities and in harmony with those of the community. [*Anderson* (1943)]

Social work is a form of professional service comprising a composite of knowledge and skills, parts of which are and parts of which are not distinctive of social work, which attempts on the one hand to help the individuals satisfy his needs in the social milieu and on the other to remove as far as possible the barriers which obstruct people from achieving the best of which they are capable. [*Clarke* (1947)]

Social work is that process which deals directly and differentially with persons who have problems relating primarily to their social situation and which endeavours, individual to individual to understand what help is needed and to assist the individual to find and utilise the help indicated. [*Friedlander* (1951)]

Social work is a professional service, based on scientific knowledge and skill in human relations, which assists individuals, alone or in groups, to obtain social and personal satisfaction and independence. [*Friedlander* (1955)]

Social work seeks two things for people: economic well-being and the deeper source of happiness, that is self-realisation, the stuff of its concern is human behaviour and relationship. Its focus of attention is the individual and his self-adjustment to a recognised reality. [*Youngdahl* (1949)]

Social work is an entity representing three clearly distinguished but inter-related parts: a network of social services, carefully developed methods and process and social policy expressed through social institutions and individuals. All three are based on a view of human being, their interrelationships, and the ethical demands made on them. [*Konopka* (1958)]

Social work seeks to enhance the social functioning of the individuals, singly and in groups, by activities focused upon their social relationships which constitute the interaction between man and his environment. These activities can be grouped into three functions: restoration of impaired capacity, provision of individual and social resources and prevention of social dysfunctions. [*Boehm* (1959)]

Social work is the art of bringing various resources bear on individual, group and community needs by the application of a scientific method of helping people to help themselves. [*Stroup* (1960)]

Social work is concerned with the interaction between people and their social environment which affects the ability of people to accomplish their life tasks, alleviate distress, and realise their aspirations and values. [*Pincus and Minahan* (1978)]

Indian View Point

"The aim of social work, as generally understood, is to remove social injustice, to relieve distress, to prevent suffering and to assist the weaker members of society to rehabilitate themselves and their families and in short, fight the five giant evils of (1) Physical want, (2) Disease, (3) Ignorance, (4) Squalor, (5) Idleness". [*Kher* (1947)\

"Social work is a dynamic activity undertaken by public or private effort in the implementation of social policy, with a view to raise the standard of living and to bring about social, economic, political and cultural well-being of the individual, family and the group with a society irrespective of its stage of social development. [*Sushil Chandra* (1954)]

Social work is a welfare activity based on humanitarian philosophy, scientific knowledge and technical skills for helping individuals or groups or community, to live a rich and full life. [*Indian Conference of Social Work* (1957)]

Social work, "help an individual in his social functioning. It is based on certain knowledge foundation, calls for skill in human relationships on the part of its practitioner, and has a set of values furnishing its philosophical base." [*Khinduka* (1962)]

Social work is a professional service based on knowledge of human relations and skill in relationships and concerned with problems of intra-personal and or inter-personal adjustments resulting from unmet individual, group, or community need. [*Mirza R. Ahmad* (1969)]

Social work is "help rendered to any person or group, who or which is suffering from any disability, mental, physical, emotional or moral, so that the individual or group so helped is enabled to help himself or itself". [*Moorthy and Rao* (1970)]

Thus it can be concluded that a social work is a profession which provides those services which help in relieving distress, preventing sufferings, removing social injustice and provide opportunities for social development.

Analysis of the Definitions

When one looks at the definition given be Alice Cheyney one finds that she has included only voluntary efforts in the social work practice whereas social work includes both voluntary and public efforts. Witmer was of the view that the main objective of social work is to remove those hindrances which are felt in the process of receiving group services or in performing the roles. According to Fink, social work provides those services which help individuals participating in social activities. Anderson's view is that social work is a profession used to raise standard of living and improving social relations. Clarke has attempted to relate the social work with environment and which makes the environment favourable for the growth of the individual.

Friedlander has given a very comprehensive definition of social work. Social work is a profession like other professions i.e. medicine, law, through which social worker, trained in dealing with human relations and having scientific outlook helps individuals for the purpose of obtaining satisfaction—personal as well as social. Youngdahl explained two objectives of social work—economic as well as social development. Konopka contends that social work provides social services through social institutions for strengthening interrelationship. Boehm has mentioned three functions of social work—restoration of impaired capacity, provision of resources and prevention of social malfunctioning. Stroup opines that social work is an art the basic purpose of which is to help people to help themselves. Pincus differs in his approach when he says that social work deals with the problems of interaction and develops abilities of interaction because it is the interaction which is the cause of every trouble in human life.

According to Kher, social work deals with physical want, disease, ignorance, squalor and idleness. Sushil Chandra defined social work as a dynamic activity undertaken to raise the socio-economic standard of the people. Indian Conference of social work suggests that social work is a welfare activity which has scientific basis in dealing with the problems of individual and society.

Khinduka stressed on the social functioning. Social work helps in adhering to the social functioning of the individuals. Mirza R. Ahmad has laid much emphasis on the role of social work to bring intra-personal and inter-personal adjustments. Moorthy has taken up the work of social work as help only to the sufferings and difficulties of individuals and is less concerned for the growth and development.

On the basis of these definitions it can be submitted that social work: (a) Is a professional service which includes specialised knowledge and skills for dealing with human behaviour; (b) Its main emphasis is on the analysis and synthesis of human behaviour; (c) Individual and social problems are solved by applying different methods and techniques; (d) Social work gives much emphasis on adjustment; (e) Its main objective is to make individual self dependent; (f) It not only solves the problems but also prevents its occurrings; (f) It also integrates and coordinates means and resources of social development, and; (h) It believes in democratic values.

Objectives of Social Work

Objectives are statements or formulations of what we are trying to do in social work. Brown has mentioned four objectives of social work—to provide physical help, help in adjustment, to solve psychological problems and make availability of opportunities to the weaker sections for raising their standard of living. Friedlander mentioned three objectives of social work—change in painful social situations, development of constructive forces and provide opportunities, for experiencing democratic and humanistic behaviour. According to Witmer social work has two objectives— to give assistance to individuals in removing difficulties which they face in utilising the society's services and utilisation of community resources for their welfare. Youngdahl explained two objectives of social work—economic well-being and self experience. According to Social Commission, Economic and Social Council of the United Nations Social Work (i) seeks to see and assist individuals, families and groups in relation to the many social and economic forces by which they are affected, and differs in this respect from certain allied activities, such as health, education and the like, (ii) social work seeks to perform an integrating function for which no other provision is made in contemporary society, (iii) social work seeks to maximise the resources available in the community by promoting social well-being.

The emerging purposes of social work, Katherine Lenroof, Chief of the Federal Children's Bureau, listed as follows:

1. Material security through economic and political organisation that will assure every individual and every family the means of satisfying basic material wants.

2. Emotional security through personal and social adjustment.
3. Social justice through fair and ordered relationships between groups, with adequate opportunities for all groups.
4. Social achievement through collective endeavour.
5. Spiritual power through philosophical or religious thoughts.

Generally social work has the following objectives:

1. To solve psycho-socian problems,
2. To fulfil humanitarian needs,
3. To solve adjustmental problems,
4. To create self-sufficiency,
5. Strengthening and making harmonious social relations,
6. Make provision of corrective and recreation services,
7. Develop democratic values,
8. Provide opportunities for development and social progress,
9. Conscientise the community,
10. Change the environment in favour of individual's growth and development,
11. Bring change in social system for social development,
12. Provide socio-legal aid.

Above mentioned area are the fields of social work in which it provide its services to the individual, group and community as a whole.

Basic Assumptions of Social Work

Clarke has described six major assumptions of social work. These are:

1. Social work is a profession, a very new one to be sure but, nevertheless, a profession. It necessitates intellectual activities accompanied by great individual responsibilities. It is not just academic but is also practical in its aims.
2. Basic to the functioning of the professional social worker is

understanding of human personality and of the world he lives in.

3. Social welfare and social work are not the same thing, although on many points they are, the former includes social institutions and the field of practice which are not social work. The latter comprises a body of practices which can be employed at many places in the large social welfare field.
4. Social work has its own processes and techniques, but it involves much more than skills. It has a point of view, a philosophy. It assumes that although personal and social conflict are inevitable and natural, social change can be helpfully directed.
5. The social worker by nature his activities must use many types of services. This means that he must have extensive information about the resources of his community.
6. The social worker is concerned with the needs of individuals and with the environment that cause personal problems. The person and his environment, or better, the interaction of person and situation is the focus of the social worker.

Social Work Knowledge

There are four areas of information with which a social worker is equipped with:

(i) Knowledge of the availability of the services.
(ii) Knowledge of people their motivations, dynamics and strengths.
(iii) Knowledge of society—its values, traditions, customs, taboos, problems, priorities, etc.
(iv) Knowledge of resources — fiscal, material and manpower.

Specialities of the Area of Knowledge

Social worker has the following four areas of specialities of knowledge:

(i) He is unique and has special knowledge and skill of communication between himself, people and system.

(ii) Social worker has depth in understanding of the person, his problems and available resources.

(iii) Social worker has special knowledge and use of relationships with individuals who need help as well as with those who can provide help.

(iv) He has different strategies in his command to deal with various types of problems.

Skills of Social Work

Social worker is skilful in interviewing and counselling, relating himself., to individuals, groups and communities, providing effectiveness as a change agent, self-scrutinising, adequate self awareness and an ability to make professional use of self. He is skilful in establishing and maintaining stable, useful relationship. He has ability of problem solving and capacity for programme and system evaluation and planning.

Tools and Techniques of Social Work

There are four major tools which are used in the practice of social work. These are:

1. Conscious use of self,
2. Constructive use of relationship,
3. Verbal interaction,
4. Programme planning and its use.

The social worker has in its command the following techniques, interviewing, listening, observing, questioning, supporting, educating, counselling, explaining, advising, agreeing, disagreeing, reviewing, preparing, reinforcing, confronting, clarifying and reassuring.

Methods of Social Work

There are six methods of social work: (i) social case work, (ii) social group work, (iii) community organisation, (iv) social welfare administration, (v) social action, and (vi) social research. Social case work means social treatment of a maladjusted individual involving an attempt to understand his personality, behaviour, and social relationships, and to assist him in working out a better social and personal adjustment. Social group work is a method through which individuals in groups in social agency settings are helped by a worker who guides their interaction in programme activities so that they may relate themselves to others and experience growth opportunities in accordance with their needs and capacities to the end of individual group and community development. Community organisation is a process by which a social worker uses his insight and skill to help communities—geographical and functional to identify and to work towards a solution of their problems. Social welfare administration is the process of transforming social policy into social services and the use of experience in evaluating and modifying policy. Social action might be described as group effort to solve mass social problems or to further socially desirable objectives by attempting to influence basic social and economic conditions or practices. Social work research is concerned with the functions of identification and evaluation of social problems and needs, the development and evaluation of service delivery systems and client treatment programmes.

Professional Role of Social Worker

Social worker plays various types of roles in serving his clients. As a care giver he counsels and supports people with problems in a therapeutic way to promote change. As a consultant he works with individuals and groups to assist in their problems and programmes. As a broker he helps people to reach the services they need and makes the system more useful. As a mobiliser he tries to bring new resources to the individual and groups. He gathers and analyses information for programme planning and evaluation working as data manager. As an evaluator he evaluates the weaknesses and strengths of individuals and groups, their needs and problems. As an advocate he works for the improvement of policies and laws in order to make system more effective. As referral agent he refers the individuals and groups to use the services available in other agencies.

Functions of Social Work

Social work operates to assist individuals in adjusting to the institutional framework of society, and attempts to modify the institutional framework itself in appropriate areas. Social work has four broad functions: curative, correctional, preventive and developmental. Under the curative function, the following services are provided: Medical services, health services, services relating to psycho-social and mental health, psychiatric services, child guidance, child welfare services, services for the handicapped and disabled and rehabilitative services.

Correction social work has 3 broad areas:

(i) Individual reform services which include prison reform, probation, parole, other related services,

(ii) Services for strengthening and improving relationship — family welfare services, school social work, industrial social work,

(iii) Services for social reform — employment services, prevention of prostitution, beggary, prohibition services and removal of untouchability.

Prevention services include Life Insurance, public assistance, social legislation, labour welfare, adult education and prevention of diseases.

Development tasks are socio-economic developmental activities, education and recreational services, urban and rural development programmes and the programmes for integration.

Importance of Social Work

Earlier poverty was known as distress and the material help was given to the people who did not have food or money or sufficient clothing and shelter. But in the early twentieth century, the distress was redefined and was known as intrapersonal and interpersonal discomfort, with this shift from poverty to psychiatric discomfort (problem of living), the will to help was assessed inefficient and the helpers needed training to provide the proper help. This occurred first in medicine and later on in social work.

Modern man is experiencing an increasing loss of a belief in God and a life after death, therefore, the distress of the current experience could not be minimised and seems to require relief. Further, the philosophy of existentialism tells us that the things that exist are only concretisation of potentials that might also lead to other concretisation. The people are dissatisfied with their concretisations and find difficult to perceive their real 'Self'. It is, thus natural for dissatisfied person to demand for help.

People find that they do not express the most desirable potential of their being and thus there is no authenticity in living. They are forced into concretisation which seems to be justifiable to their parents, spouses, employers or society as such who are powerful than they. For this struggle to relieve stress and tension social work comes to their rescue.

Man's awareness of his mortality makes the experience of living one of running towards one's own death. This results in the experience of worrying. To alleviate this worry an element of urgent efforts makes the profession of social work more essential.

Due to economic hardships and industrialisation the members of 'socialisation group' have gone away from the scene. The entrance of women into the labour market and the increasing participation of women in the professions have separated spouses not only in time but frequently in geographical space. Under such conditions many persons experience loneliness to an unprecedented degree. Here social work becomes first and foremost a process rather than a production. He who gets social work services, comes out of distress (production) as well as fortifies against new distress (process). Therefore, what social work can provide is not freedom from discomforts, rather, it can provide change of discomforts.

Misconceptions of Social Work

Social work as a profession is of recent origin and therefore, people are not aware about the real meaning of social work. They define in their own terms and knowledge. The following are the few areas which are generally known as the fields of social work.

Social Work as an Aim-giving Activity

It is a traditional concept. The desire to help the needy fellow men has been present from the very inception of human society. Such a desire was generated by the feeling of belongingness. It was a religious duty of a man to provide care and protection to the people suffering from various kinds of distresses. In India alms-giving was considered as a path of *moksha.* Still today alms-giving to the poorer is considered a social welfare activity and therefore, it is called social work. But alms-giving is not social work because the aim of help in social work is to solve client's problems scientifically. Social worker attempts to regenerate self confidence and self-dependency. Causative factors are investigated and diagnosis is confirmed. Later on therapeutic models are pushed into service.

Sharmdan as a Social Work

Voluntarily to provide physical help to any individual, group or community is known as *Shramdan,* i.e. construction of public roads, public sanitation, help to flood victims, etc. But this is not social work because in such activities labour is given without any remuneration whereas in social work activities, worker is paid. There is no need of training in *Shramdan* whereas social worker is a trained person. Adjustment problems are not taken up in *Shramdan* but the basic aim of social work is to solve adjustmental problems. This is an absence of scientific methodology in *Shramdan* but in social work problems are solved scientifically.

Leadership Activities are Social Work

Leaders are known as social workers. Even national prizes are given to them as social workers. The political worker and social worker have become interchangeable terms. It is detrimental of social work. The process of clarification is urgently needed. Political workers are not social workers because they are neither trained in social work profession nor use social work methodology in their practice.

Work in Voluntary Welfare Agencies is a Social Work

Few people think that a person working in voluntary welfare organisation is a social worker and his service rendered in such an institution is social work. But it is not social work because these services are not based on scientific knowledge and values of social work.

Social Work & Social Welfare

The term social welfare expresses a changing concept. It means not only to provide financial assistance and other services to the poor and the disadvantaged but it also refers to the collective responsibility to meet the needs of all the people in general. Elizabeth Wickenden defines social welfare as "Including those laws, programmes, benefits, and services which assure or strengthen provisions for meeting social needs recognised as basic to the well-being of the population and the better functioning of the social order. Social welfare is concerned with all those forms of social intervention that have a primary and direct concern with promoting both the well-being of the individual and of the society as a whole. Social welfare includes those provisions and processes directly concerned with the treatment and prevention of social problems, the development of human resources, and the improvement in the quality of life. It involves social services to individuals and families as well as efforts to strengthen or modify social institutions.

Changing Concepts of Social Welfare

Here are discussed major concepts of social welfare which have been recognised in the process of social development. Romanyshyn has described the following concepts.

1. From the Residual to the Institutional Concept

Residual concepts of social welfare hold the view that social welfare activities should come into play only when the normal structures of society break down. Welfare programmes exists to meet the emergency needs of individuals when they are incapable of providing for themselves through the normal institutions of the family and the market. The poor, dependent children, the aged, is handicapped have been some of the recipient of welfare services. In such a situation society intervenes through public or voluntary means to assure some of minimum level of personal well-being and social functioning.

Institutional view of welfare is predicted on the assumption that a modern industrial society requires a variety of services as first line supports to enable individuals to cope successfully with a changing economic and social environment and to assure the stability and development of social institutions.

2. Charity to Citizen Right

Charity, philanthropy, relief, and help to the disabled and deviants have been the traditional way of welfare. But gradually and gradually this concept got changed and receiving welfare services became the citizen's right. Social rights make up the dominant theme of the present century. The notion, of such rights is implicit in the concept of the welfare state.

3. Special Universal

One tends to think of social welfare as consisting of special services for the poor. Increasingly, however, social welfare programmes are developed to meet universal needs of the population. Such universal programmes tend to focus on certain common social contingencies that are consequences of living in an industrial society, with such related risks as unemployment, old age, disability, loss of the bread winner, the high cost of medical care, and so forth.

4. Minimum to Optimum

Social Welfare services are not restricted now to minimum capacity and resources to be made available to individuals. Attention is focused now to make available to all children to those optimum conditions that may make it possible for them to develop to the fullest of their capacities.

5. Individual to Social Reform

Now one believe that problems are not due to individual's weakness or his moral defects but they are structural and result from defects in institutional arrangement. Consequently reform of the society is more important than that of the individual.

6. Voluntary to Public

Social welfare services have been provided since time immemorial but most of these services were by volunteers and voluntary agencies. New government have realised its responsibility and public departments are now more active in this field.

7. From Welfare for the Poor to a Welfare Society

The basic problem of philanthropy has changed from that of caring for the physical needs of a relatively few destitute people living in a simple society in attempting to meet the physical, social and psychological needs of total population in highly complexed society. The emphasis is now being placed on securing a better, happier, or healthier world for all.

Social Functions of Social Welfare

Social welfare programmes may be understood in terms of the social functions they perform. They are (i) social provisions, (ii) social services, and (iii) social action. Social provision are public assistance, social insurance, public housing, medical care, etc. The ideal goal of social provisions is social security and social justice, social services may be seen of four types: developmental, remedial, supportive and substitutive. Education services are developmental, family counselling and child guidance services are remedial, day care and nutritional services are supportive and foster services are substitutive.

Social action is concerned with the system change, while services are concerned with changing people. Social action seeks to alter the structure of roles and the distribution of power, prevent problems, expand opportunity and enhance the quality of life. In general system change is brought through violence or revolution but in social welfare, violence or revolutionary tactics are not considered part of social welfare methods. Social action may be defined as an organised effort with the aim of securing social progress and of solving mass social problems by influencing social legislation or the administration of social services.

Social welfare and social work are historically related and are sometimes still used synonymously. The distinction between the two is of recent origin. When Devine wrote about social work in 1922, he did not make the distinction. He wrote, "Social work is the sum of all efforts by society to take up its own slack", to provide for individuals when its established institutions fail them, to supplement those established institutions and to modify them at those points at which they have proved to be badly adapted to social needs. It may have for its object, the relief of individuals or the improvement of conditions. It may be carried on by the government or by an incorporated society or by an informal group or by an individual, or it may be temporary growth on some older institution which exists primarily for some other function .... It includes everything which is done by society for the benefit of those who are not in a position to complete on fair terms with their fellows, from whatever motive it may be done, by whatever agency or whatever means, and with whatever result.

Both social work and social welfare have common stages of development as noted by United Nations Department of social affairs. Training of Social Work, "... the stages through which social work has passed in many of the countries in which it is today fully developed, may be broken down into three major categories:

(a) social work as individual charity;

(b) social work as organised activity, under governmental and non-governmental auspices, directed towards the solution of problems associated with economic dependency, and

(c) social work as professional service, under governmental and non-governmental auspices, potentially available to every member of the community, irresponsive of his means, to assist him in achieving his full potentialities for productive and satisfying living.

Social work stands in relation to social welfare as the medical profession stands in relation to the field of health. Social work seeks to enhance the social functioning of the individuals, singly and in groups, by activities focused upon their social relationships which constitute the interaction between man and his environment. These activities can be grouped into three functions; restoration of impaired capacities, provision of individual and social resources and prevention of social dysfunction. Social work is a form of professional service having composite of knowledge and skills which attempt on the one hand to help individuals satisfy their needs in social milieu and on the other hand to remove barriers which obstruct them from achieving the best of which they are capable.

Social welfare is an organised system of social services and institutions, designed to aid individuals and groups to attain satisfying standards of life and health. Social work is a professional service based upon scientific knowledge and skill in human relations, which assists individuals, alone or in groups, to obtain social and personal satisfaction and independence.

Social welfare is specialised work for the benefit of the weaker and more vulnerable sections of the population and would include social services for the benefit of women, children, the physically handicapped, the mentally retarded and those specially handicapped in many ways. "Social work is a professional service based on knowledge of human relations and skill in relationship and concerned with problems of intrapersonal and/or interpersonal adjustments resulting from unmet individual, group or community needs.

Social welfare aims at providing services to the weaker sections of the population who because of various handicaps, physical, mental, economic and social, are unable to make use of social services provided by the society or are traditionally denied these services. The aim of social work is to remove social injustice, to relieve distress, to prevent suffering and to assist the weaker members of society to rehabilitate themselves and their families and, in short, fight the five giant evils of (1) Physical want, (2) Disease, (3) Ignorance, (4) Squalor, (5) Idleness.

Social welfare is basically secured through the institutional organisation of society, and its activities are directed towards the improvement of that organisation, while the activities of social work are directed towards assisting individuals in their use of social institutions.

Social welfare is a constructive approach to assist and aid the people to understand their ails, acquire necessary skills and establish or organise productive centres, craft centres, schools, etc. for the fulfilment of their needs. It is all done on planned lines with the aid of government machinery. Social work refers to an occupation and profession concerned with improving social relationships. The activities of the social workers are oriented towards "almost every major social institution. That is, public assistance is oriented towards the economic functioning of individuals; family and child services are, of course, concerned with the family; probation, parole, correctional social work is directed to the relationship between the individual and the law; school social work is concerned with the relationship between the educational institution and the individual whereas medical social work is oriented toward the relationship between the individual and health institutions.

In social work, a personal identity, rather rapport, is established between social worker and his client whose rapport or identity of interest is neither required nor relevant in any kind of social welfare activity.

Social work is a professional service but social welfare is general service. Social worker has scientific knowledge and skills in human behaviour whereas social welfare activities can be carried on by any individual. The basic aim of social work is to solve adjustmental problems but social welfare activities are mainly directed to solve socio-economic problems. The clients in social work have choice to select their own paths for the solution of their problems but in social welfare such type of freedom is not given.

Social Service and Social Work

Social services are those organised activities that are primarily and directly concerned with the conservation, the protection and the improvement of human resources. One mean by it (social services) those efforts to restore, maintain, and enhance the social functioning of individuals and families through (1) enabling social resources (e.g. day care and a home-maker services) and (2) processes that enhance the capacity of individuals and families to cope with stress and with the normal demands of social life. The ideal goal of the social services is the enhancement of social competence. Changes in the individuals are not brought directly to modify their behaviour but through modification or alterations in their social environment.

Social work is an entity representing three clearly distinguished but interrelated parts; a network of social services, carefully developed methods and processes, and social policy expressed through social institutions and individuals. Social work is that process which deals directly and differentially with persons who have problems relating primarily to their social situation and which endeavours individual to individual to understand what help is needed and to assist the individual to find and utilise the help indicated. Thus, helping the helpless in social service, helping the helpless to help themselves is social work.

Social services are essentially "people changing institutions (developmental, remedial, supportive or substitutive). Their main aim is to equip individuals with the competence and resources essential for effective social participation. Social work fulfills the objectives of social services.

Social Reform and Social Work

Social reforms by definition entail change or replacement in the institutions, which have become functionally irrelevant (totally or partially) to the contemporary social order causing loss of quality of life, deprivations, unrest and misery to sizeable sections of the society. The reforms are initiated by a group of promoters having the belief that the social improvement can only be accompanied if the institutional structure is suitably modified or altered as per the exigency of the situation.

Social reform is concerned with the change in community that affects the whole life including values and social institutions. It brings change in social institutions and create favourable conditions for the social progress for those who are continuously suffering from discrimination and social neglect. Struggle for women's rights, improvement of conditions of the Harijans, community service centres in slums, etc. are social reform activities. The aim of social work in the present context is to counteract the effects of an oppression, to assist people to understand their alienation in terms of their oppression, and building up their self-esteem.

Social reform is movement motivated by an urge to uproot traditional values of social life and institutions and bring about instead new values and pattern of social life.

Social work is neither a movement nor it attempts to change values of institutions, social work provides services without touching the existing set of values. It is intended to enlighten and assist one to know one's misery and help oneself to be free from that misery.

Social reform does not have personal touch whereas social work is practiced on the basis of personal touch and personal relationship is the medium of practice. Social reform does not need any skill whereas social work is practiced on the strength of professional skill to help the client. Social reform involves radical change in social system but social work is concerned with assisting the individual in freeing himself from his maladjustments in social life.

Social work has a historic identification with social reform but it often has been constrained to be more conservative than innovative. But with the changes in social set up, important changes have been taking place in social work practice with an increasing emphasis on developing skills and modes of practice for system change as well as for more effective delivery of social services. Recognising the social problems results from system defects as well as individual maladjustments, greater attention is being given in professional schools to preparing people who can be agents of social change.

Social Security and Social Work

Social security can be understood as the security that society furnishes through appropriate organisations against certain risks to which its members are exposed. It is a programme of protection provided by society against those contingencies of modern life—sickness, unemployment, old age dependency, industrial accidents, and against which the individual cannot be expected to protect himself and his family by his own ability or foresight. The work of social security is done through public assistance, social insurance, health and social welfare services etc. Social work consists of social security in its programme activities so that individuals may lead a happy life. Social workers are supposed to know the social security programmes so that he would use them in helping the client.

References

Anderson, J.P., *'Social Work as a Profession'* in Social Work Year Book. National Association of Social Workers, New York, 1945.

Bison, Herbert, The Philosophy of social work, *Public Affairs,* Washington D.C. 1952, p. 72.

Boem, W.H., *Objectives of the Social Work Curriculum of the Future, Vol. 1.* The comprehensive Report of the Curriculum Study, Council of Social Work Education, New York, 1959, p. 54.

Brown, E.L., *Social Work as a Progression,* Russell Sage Foundation, New York, 1942, p. 24.

Cassidy, Harry M., *Social Security and Reconstruction in Canada,* Quoted by Friedlander, W.A. *op. cit.,* p. 4.

Chaudhary, D. Paul, *A Handbook of Social Welfare,* Atma Ram and Sons, New Delhi, 1966, p. 194.

Cheyney, Alice, *Nature and Scope of Social Work,* American Association of Social Workers, New York, 1926.

Clarke, Helen I., *Principles and Practice of Social Work,* Appleton Century Croft. Inc., New York, 1947, p. 16.

Definition given by International Labour Organisation and quoted by Chaudhary, D.P. in *Hand Book of Social Welfare,* Atma Ram and Sons, New Delhi, 1966, p. 194.

Devine, Edward T., *Social Work,* Macmillan, New York, 1922, pp. 21-22.

Friedlander, W.A., *Introduction of Social Welfare,* Prentice Hall, Inc. New York, 1955, p. 4.

Friedlander, W.A., Social Work Journal 1951, Vol XXXII, No. 1, p. 43.

Government of India, Planning Commission, *Social Welfare in India,* 1955, Preface.

Hamilton, Gordon, *Theory and Practice of Social Case Work,* Columbia University Press, New York, 1947, p. 192.

Kher, B.G., Quoted in United Nations, *Training for Social Work; An International Survey,* 1947, p. 108.

Khinduka, S.K., *Social Work in India,* Sarvodaya Sahitya Samaj, Jaipur (India) 1962, p. 1.

Kidneigh, John C., "Administration of Social Agencies". *Social Work Year Book,* 1955, p. 76.

Konopka, G; and Edward C. Lindeman; *Social Work Philosophy.* The University of Minneasora Press, Minneapolis, 1958, p. 83.

Mirza R. Ahmad, *Samaj Karya—Darshan Avam Pranaliyan,* British Book Depot, Lucknow, 1969, p. 4.

Moorthy, M.V., *Social Work—Philosophy, Methods, and Fields,* Karnatak University, Dharwar, 1974, pp. 2-5.

Pincus, Allen and Minaham, Anna, "A Model of Social Work Practice" Specht, Henry and Vickery, Anna *(ed.), Integrating Social Work Methods,* George Allen and Unwin, London, 1978, p. 78.

Romanyshyn, J.M., and Romanyshyn, A.L., *Social Welfare, Charity to Justice,* Random House, New York, 1971, p. 3.

Romnyshyn, John. M. and Romanyshyn, Annie L., *Social Welfare: Charity to Justice,* Random House, New York, 1971, p. 356.

Ross A.D., "Philanthropy" *International Encyclopaedia of Social Sciences,* Macmillan Co., New York, 1968, p. 80.

Ross, M.G., "Conceptual Problems in Community Organisation" *The Social Service Review,* June 1956, p. 180.

Social Commission Economic and Social Council, United Nations: Training Social Work; An International Survey, United Nations, New York, 1958, Mimeo, pp. 18-20.

Solender, S., "Social Action" in *Social Work Year Book* 1957, pp. 517-518.

Srivastava, S.S., "Social Reforms and Social Sciences" Paper presented in a national *Seminar on Reforms and Change in Indian Society.* Institute of Social Sciences. Agra, 1958.

Stack Mourice, "The Meaning of Social Security" William Haber and Wilpur J.C. (ed.) *Reading in Social Security,* Prentice Hall, New York, 1948, p. 41.

Stroup, H.H., *Social Work—An Introduction to the Field,* American Book Co., New York, 1960, pp. 1-2.

Trecker, H.B., *Social Group Work—Principles and Practices,* Association Press, New York, 1955, p. 5.

U.N. Department of Social Affairs: *Training for Social Work, an International Survey, United Nations,* New York, 1950.

Wickenden, Elizabeth, *Social Welfare in a Charging World* U.S. Dept. of Health, Education and Welfare, Washington, D.C. 1965, p. VII.

Witmer, Helen I., Quoted by Modan, G.R., *Indian Social Problems,* Allied Publishers, Bombay, 1973, p. 15.

2

Philosophy of Social Work

According to Leonard, "philosophy is more than a conceptual expression of different world views.... apart from its ideological character, it also reveals certain fundamental truths concerning the relations of man with other men and of men with the universe. According to *Webster's New International Dictionary*, philosophy is, "The science which investigates the most general facts and principles of reality and human nature and conduct: specially, and now usually, the science which comprises logic, ethics, aesthetics, metaphysics, and the theory of knowledge," According to John De Wey. "It is concerned with problems of being and occurrence from the stand point of value, rather than from that of mere existence.

Social work like other professions grew out of certain needs of human beings. In the beginning social work served mainly the poor, but with the changing situations and conditions it became a different service. Now it is mostly concerned with the problems wherever human institutions or human relations either break down or threaten to break down or are not at the stage of maximum potential. Therefore, it becomes essential to clarify the philosophical foundation and of social work. Social work has not produced great philosophers. Therefore, it has had to use the thought of others and concern itself mainly with its methods. Edward C. Lindman was the first social worker who consciously emphasised philosophical base of social work.

Social work is an entity representing three clearly distinguished but interrelated parties; a network of social services, carefully developed methods and processes, and social policy expressed through social institutions and individuals. All the three are based on a view of human beings, their interrelationships, and the ethical demands made on them.

Since the very beginning, social work has been based on certain assumptions about man and society (theory) and their moral obligations to each other (Philosophy). The philosophy and social work is based on humanitarianism, liberalism, and democracy. Except from devotion to welfare of human beings, social worker has to find a method of enabling those who are assisted to regain their confidence in themselves for the proper adjustment to normal life. "The introduction of the concept and philosophy of democracy further strengthened the need to recognize every human being as an individual, worthy of respect and recognition, the individual being given the rights as well as responsibilities of an equal citizen in a democratic society. The consent of the governed, rule of the majority, respect for the creative minority, freedom of assembly, speech and religion supported the development of the individual in his own right. Underlying these factors lay the social philosophy of justice, liberty, equality and fraternity. It is in the background of this philosophy of life that the methods of social work have been developed by the practitioners."

In education for the Public Social Services, the American Association of Schools of Social work has set down a statement that maybe said to represent the current philosophy of Social Work.

"Social work accepts as its main objectives the adjustment of the individual in society. It views this adjustment as dynamic and changing as individual development takes place and as the social setting is modified. It views the lack of adjustment as originating in the physical, mental, and emotional make up of the individual and in the environment which conditions his behaviour. Thus the profession of social work functions in both areas, utilising certain skills for service to the individual and others for the control of the environment." The concern of social work is the individual, in the understanding of his needs and in his adjustment to his environment.

Social workers enter people's lives in a very practical and intimate way, they necessarily become involved in issues which have an inescapable connection with the philosophy of human being. Social workers are precipitated into philosophical considerations that take on practical importance when we consider of what it is that our practice consists. Questions about the nature of the self and other selves, the nature of reality, of consciousness, of determinism, of science, of reason, and of the function of the will cannot be evaded, because we are technicians who work with people and people live in a social world, in world of change, of community, and of habit.

Herbert Bisno has described the philosophy of social work in details in his book *The Philosophy of Social Work.* He has narrated the philosophic tenets of social work in 4 areas:

1. The nature of the individual,
2. The relations between groups, groups and individuals and between individuals,
3. The functions and methods of social work, and
4. Social maladjustment and social change.

I. The Nature of the Individual

Bisno has explained the following basic tenets, of nature of individual, which are the basis of the foundation of social work.

(i) Each individual, by the very fact of his existence is of worth. It is the firm conviction of social work that life in itself is socially desirable. The most fundamental premise of all which permeates social work is, "for belief in the inherent worth of the individual is the focus of several cardinal principles: equality of opportunity, the rights of minorities, the rights of free expression."

(ii) Human suffering is undesirable and should be prevented, or at least alleviated, whenever possible. Social work rejects the doctrine of the value of 'suffering for suffering's sake'.

Social work believes that sufferings are the results of weaknesses of the social system and therefore, man should be helped in alleviating and preventing sufferings whatever form it appears.

(iii) All human behaviour is the result of interaction between the biological organizm and its environment. Social work, conceives personality as a unit in which both emotional and physical factors are inextricably involved in some malfunctioning of the organizm. No particular behaviour can be attributed to any single factor because the behaviour results by the interaction of original nature, unique experiences, and the culture. It is also acknowledged that human choices are always limited and conditioned by psychological, physical, economic, social and other factors.

(iv) Man does not "naturally" act in rational manner. It is now understood that the fact that a human being is human, with all the usual attributes, does not mean that he will act, or "be able" to act, rationally. There is no innate rationality, nor is there an inherent recognition of that which is rational. Basically, the ability to act in rational and constructive manner is largely dependent upon an individual's life experiences. Certain conditions must obtain if a person is to be able to achieve mastery over his irrational emotions.

(v) Man is a moral and social being at birth. It means that man at birth neither moral or immoral, social or antisocial. He is neutral. Behaviour is the result of many forces and human beings are interdependent and the full development of the individual is possible only in a social setting. Though there are common elements in human behaviour, the behaviour itself is the result of an interaction of forces in a given social setup.

(vi) There are both individual and common human needs. The existence of certain physical and emotional needs which human being have in common is well recognized. However, in addition to these needs, every individual also has other needs and desires which are uniquely his. The social worker believes that it is essential for individuals to have an opportunity to express these needs and desires in a satisfying and socially useful manner. The failure to provide these motivating forces with such an opportunity for constructive expression may be reflected in an irrational and/or antisocial behaviour.

(vii) There are important differences between individuals and they must be recognized and allowed for. The present practice of social work acknowledges both similarities and differences. Social work places paramount importance to individualisation. Recognition of individual difference is the fundamental equipment for the therapeutic relationship in case work.

(viii) Human motivation is complex and frequently obscure. Human behaviour is the result of certain needs which motivate it, thus behaviour is the symptom of these causes. When needs are hot fulfilled, he feels frustrated and abnormal symptoms appear in his behaviour.

(ix) Family relationships are of primary importance in the early development of the individual. The importance of the family relationship in the development of the personality has been stressed by psycho analytical psychologists and accepted by social workers. The type of family, its atmosphere and emotional maturity, all have direct impact on individual's personality. Ridicule, suppression and the lack of realistic outlets may turn the normal behaviour into an unstable and destructive one.

(x) Having experience is an essential aspect of the learning process. An individual develops social traits by experiencing in social world that starts within the actual experience of the group and encourages the growth of a sense of social responsibility to the larger whole.

II. The Relations Between Groups and Individuals and between Inividuals

(i) Social work rejects the doctrine of *laissez faire* and survival of the fittest. Social work believes that each individual by the very fact of existence, is of worth. The unfit person has the same fundamental needs and desires as do his more fit fellow men. Each person should be given the fullest opportunity to cope with his environment in the best possible manner.

(ii) The rich and/or powerful are not necessarily 'fit' while the poor and/or weak are not necessarily 'unfit'. Acquisition of wealth and power is considered as the symptom of fitness but the researches show that relatively few members of the present upper class have achieved their status through their own industry. Social work has rebelled against the acquiring of wealth and power with fitness and superiority. The democratic relationship between client and worker, the protection of the rights and the dignity of the needy represent the application in the practice of the denial of the doctrine that only wealthy and powerful are fit.

(iii) "Socialised individuals" is preferable to "rugged individualism." Social worker does not believe in rugged, but in socialised individualism. The social workers support the right of every individual to attain the fullest, personally and socially constructive development of which he is capable. This development is achieved through a planned social organization. That is why social work believes that the participation in group living and in group experiences is the chief instrument of personality development.

(iv) A major responsibility for the welfare of its members rests with the community. It is because that the pathological conditions in any part of the community react adversely upon the entire community. The facilities of the community must be utilised for dealing with the existing problems for the purpose of prevention of spreading in others.

(v) All classes of persons in the community have an eqûal right to the social services; there is a community responsibility to relieve adequately and without discrimination among the members of the community. The philosophical foundation of the belief in assistance as a 'right' is embedded in the theory of community responsibility and in the assumptions, about the nature of man and the individual's relation to society, that underline it.

(vi) The federal government is thought to have an important responsibility in providing for health, housing, full employment, education and various types of public assistance and social insurance programmes.

(vii) Public assistance should be based on the concept of need. Social work believes that needs should be scientifically examined and after finding their validity, assistance should be given.

(viii) Organized labour makes a positive contribution to community life and should be accepted as a constructive, rather that destructive force. It is a new philosophical orientation that has recognized the role of organized labour in the process of development.

(ix) There needs to be complete social cooperation of all races and ethnic groups, on the basis of complete equality and mutual respect. This view is grounded in two beliefs; (1) that the potential capacities of all races are equal, and (2) that cultural diversity has positive value.

(x) Freedom and security are not mutually exclusive security and freedom are part of the same problem. Freedom with security is the freedom to starve, the freedom to be homeless, dependent, or sick. Security without freedom is the security of the prison and the concentration camp.

III. The Functions and Methods of Social Work

(i) Social work has a functionally dualistic approach. It has distinctly two methodologies: The case work on one side and the social action on the other. Social work operates to assist individuals in adjusting to the institutional framework of society and also attempts to modify the institutional framework itself in required areas. Community organization and group work operate as a mediating 'Third force' between the above mentioned polarity of functions.

(ii) The social worker relies on the 'development of insight and/or environmental manipulation for the purpose of modifying behaviour or furthering social growth rather than on 'ordering', 'forbidding' or 'exhortation'.

(iii) Social work services should be provided by professionally trained workers in both public and private agencies.

(iv) Social work accepts democracy as 'the method'. Social work is so interwoven into the fabric of its democratic matrix that it can hardly be understood if viewed apart from it. Social workers have a peculiar responsibility to tend their support to the attainment and full maintenance of all civil rights. Their basic professional concepts are founded on a belief in the value of the individual, his right to the opportunity for employment, self-maintenance and self-development, and his right to hold and to express his own opinions and beliefs and to act upon them, so long as by doing so he does not infringe upon the equal rights of others or abuse his professional relationship to those he serves or supervises.

IV. Social Maladjustment and Social Change

(i) There are serious political, economic and social maladjustment in our culture. The co-existence of serious social psychological maladjustments and such permeating social myths implies that there is an urgent need for new ways of social thinking, that the gap between social facts and social values must be bridged.

(ii) Evolutionary type 'reform' is both possible and desirable in our society. It is based on the belief that our institutions are, potentially possessed of enough flexibility so as to allow for necessary adaptations to changing needs and circumstances.

(iii) There is a need for social planning. Social workers believe in the possibility of the intelligent direction of social change, in other words, they recognize the need for and feasibility of social planning. Social planning is essential with two fundamental purposes of social work; (1) to stimulate people to use their power for the cooperative improvement of group life, and (2) to assist in the development of the process by supplying the technical services required. But planning for welfare must include planning for freedom.

Gandhian Philosophy of Social Work

Gandhiji had his own vision of the new society and visualised that with genuine lead and guidance that young men and women can fruitfully be employed for eliminating the social evils and re-instalment of higher moral values in the society. Tackling of dowry menace, elimination of age old caste taboos and other discriminatory practices, discouraging child marriages and ill treatment of widows are some of the glaring examples to be tackled for proper social development.

Mahatma Gandhi suggested and practiced two fold strategies to resolve community problems. The first component is non-violence. It means non-appreciation and abhorrence of power for domination, control and profit. The society based on the principles of non-violence seeks *antodoya* as the main aim. It concentrates on the development of the majority. Through non-violence all the problems of society can be solved, stressed that truth and non-violence are not matters for mere individual practice but for the practice by groups, communities and nations. The second component is *Satyagrah* which means the use of truth as a force to achieve one's goal. *Satyagrah* is a long protracted struggle, persuasion, setting examples through suffering for one's convictions. These qualities are necessary for social workers.

Value of Individual

Gandhiji considered the individual as the pivot of all social concerns. He should be central focus of all social services for the alleviation of his sufferings. He believed that once the individual is perfect, he will acquire an enlightened state of perfection, called *'Ram Rajya'*. His concept of individual perfection does not confine to a state of utmost comfort and happiness by acquisition of material benefits to an individual but also extends to the achievement of moral and ethical standards in one's life. He believed in holistic perspective in regard to an individual. The various facets of human life are not to be treated as unrelated compartments and that these can never be tackled in an isolated way. Any change in human being that is being induced, manipulated or planned, will involve the consideration of multiple factors.

The Concept of Help

Gandhiji never used the word 'help' for the solving of the people's problems. Instead he used 'service' *(lok seva)* which meant nothing less than social, moral and economic independence of the people. For Gandhiji constructive work and programmes are only means by which the strength and the will of the people, are sought to be generated. He formulated 18-point programme for constructive work on different aspects of social life: communal harmony, removal of untouchability, prohibition, *khadi, gramodyog, nai talim,* adult education, village hygiene and sanitation, service to backward classes, emancipation of women, health education, encouraging national education, nature cure, removal of economic disparity, establishing organizations for farmers, labours and youth, self-purification, *sarva dharma sambhav* (religious tolerance) and physical labour.

These programmes enabled-people to be aware of new dimensions to their capacity and strength. Its aim was to bring a total change in the society by generating will and strength in the people themselves. Gandhiji felt that the involvement of constructive organizations would serve two basic purposes. Firstly, these programmes would substitute dependence on government for socio-economic development with reliance on people themselves, and secondly, voluntary organizations would be able to win the support and sympathy of all sections of society and thus would help in creation of necessary climate for socio-economic development of the people.

Ashram institutions were established to prepare the personnel for the development activities to be pursued in constructive work programme. An *ashram,* placed under the charge of a person acting as its leader and possessing a father image for the trainees was required to inspire a community life based on the well known eleven vows: truth *(Satya),* non-violence, non-possession *(Aparigrah),* control of palate, non-stealing, fearlessness, removal of untouchability, bonded labour equality of different religions and the use of home made goods. Thus, it may be of interest to emphasise that Gandhiji's constructive work programme came closer to many popular concepts of professional social work.

Gandhiji emphasised the spiritual nature of man as basis of change and development. He used spiritualism as a technique and tool of constructive work in refashioning the prayer meetings, emphasising *mantras* and vows for constructive workers. He stressed the need for inculcation of scientific insight of the workers into the social and psychological aspects of human life. The Gandhian concept of social work looks to spiritual nature of man as the main key to the unfoldment of the potentialities of growth.

With the inspiration of Gandhi's thought on spiritual nature of man, social work education in America in the sixties and seventies emphasised upon man's spiritual nature. It is believed that "Man is a physiological, intellectual, emotional, cultural, social and spiritual being. All these aspects must be understood in order to understand the whole person as revealed in his social functioning.". Religious content in Social Work Education under the auspices of Council of Social Work Education, USA. has found the spiritual content of man as important conception in Social Work Education.

Concept of Swadeshi

Using *Swadeshi* as an 'umbrella term' Gandhiji emphasised economic, cultural, social and political dimensions of the development of society. In opinion the concept of *Swadeshi* would promote dependence on the goods produced in one's neighbourhood rather than in remote areas. It included non-possession or voluntary poverty, simplicity in life and resource conservation. At latent level, the *Swadeshi* movement helps in the growth of cottage industry and circulation of self-employed workers. This movement was fulfilling the aim of social work i.e. self-dependency.

Concept of Charkha

The idea of spinning wheel was linked with the process of decentralisation. Gandhiji wanted every village to become 'self-autonomous' capable of producing enough to meet its own requirements and then to have little surplus as contribution to the requirement of cities.

Gandhi's concept of social work, his priorities, his field of action and techniques differed significantly from those of the professional social workers. But Gandhi's contribution has been to prepare the background, for the establishment of the profession of social work in India. Gandhi's philosophy as well as the plan of social work were grounded on a broad strategy of total social development resulting from a radical transformation from within the case of the individual and of the community in which he lived. Social work was not to be directed merely to corrective or ameliorative activity, although this was important. It has to be geared to radical transformation, not merely to dealing with the consequences of an inequitable social order. Thus it can be summarised that Gandhian philosophy of social work is not an individual problem oriented, ameliorative, but a community oriented process of rural development.

Leonard thinks that "philosophy is more than a conceptual expression of different world views...... apart from its ideological character, it also reveals certain fundamental truths concerning the relations of men with other men and of men with the universe ..... .human science will have to be philosophical in order to be scientific."

Butrym believes that, "social work has to be philosophical in order to be real."

William James was right in maintaining that every human being has a philosophy and that it determines the perspective in his several worlds. To him, each man's philosophy represents, "our more or less dumb sense of what life honestly and deeply means." Social work, as we know, has a deep concern with the quality of human living. This concern "cannot operate in a moral vacuum, but on the contrary must be based on certain beliefs regarding what constitutes 'a good life' and also on ethical considerations in relation to ways by which such a good life can be sought and promoted."

It is in this light that we shall discuss the philosophy of SOCIAL work. This will include a synthesis of the concepts, attitudes, and values of professional social work. Some of these will be found to be universally accepted; others will appear to have an air of controversy around them. The controversial aspects of social work philosophy are related to controversy regarding what life honestly and deeply means, to the perspective on world, to our concepts regarding relations of men with other men, to the shape and form of the social and economic system in which were live. The philosophy of social work in every country bears the hue of the particular culture, rather of the socio-economic system that prevails there and has the impact of unique realities of the as they obtain. That is why, we find differences in the statemen of the philosophy of social work and also differences in the interpretation of the same philosophical tenets. However, there is a basic core of social work philosophy that is universally accept irrespective of the socio-economic system and cultural configuration.

That "social work is humanitarianism in search of a method, he cannot be denied. Even after social work became a scientist profession based on developments in the various social sciences, concern for the underdog, the downtrodden, the destitute and the dying remained the mainspring of all social work activity.

No practising profession can afford to be value-free. A profession like social work which is concerned with effecting personal and social change must have a set of attitudes and values on which to operate. These sets of values and attitudes are also instrumental in shaping the very personality of the social worker before the social worker attempts to effect personal and institutional intervention and change. For a social worker it is not enough to acquire the knowledge of social work methods and techniques; what is equally important for him is to develop a personality that is characteristic of a social worker—a personality that is based on the concepts, tenets, attitudes and values of social work. The social worker must develop a sound perspective on life before helping others with their "problems of living"—a substitute term used by Thomas Szasz for what is commonly called mental illnes. C. Marshall Lowe attributes the role of a secular priest to the therapist in the sense that his job is to guide people in the solution of their "problems of living"—a task involving assistance in resolving value conflict and in jettisoning and choosing values. He agrees with Charlotte Buhler who maintains that the indecision of the contemporary individual is a sign not so much of failure in ego functioning as an indication of the ambiguities inherent in the contemporary value systems.

Williamson thinks that counselors typically deal with problems arising from processes of growth and development, many of which arise from conflicts among the different life choices open to the patient. He believes that the counselor in vocational and educational counseling must also help the client select a moral life style in which choice of goals becomes an expression of the clients' personal values. Samler doubts that the counselor can divorce his personal values from his professional concern with helping clients develop and understand their own characteristic life patterns. He suggests that the counselors should help the client to find his personal values from the counselor's attempts to help the client atriculate integrated picture of himself and of his various roles.

When we talk of social work philosophy we must bear in mind at the same time that there is no complete unanimity about it. Dr. Bruno thinks that social work *is* a practice with "a common techniques, but not a common philosophy."

However, there is a basic core of social work philosophy which is almost universally accepted. Kohs has divided the values of social work into primary and secondary values. He enumerates ten values as the primary values of social work. As we shall see, these values appear to be universally accepted and yet there can be divergence in their interpretation, and, consequently, in the techniques that are to be adopted for their attainment. Pumphrey has classified values into abstract values and instrumental values. The first means what ought to or should be. The second concerns the means to achieve those values. Despite agreement on abstract values, when it comes to "instrumental values, wider divergence of opinion occurs; interpretation becomes more difficult...... For example, such questions arise as 'Is a 'good' family ever a 'divorced family'? 'Does a 'good' government prevent bloodshed at the cost of individual social participation?" Throughout this chapter we shall find at many places divergence of meaning as we proceed from abstract to instrumental values. This divergence is natural considering the situational differences as well as differences in cultural background, political beliefs, group aspirations and scientific principles. The ten values which Kohs regards as the primary values of social work are as follow:—

1. The worth and dignity of man.
2. The capacity of human nature to achieve full human potential.
3. Tolerance of differences.
4. Satisfaction of basic human needs.
5. Liberty.
6. Self-direction.
7. Non-judgmental attitude.
8. Constructive social cooperation.
9. Importance of work and constructive use of leisure.
10. Protection of one's existence from the dangers caused by man and nature.

Although no social worker will deny any one of these values, yet discrepancies may arise with respect to the interpretation of some of these when some of these abstract values are converted into instrumental values. Take, for instance, the 4th value— satisfaction of basic human needs. The application of this value in a developing country like India, where according to the 32nd round of national sample survey for the period July 1977 to June 1978, as much as 48.13 per cent of the total population is estimated to have been living below the poverty line in 1977-78 (the poverty line in India at 1977-78 price has been worked out to Rs. 65/- per head per month for the rural areas and Rs. 75/- per head per month for the urban areas), where people in several rural areas in a state subsist on roots and leaves owing to acute scarcity conditions, where in one state of West Bengal fifteen million people in the rural areas were found to be either "starving or living on one meal a day," will have different implications than the implications it would have in a country like the U.S.A. where the poverty line is around Rs. 900/- per head per month. The strategy to be adopted in suck a situation will be different and will involve, in the words of Mr. Robert Mc Namara, a more egalitarian distribution of economic and political power. It may involve a radical change in the social and economic system—a change that will mean greater control of the state over the means of production and a greater restriction on the free interplay of market economy. It will imply, in the words of Romanyshyn, the substitution of "intelligent political direction for the invisible hand of the free market and social responsibility for economic individualism."

In other words, *this value in our social sitting will mean that social work believes in the redistribution of economic and political power is. a more egalitarian manner so* that it may no more be possible for the top ten per cent of the Indian population to have a 36-5 per cent share in the national income leaving a minuscule 1.8 per cent share for the bottom ten per cent.

Similarly, there might be differences in the interpretation of the 10th value enunciated by Kohs when it is converted into instrumental value. How is one to be protected against the dangers or harms caused by other men? In a setting like ours this will mean a commitment of social work to oppose all kinds of exploitation of man by man. This will concern us with the exploitation of the toiling masses of our country by the unconscionable axis between the kulaks, the big business and the political bosses. This value will imply that social work is opposed to the exploitation of the poor and the downtrodden by the opulent class consisting of the kulkas, the business tycoons and the political thugs. This value, when converted into an instrumental value, will imply a different strategy for social intervention, one that is directed towards breaking the hegemony of the opulent minority over the indigent majority. The seemingly non-controversial value of liberty, placed at number 5 by Kohs, is also open to conflicting interpretations when it comes to instrumental value. One interpretation may be that man is free in the social, political as well as economic sphere to do as he deems fit for his personal interest. While all may agree with respect to man's social and political freedom, it may not be possible to agree on absolute freedom in the economic sphere. The implications of economic freedom have been discussed at greater length in the chapter on "Social Work and Socio-economic Development" while dealing with the concept of Social Justice. The 'justice as respect view' of social justice does not allow absolute freedom in the economic sphere, subordinates the economic freedom of the individual to the larger interests of society and regards human welfare as more important than human liberty. *This calm will, therefore, mean that social work believes in the social feasibility of production and in the subordination of production to social purposes.* Kohs maintains that there might be differences among social workers about the secondary values of social work and that these differences may be based on the social class, national background, political beliefs, cultural and family background, group aspirations and standards, individual experiences and different scientific principles of the social workers.

We hive already seen how even with respect to the interpretation of some of the primary (abstract) values there might be and are differences among social workers when it comes to instrumental values. Those inclined toward Western (capitalistic) democracy will like to interpret the 4th, 5th and 10th primary values in a manner that involves supporting the *status quo* and upholding the establishment, just doling out certain fringe benefits to the needy and keeping them at their places by allurements and appeasements now and then. In other words, they will try to coax the underdog to believe that change within-the-system will be sufficient and that they should aquiesce in the established social order. This will stand out in sharp contrast to the liberal-radical position which has to be taken in developing countries like India as mentioned above. Konopka has enumerated only two primary values of social work:

1. Respect for every person and the right of each person to the fullest development of his/her potential.
2. Mutual dependence of individuals and responsibility towards each other according to their abilities.

Herbert Bisno has given a most extensive treatment to the values of social work in his book. The Philosophy of Social Work. He has distributed social work values over four areas— Nature of the individual, the relations between groups, groups and individuals and between individuals, functions and methods of social work and lastly, social maladjustment and social change.

In the first area he includes one of the cardinal valuesr of social work; Each individual, by the very fact of bis existence, is of worth. This value is indeed the cornerstone of all social work philosophy. Especially, for an invidiously stratified society of soars it has vital significance in bringing all people on an equal plane and in welding then into an unsunderable bond of national unity and brotherhood. Unless this is. done no social or economic development is possible. The 'justice as respect view' based on the philosophy of Martin Luther King and Emanuel Kant regards people as ends in themselves and not as means to an end. Since equal integrity of each person is accepted it is considered to be the duty of society to provide equally for each person's pursuit of happiness. Equalisation of income for all persons is favoured by this view. This view, therefore, strongly corroborates the first value enunciated by Bisno.

The second value propounded by Bisno is that human suffering is undesirable and should be prevented, or at least alleviated, whenever possible.

This, again, is the mainspring of all social work activity and has immense importance for social work. Bisno has enumerated eight more values in the area designated as the The Nature of the Individual.

In the chapter on The Relations between Groups, Groups and Individuals, and between Individuals, the first value presented by

Bisno is: Social Work rejects the doctrines of Laissez-faire and survival of the fittest. This brings us to a new concept of the "Service State" beyond the concept of the Welfare State. Frank argues that, "The Service State, not to be confused with the welfare state with its aura of charity and philanthropy, is oriented to the enhanced 'well-being' of everyone, as Halbert Dunn has expressed it. It marks the acceptance of human conservation as the basic democratic task." As already stated, social work believes in the substitution of "intelligent political direction for the invisible hand of the free market and social responsibility for economic individualism." Bisno has presented nine more values in this chapter. The eighth value enunciated by Bisno is also of special importance for a country like ours where the organized labour movement is weak and does not have the power to counter the organized barons of industry with their unconscionable political nexus. This value reads as follows:

Organized labour makes a positive contribution to community lift and should be accepted as a constructive rather than destructive force.

Again, this value is of crucial importance for a country like ours where organized labour forms a minuscule part of the total labour force. However, even in America a great number of social workers have allied themselves directly with the objectives of trade unionism and labour. Some social workers have already spoken of the "alliance of labour and social work" as one of the major developments within the profession. Social workers and labour unionists have realised that they have essentially the same objective, that is, "a decent and satisfying life for each individual here and now." Besides they also agree that "social class and caste are not valid bases for the allocation of special privileges." In an invidiously stratified, inegalitration society of ours where privileges are mostly given on the basis of caste loyalty and not on the basis of one's achievement, this value has a unique significance. Hoselitz believes that in less-developed economies important economic responsibilities are distributed on the basis of a very particular system of values. He thinks the Indian Caste System implies a rigid separation of social classes and the inheriting of privileges and even trades within each group. In contrast, he maintains, the Western Society allots resources in the most efficient way to ensure maximum production. The objective if achieved through rational planning based on a universal standard of values.

In our own setting we can say that *social work believes that economic roles should not be assigned by ascription, or according to status, but by the standard of achievement.* "The system of diffused economic responsibilities must be replaced by better defined labour tasks. Self-interest of the ruling elite must be replaced by group interest."

Case Con, a radical organization of social workers in the U.K. believes that social workers must organize independently of the state and in the interests of the working class. They believe that "until this society, based on private ownership, profit and the needs of a minority ruling class, is replaced by a worker's state, based on the interests of the vast majority of the population, the fundamental causes of social problems will remain. It is, therefore, our aim to join the struggle for this workers' state." Social work in India finds itself very close to this ideological stance of Case Con.

In the chapter on the Function and Methods of Social Work, Bisno has presented six values of social work. The first of these is that social work has a functionally dualistic approach. This means that whereas on the one hand social work assists individuals in adjusting to the institutional framework of society, on the other it attempts to modify the institutional framework itself in appropriate areas. Bisno quotes Hamilton who thinks that, "critics of social casework suspect in the word 'adjustment' an attempt to make the client accept, in the sense of acquiescence, a harsh, depriving, and unjust society. This is not true. The caseworker may, however, help the client sort out what is real in the external world, whether he or anyone else chooses to acquiesce in it or not."

Bisno concludes that both casework and social action are legitimate and important methods of social work and that they are complementary rather than conflicting. He suggests seven avenues through which social workers may participate in social action.

"These are:

(1) Individual activity.

(2) Action through professional organizations,

(3) Action through semi-professional organizations (Such as the National Conference of Social Work).

(4) Action through social agencies.

(5) Action through non-partisan, non-social work associations.

(6) Action through politically partisan non-social work associations.

(7) Action through politically partisan social work association.

Bartlett speaks of social intervention in a variety of ways. "In interventive action, some social workers will place greater emphasis on giving direct services to the people coping with problems and others will emphasise bringing about changes in the social environment (including social institutions), but all must be continually aware of and concerned with the people and their environment in interaction with each other because this is the nature of social work." One type of intervention, which involves direct service, is often described as "clinical", while the other is variously described as community practice, social welfare service, social planning, or some similar term."

Of course, there might "be constraints involved in initiating institutional intervention for social workers who are employed by some agency. Bartlett mentions that some professional social workers have taken the initiative to establish agencies and programmes themselves. Such leadership has been taken by a number of schools of social work to provide teaching centres for their students. Another example is a special correctional unit developed under social work leadership. Thus social workers are freed from many restraints that inhibit them under traditional agency auspices.

In the chapter on Social Maladjustment and Social Change Bisno has mentioned three values, the first of which is that "there are serious political, economic, and social maladjustments in our culture." "The 'Boom and bust' tendencies of our economy, the inequalities and injustices that characterise the functioning of our socio-economic institutions, the political incompetencies and intolerances, the international tensions and conflicts, the interpersonal hostilities and maladjustments; all of these conditions accentuate the need for the controlled use of social intelligence in working for constructive social changes in overcoming the pressing 'cultural lags' of our day." Bisno is not alone in his disenchantment with the American social system. Professor Galbraith has quoted Ludwig Von Mises in his book. The Affluent Society, "The men whose research has given rise to new methods of production hate the businessmen who are merely interested in cash value of their research work. It is very significant that such a large number of American research physicists sympathise with socialism and communism. . . .university-teachers of economics are opposed to what they disparagingly call the profit system.. . ." Professor Robert H. Bork agrees with the conclusions drawn in the recent book entitled 'the Divided Academy' by Ladd and Lipset to the effect "that professors, particularly those from the most prestigious universities, tend rather strongly to be left liberals and to prefer more government regulation in economic and social matters."

What is true of America is far more true for a developing (poor) country like India which is plagued by crass social inequalities based on the caste system, by the inhuman economic inequalities perpetrated by the kulak-industrial-bureaucratic-political axis manipulated by the mighty few to the utter disadvantage of the emaciated many, and by the lack of opportunities for effective political participation for the masses. The mixed economy has proved a bane for our country. The private sector is thriving at the cost of the public sector and is building and expanding its empire to the detriment of the larger mass of society.

Mr. P. Ramamurti, a member of the Indian Parliament, is of the opinion that, "with the present socio-economic framework, it is impossible to find any solution. The so-called planned mixed economy (really a misnomer for developing monopolies with the help of the public sector) is ruinous for a developing country."

Professor A.N. Oza of the Department of Economics, Bombay University writes, "The fact that for the last five years we have been facing the paradoxical situation of, on the one hand, food stocks piling up and foreign exchange reserves swelling up, and, on the other, of the incidence of poverty and unemployment increasing, itself shows how planless our so-called "planned" economy is."

Commenting on the strategy for rural development adopted by the present government, Ramamurti says, "you talk of village industries, but who is going to buy the products made by them? When the rural poor do not have enough money even to buy food, how will thye buy other products? The benefits of janta policy will only go to the rich farmers who do not want to buy things made by village industries—they want Mercedes cars and Terylene shirts." The declared goal of our Constitution is the establishment of a socialist state, but the facts are otherwise. The private sector is being helped to thrive at the cost of the public sector. Consequently, the private empires of the industrial tycoons are expanding while at the same time the number of those living below the poverty line is going up.

Ruddar Datt coments, "In the business world, there is a common saying: A businessman cannot become a millionare unless the declares himself bankrupt seven times. In several cases, the Government at a very late stage discovered that sickness was contrived, but the private business was successful in abandoning the sick child, which has been deliberately starved by it, in the lap of the state. The function of blood transfusion was then given to the Government to save sick child from death. In other words, for the sins of the private sector, the public exchequer is called upon to pay, which in the ultimate analysis means the poor people." George Fernandes is reported to have angrily remarked, "profits should go to the private sector for them to sustain their five-star culture. Losses should be borne by the state—which means by the poor peple of our country."

Datta reports that the big business in India is getting finances from public institutions or ordinary share-holders. "For instance, the asses of TISCO total Rs. 300 crores, of which Rs. 175 crores is contributed by share-holders and the balance is based on loans from public financial institutions. The Tatas have applied for a loan of Rs. 400 crore so that they can modernise their plant. If the State has to finance the development of the private sector, then, the protagonists of nationalisation consider it better that the state should run the enterprise."

So far as the comparison between the performance of the public sector and private sector is concerned, a Reserve Bank of India Study of 404 selected large, non-government, non-financial limited companies (each with a paid-up capital of Rs. 1 crore or above), revealed that during 1975-76 and 1976-77, 33 per cent of large companies in the private sector were incurring losses, whereas among the public sector undertakings under the Central Government, only 28 per cent were incurring losses. And this is the condition when the private sector is sucking the blood of the public exchequer. One of the main reasons for the losses incurred by public sector undertakings is that the money from the public sector is drained off into the private sector by legal as well as illegal means (corruption) in order to help building private empires. If the private sector is altogether abolished the black money will not find a place to hide and to run an almost parellel economy.

Recently, the Government have enacted the Taxation Laws (Amendment) Act, 1978 which came into force on April 1, 1979. Under the Act, the Government have decided to exempt political parties from wealth tax. They "have also been exempted from income-tax regarding income derived from investments, house property, other sources and donations. It would not be obligatory for political parties to keep or maintain a record of such voluntary contribution that singularly is not in excess of Rs. 10,000 at a time."

Mr. Sood apprehends that, "all such political parties already possessing huge black money will be able to legalise the same under the shelter of this Amendment Act. They would cover it by showing it as 'donations' received merely by giving the narration that each donation did not exceed Rs. 10, 000, record of the sources has not been maintained and thereby their problem whatsoever about the old black money would be conveniently over for good. ...and the pity would be that the non-political tax evaders may also exploit the new provisions in connivance with such political parties and politicians. They can take the stand that the amount detected and found with them even during any search and raid represents donations to their political party and that such donations have been collected by them and are made up of contributions of not exceeding Rs. 10,000 each for which no record of the sources has been kept or maintained as provided for under the law."

It was probably in the light of the cancerous growth of monopolies in India that the President of India Mr. N. Sanjiva Reddy strongly advocated "ceiling on wealth along with ceiling on land" to achieve socialism in the country. Inaugurating the Golden Jubilee celebrations of the Andhra Pradesh University the President is reported to have said that, "unless the big money was controlled it will be dangerous for the country." He is further reported to have said than 45 families in the country had assets ranging from Rs. 100 crores to Rs. 1,000 crores. "Like land ceiling", he said, "there must be a ceiling on wealth and money." Mr. Reddy is also reported to have said that even the late Pandit Nehru had told him, when he was the Congress President, that the economy of the country was being controlled by 200 families and "it (economy) will be' crippled if they go unchecked."

In the light of the above we can say *that social work believes in remoting economic imbalance by plugging the sources of black money, protecting the public sector from the onslaughts of the plicate sector and taking sincere and. honest measures for the establishment of a socialist state.* The process whereby the private sector is nurtured by the public sector should be immediately stopped. A process should be immediately started whereby the area of operation of public sector should start expanding and that of private sector should start shrinking.

The third value presented by Bisno in his chapter on Social Adjustment and Social Change is: There is need for social planning.

According to Sidney Hook social planning is that which is "organized for the social welfare of the great masses of producers. The undesirable fact is that planning under capitalism, like all other forms of technical rationalisation, aims primarily at the retention of the rate of profit. Human values are- subordinate." Bisno holds that all planning is not alike; there may be non-democratic planning, coercive planning or planning that tends to curb certain cherished freedoms. He thinks that social workers do not accept such plannings. Social workers ia his view, accept, democratic planning that is experimental, tentative, and non-authoritarian—only then it becomes social planning. To those who talk in terms of freedom vs. planning, Bisno remarks that real freedom does not mean simply absence of legal constraints but the presence of resources and capacities. "You cannot really be free when you are badly clad, underfed, wretchedly housed, without education, without money for medicine, living at a miserable wage, or haunted by fear of war, unemployment, or a penniless old age. The material and cultural means to freedom cannot be realised without democratic planning and organization. Hence, freedom without organization is a delusion, just as organization without freedom is a strait jacket."

In our country that is beset with conditions of dire want and scarcity of resources, we can no more afford the free play of market forces for the profit of a privileged elite to the detriment of the huge mass of underprivileged have-nots. Social planning does not fit in with either a capitalist structure or a mixed economy where the capitalist class always gets the upper hand and exploits the public sector (people's money) for its own ends.

Social work, therefore, believes in social planning that is organized for the welfare of the great masses of people in a socialist economy.

Social work believes in the service-state which is oriented to the 'well-being' 'of everyone and marks the acceptance of human conservation as the basic democratic task. It is different from the welfare state with its aura of charity and philanthropy. Horowitz remarks that, our welfare state is "....an attempt to 'cool out' the marginal underclass and minimise the potential danger it poses. It is an attempt to avoid the consequences of large-scale marginality without making any social structural changes."

In the words of World Bank President, Mr. Robert McNamara, when the "highly privileged are few and desperately poor are many— and when the gap between them is worsening rather than improving— it is only a question of time before a decisive choice must be made between the political cost of reform and the political risk of rebellion."

"The fatal error", in the words of Romanyshyn, "is that time is running out and the underclass, or at least a significant militant minority, plus other dissident groups now challenge the legitimacy of existing institutions."

Social work believes in social development which involves structural changes that allow for citizen participation in new economic, social, and political roles. Participation in this sense means "participation in every dimension of life, of culture, of our economy, our educational system, our political system, our decision making process. It means full enfranchisement with respect to the totality of society's activities."

Social work believes in distributive value as against aggregate value. Aggregate value means a good to be maximised for society even though it may not be maximised for each individual within the society. A distributive value is one which is to be maximised for each individual, though not necessarily for the society as a whole.

Romanyshyn thinks that, "much of the social welfare effort is in behalf of distributive values. "Ultimately the test of social development is the development of man, of all men, and of our highest capacities as human beings. Institutions exist to serve the needs of man. When they no longer function adequately men have the right and the obligation to change them."

Social work believes in social justice. There are three views of social justice that merit consideration.

(1) The social contract view associated with Hobbes, Rousseau, and John Rawls.

(2) The utility view which is based on the philosophy of Mill and Bentham, and

(3) Justice as respect view based on the thoughts of Kant and Martin Luther King, Jr.

The first view of social justice supports political liberty and equality but accepts inequality on the basis that this will enable people to produce more and will enable everyone to enjoy more.

The second view accepts the sacrifice of the happiness of some individuals or groups for a greater totality.

The third view, i.e., the justice as respect view regards that society as just which obtains and maintains respect for persons through social arrangements that are in the common interest but not to the greater advantage of some than others. Since equal integrity of each person is accepted, it is considered to be the duty of society to provide equally for each person's pursuit of happiness. Equalisation of income for all persons is favoured by this view. It regards human welfare as more important than human liberty and treats people as ends in themselves and not as means to an end.

Social work believes us *distributive justice which implies that the rewards should be commensurate with the contributions made by an individual to society.* This view of distributive justice is different from the one taken by John Rawls of the U. S. John Rawl's concept of distributive justice is essentially based on a new version of a social contract. This concept takes for granted basic inequalities and is a clever maneuver to gain society's approval for basic inequalities under the pretext of furthering the advantage of the less fortunate.

Rawl's view of distributive justice is, thus, different from the view of distributive justice in which rewards are to be commensurate with the contribution a person makes to society. It means a restructuring of the entire stratification system. This concept is applicable to a social system in which the means of production are in the hands of the state and where inequalities are minimum and human.

Kozlov maintains that "distribution according to work exists primarily because production is carried on under the undivided sway of socialist ownership of the means of production, and nobody, consequently, is entitled to appropriate the results of another's work...... ..society has to distribute the resources of consumer goods available among working people in accordance with their contribution to social production. The material remuneration of each working person, therefore, varies with the quantity and quality of his or her work for the benefit of society. The application of this concept requires a social structure when there are no industrial tycoons and landed barons to exploit and suck the blood of the toiling masses and the contributing intellectuals including, scientists and members of the professions, and where there are no parasites to hold the society at ransom by their unconscionable machinations that are devoid of any construction contribution to society. The application of this principle of eliminate all financial vampires and enable the really worthy make their fullest contribution and earn a commensurate reward This principle, in fact, implies, "From each according to the abilities, to each according to bis work" and is a powerful stimulus for raising labour productivity and enabling individual and public interest to be combined."

Social work believes in religious, political and scientific de-encapsulation.

In order to understand the real import of the term deencapsulation it is imperative to understand the word encapsulation. The term encapsulation has been used by Royce in the sense of a process through which a culture imposes the blinders of a limited world outlook on everyone who is a part of that culture. Because of encapsulation man's perception of things is determined by the dominant value orientation of the day. Royce believes that the periods of important historical and social transition are periods of deencapsulation.

He thinks that deencapsulation requires the acquisition of insight into the extent of one's entrapment within existing modes of thought. Encapsulation can be further mitigated if a person expands his awareness by becoming aware of alternative morals and values.

Lowe thinks that "modern man now seeks a New Truth which lies as much beyond science as it does beyond theology and philosophy. If he is to find it, he must have the freedom to interrelate the overlapping concerns of science and religion in new and creative ways.... the new freedom from older thought forms offers the other-directed individual the best chance to become the unencapsulated man."

Religious deencapsulation—The word religion has emanated from religare, meaning to tie back, to bind together, to unite the disparate elements of culture into a homogeneous unity. Lowe thinks that the cohesive force of primitive religion comes from the traditions of society. It rationalises its beliefs on the basis of sanctions derived from society's belief in supernatural. In Lowe's view "now religion is more a personal matter and to an increasing extent, it is becoming more meaningful to describe it psychologically as man's own highly personal experiencing of what he regards as his highest good." Robinson describes the basic value of the new morality as "the fact that persons matter and the deepest welfare of these particular persons in this particular situation matters more than anything else in the world."

Political deencapsulation.—Political deencapsulation increases the moral freedom of man by combining the scientist's inherent skepticism of any closed system of thought with the clinician's sensitivity to individual need.

Scientific deencapsulation.—Lowe thinks that even modern science has often produced beliefs which become dogmatic and closed to possible revision. "When the therapist deencapsulates himself from inappropriate scientific models, he creates a new spirit of questioning which may spread to older, closed types of scientific knowledge..... .the therapistcan develop these qualities (of passion, commitment, and conviviality) in the scientific investigator by helping him create an openness which, in turn, can invite new types of discovery."

Discussing the distinction between the open and the closed systems Rokeach and Restle assert that "the more closed the system, the more is the acceptance of a particular belief assumed to depend on irrelevant internal drives and/or arbitrary reinforcements from external authority.... On the other hand, the more open the system, the more should the person address himself to objective structural requirements—that is, logical relationship—and the more should he resist irrelevant motivational or reinforcement pressures." They further hold that when a variety of information comes from an external source, the relatively closed person is forced to accept all or reject all in a 'package deal'. For the relatively open person the power of authority is still there, but depends upon the authority's cognitive correctness, accuracy, and consistency with other information he has about the world. They maintain that, "the more closed a person's belief system, the more he should evaluate others according to their agreement or disagreement with his own system; also, the more difficult should it be to discriminate between and separately evaluate a belief and the person holding the belief."

References

"Coordinated Services", *Children,* Vol. 14, No. 3 (May-June 1967), p. 125.

"Professors and Public Policy—A round table discussion". *The American Review,* Spring 1979, p. 101.

Austin, L.N.: 'The Evolution of our Social Case Work Concepts' *The Family,* 20; 43, April 1939.

Bartlett, Harriett M., The Common Base of Social Work Practice. New York: National Association of Social Workers, 1970, p. 162.

Biestek, F.P. : *The Case Work Relationship,* Loyola University Press, Chicago, 1957, p. 100.

Bisno, Herbert, *op. cit.,* p. 123.

Bisno, Herbert, *The Philosophy of Social Work.* Washington D. C.: Public Affairs Press, 1952.

Bisno, Herbert: *The Philosophy of Social Work,* Public Affairs Press, Washington, D.C. 1952, pp. 1-125.

Brown, E.L.: *"Social Work as a Profession,* Russell Sage Foundation, New York, 1942, p. 185.

Buhler, Charlotte, *Values in Psychotherapy*. New York: Free Press, 1962.

Butler, Ruth M.: An Orientation to knowledge of Human Growth and Behaviour in Social Work Education, p. 24, in Sugata Dasgupta's *Towards a Philosophy of Social Work in India.* Popular Book Service, New Delhi, pp. 199-200.

Butrym, Zofia T., *The Nature of Social Work*. London: Macmillan Press Ltd., 1976, p. 42.

Cahn, E.S. and Cahn, J.C.: "Citizen Participation" in Spiegel (ed.) Citizen Participation in Urban Development. Washington, D.C. NTL Instt. for Applied Behavioural Science, 1968, p. 223.

Clarke, Helen I., *Principles and Practice of Work*. New York: D. Appleton-Century Co., Inc., 1947, p. 434.

Cohen, Nathan, *Social Work in American Tradition*. New York: The Dryden Press, 1958, p. 3.

Datt, Ruddar, "Income Inequality and Consumption Pattern in India", Mainstream. May 4, 1974, p. 15.

Datta, Ruddar, "Nationalisation-Facts and Fancies", *Mainstream*, Vol. XVII, No. 30, March 24, 1979, p. 12.

De Marco, Joseph P. and Richmond, Samuel R. "Equality and Justice", *American Review*, Autumn 1977, p. 88.

Dwey, John: *Philosophy, Encyclopaedia of the Social Sciences,* Mac Millan, New York, 1935, p. 122.

Elliot, Studt, *et al.,* C-Unit: Search for Community *in* Prison. New York: Russell Sage Foundation, 1968.

Frank, Lawrence K., "The Need for a New Political Theory", *Daedalus,* 96 (Summer 1967).

Frank, Lawrence K., "The Need for a New Political Theory", *Daedalus*, 96 (Summer 1967).

Ganguli, B.N.: Ideal Social Order, pp. 20-30 Quoted by Shankar Pathak. *Social Welfare,* Mc Millan Company, New Delhi, 1981, p. 108.

Green T.F., "Schools and Communities: A Look Forward", Harward Educational Review, 39 (Spring 1969), pp. 221-252.

Hamilton, Gordon, *Theory and Practice of Social Casework*. New York: Columbia University Press, 1940, pp. 14-15.

Hamilton, Gordon: *Theory and Practice of Social Case Work,* Columbia University Press, New York, 1940, p. 15.

Hathway, N: *"Social Action or Inaction: The Challenge"* in Training for Social Work in the Department of Social Science, University of Toronto, 1914-1940, p. 33.

Hook, Sidney, "The Philosophical Society, Yesterday, Today, Tomorrow — A Symposium. Mackenzie, F. (ed.). New York: Prentice Hall, 1937, p. 668.

Horowitz, Irwing Louis, *Professional Sociology*. Chicago: Aldine Press, 1968, p. 124.

Hoselitz, B. F., *Sociological Aspects of Economic Growth*. Bombay: Vakils, Feffer & Seimons, 1960, p. 14.

James, William, Pragmatism. New Delhi: Eurasia Publishing House (P) Ltd., 1975, pp. 17-18.

Jones, quoted in Bisno, Herbert, *The Philosophy of Social Work*. Washington, D. C.: Public Affairs Press, 1952, p. 61.

Klein, Philip, "The Social Theory of Professional Social Work". Barries, H. E., *et al.* (*ed.*). *Contemporary Social Theory*. New York; D. Applelon-Century Co., 1940, p. 758.

Kohs, S. C., *The Root of Social Work*. New York: Association Press, 1966.

Konopka, G., Edward C. Lindeman: *Social Work Philosophy,* The University of Minnesota Press, Minneapolis, 1958, p. 83.

Konopka, Gisela, *Eduard C. Lindeman and Social Work Philosophy*. Minneapolis: The University of Minnesota Press, 1958, p. 178.

Leonard, P, 'Social Work: Science or Mystique", Lecture given at a study conference held under the auspices of the National Institute of Social Work (1969).

Leonard, P.: *Social Work: Science or Mystique,* lecture given at study conference held under the auspices of the National Institute of Social Work, USA, 1969.

Lowe, C. Marshall, *Value Orientations in Counseling and Psychotherapy*. California: Chandler Publishing Co., 1969, p. 16.

Majumdar, A.M.: *Social Welfare in India.* Asia Publishing House, Bombay, 1964, p. 155.

Mises, Ludwing Von., *The Anti-Capitalistic Mentality*. Princeton: Van Nostrand, 1956, p. 20.

Nanavati, M.C.: *Origin and Growth of Professional Social Work-Historical Aspects,* S. Dasgupta (ed.); Towards a Philosophy of Social Work, Popular Book Services, Delhi, 1967, p. 24.

National Herald, September 20, 1974, reporting the Statement of the then Relief Minister, Santosh Roy.

National Herald, September 36, 1972, speech of World Bank President Mr. Me Namara at the World Bank International Monetary Fund Annual Meeting at Washington.

Oza, A.N., "Our Economy: Sick or Healthy?", *The Illustrated Weekly of India,* February 25, 1979, p. 9.

Pumphrey, M.W., *The Teaching of Values and Ethics in Social Work Education,* Vol. XIII, New York; CSWE, 1959, p. 40.

Ramamurti, P., "Our Economy: Sick or Healthy?", *The Illustrated Weekly of India*, February 25, 1979, p. 8.

Robinson, Virginia: *A Changing Psychology in Social Case Work.* University of North Carolina Press, Chapel Hill, N.C. 1930, p. 34.

Romanyshyn, John, M., *Social Welfare—Charity to Justice*. New York: CSWE, 1971, p. 379.

Royce, Joseph R., *The Encapsulated Man.* Princeton: Van Nostrand, 1964.

Samler, Joseph, "Change in values: a goal in counseling", *Journal of Counseling Psychology,* 1960, pp. 32-39.

Sood, J. K., "Tax Laws Generate Black Money", *Pioneer*, April 14, 1979.

Szasz, Thomas S., " The Myth of Mental Illness", in Dinitz *et al. (eds.), Deviance*. New York: Oxford University Press, 1969, p. 429.

Towle, Charlotte: *Common Human Needs,* Federal Security Agency, Washington, 1945, p. 3.

Willlamson, E. G., "Value Orientations in Counseling", *Personnel and Guidance Journal,* 1958, pp. 520-28.

3

Social Work: Nature and Scope

Social work is characterised by the goals which it seeks to attain in society. From this point of view social work consists of a complex and organized effort to obtain the highest personal and social satisfactions for individuals, groups, and communities. The emphasis is on the good which is sought, the goal which is to be achieved. Such a view lays less stress on the specific methods and techniques which social workers themselves employ; it is concerned primarily with objectives. The goals with which such a definition of social work is concerned are closely related to religious categories. In general "the good life" is the aim, and how the good life is defined rests ultimately on the philosophic perspective of the definer. Obviously, such a goal is not seen as a present reality; it is, instead, a future possibility toward which men are expected to strive.

One more definition of social work lays the basic emphasis on the motives of those who do social work. From this standpoint social work is much older than its modern and professional phase. According to this definition, the intended goal does not matter as much as the spirit of charity, helpfulness, or personal responsibility. Simple neighborliness is as important as a specific set of professional techniques. Like the first point of view, this definition rests on spiritual or philosophic foundations.

There are other definitions of social work. The one which seems to predominate among social workers today defines social work as certain social processes applied to individuals, groups, and communities. Social work, from this viewpoint, is not a "cause"; it is a social function. Such a definition does not preclude goals and motives; it only seeks to define social work according to what social workers do.

Let us say that social work is the art of bringing various resources to bear on individual, group, and community needs by the application of a scientific method of helping people to help themselves. Social work, in this sense, is of rather recent origin. There were long periods in history when men did not apply objective methods to interpersonal problems; in fact, according to a number of social workers, scientific social work began only recently and is not yet wholly scientific in its methods. It depends to a marked degree on the development of exact knowledge among the various social sciences, but as yet these have not become fully scientific either. Wherever possible, however, social workers try to apply the results of objective investigation, particularly in the social sciences, to human problems, and they attempt to maintain an unemotional and critical attitude in their own work.

Social work is scientifically oriented in the knowledge and methods it uses, but it also involves certain elements of skill which make it akin to an applied or practical art. As a subject, social work is scientific; as a practice, it is an art.[1]

One of the best ways to understand the meaning of social work is to analyse the way it helps individuals, groups, and communities.

Social Work Helps Individuals

Social Casework

Social work as a particular aid to individuals is commonly called *social casework*. Social casework is practiced by a variety of agencies and organizations in the community. As a process it aims primarily at helping individuals, on a person-by-person basis, to attain the fullest degree of personal development. To the extent to which this aim is achieved, a social value is created; therefore, social casework is connected with the increase and maintenance of social welfare generally.

Social casework as it deals with individuals has traditionally been concerned with those persons who have been unable to achieve a fairly normal adjustment to life and who need some outside support. Today, however, it is becoming increasingly evident that social casework can benefit all people. Many persons who have a generally normal adjustment to life may face a problem with which they need help. An analogy to the work of the physician will clarify this point. The physician is concerned not only with the chronically ill but also with persons who may enjoy generally favourable health with occasional medical needs. So social casework currently aims at assisting not only those persons who cannot maintain a normal adjustment to their human environment but also all people who may be in circumstances of particular need. Every person can profit by casework services at one time or another.

Concern with Individual and General Welfare

Social casework, then, is concerned both with the individual and his adjustment to life and with general social welfare. It is not responsible for either in an exclusive way. It does not concentrate on the individual to the exclusion of the social factors which have contributed to his situation. Nor does it seek social improvements without cognizance of the needs and aspirations of the individual. In other words, the basic objective of social casework is social welfare, with the fundamental focus on the individual. It is a personal-social treatment process which involves the release of individual ability and the alleviation of environmental pressures.

Present-Day Crises Create Needs

Each human being has a wide array of needs requiring satisfaction. In our time these needs must be satisfied in a complex and oftentimes confused society. The impact of numerous public crises, such as war and depression, upon the well-being of individuals is often highly frustrating. Because of their own inherent strength or the milder nature of their problems, many individuals are able to withstand disorganizing pressures and to maintain fairly satisfactory lives. But others, who are not so fortunate, because of their own inabilities or the seriousness of social pressures fall by the way. It seems that social change in our society is so great and so fraught with personal disaster that most people at one time or another need the kind of alleviating support which social caseworkers are able to provide. There is no sign on the horizon, moreover, which suggests that social casework will be needed to a lesser degree in the future.

Implicit in social casework is the moral conviction that individuals are important, that they are entitled, simply because of their humanness, to respect and to aid when it is needed. This valuative element in social casework finds ample support in the Christian ethic, Kantian moral idealism, humanitarianism, and other motivating ideologies.

Development of Social Casework Theory

The development of social casework theory will be presented in this chapter.

Early Beginnings

It is impossible to date the actual beginnings of social casework theory. The founding of the first professional school of social work, the New York School of Social Work, in 1898, can be a suitable starting point for the purposes of the present study. The establishment of this institution indicates that the theory of social work had become so definite and large a body of knowledge that it properly was the subject of a special professional school. In fact, in the years immediately following the turn of the century, other professional schools were founded with much the same motivation. Of course, these schools also expressed the growing need for better-trained personnel as more and more complicated problems arose which could not be adequately handled in traditional ways.

Impact of First World War

Prior to the First World War, the major emphasis in social casework was on the social factors which influenced individuals who had problems. Many people believed in social and economic determinism. The causes of human misery were found in the environment. There was a recognition of the importance of the larger social and economic pressures under which people lived; economics, especially, was looked upon as supplying a basic context for social workers. Such smaller, though not less significant, factors as the family, the play group, the school, and the various stimuli of the neighborhood, were not neglected. Social caseworkers during this period found in all of these the primary basis of human behaviour.

The First World War made a definite and widespread impact on social casework theory. Psychiatry in this period became increasingly important. The contributions of Freud and his followers were making their impression, and to some extent sociological explanations gave way to psychological and even psychiatric ones. The acceptance of this orientation had its effect on the methods employed by caseworkers in their dealings with persons in need. The child guidance clinic movement, with its stress on early treatment and prevention of mental problems and delinquency, encouraged the trend to psychological orientation.

Gains in 1920's and 1930's

In the later 1920's, it was seen that acceptance by the worker of the client and his values was essential to successful casework practice. The previous planning done by social caseworkers for the benefit of their clients was often found to lead nowhere, because the clients themselves had not really been allowed to help themselves. At this time social caseworkers realized that in order to respect the rights of clients as well as to be effective they were obliged to place more responsibility on the clients for making life decisions.

Such gains in social casework theory were carried over into later periods. By the early 1930's the conception of a relationship between worker and client, which previously had engaged the attention of social caseworkers, again became important but with a refinement derived from experience. Certain psychoanalytic contributions, such as the value of catharsis and free-association interviewing, also came more to the foreground.

The depression of the 1930's caused the modification of many features of social casework. Most of the voluntary agencies were forced to reconsider their function in the community, to devise new techniques of helping people without delay, to co-operate with fresh-born government agencies, and to face a different type of problem presented by their clients.

Gradually, a more conscious application of psychological theory occurred, but social caseworkers were unable to agree on which theory of psychology should guide them in their activities. As a result several schools of thought developed, such as the "organizmic" and the "functional", with many points in common and yet a number of differences. These schools were based on the teachings of Sigmund Freud and Otto Rank. In addition, "Thomistic" social casework theory grew out of the appreciation of many Roman Catholic social workers for the general contributions to human understanding made by Saint Thomas Aquinas (1225-1274 A.D.).

Advances During Second World War

Social casework, like other branches of human knowledge and action, was greatly influenced by the events of the Second World War. Many of the advances which characterise modern practice were initiated or strengthened by wartime experience.

During the war social agencies witnessed an increase in personal problems on the part of clients in contradistinction to material problems. It is true that the disruptions of war caused many persons to suffer financially, but it was mainly the emotional problems that increased. To meet this need the counseling responsibilities of family agencies were enlarged. This development, moreover, gave social caseworkers reason to examine the nature of their services to individuals with personal problems and to "grow in wisdom and stature" as a result.

The war also made social work known to large numbers of people who previously had not been acquainted with it at all or who had been familiar only with particular aspects of it. Since social caseworkers were widely represented on selective service boards, they were brought into contact with the lay people on the boards and with the young men who were examined by them. The recognition by the armed services of a definite social work category in personnel also directed attention to social work. Medical and psychiatric social workers were especially in demand during the war. In the armed services many men and women came to know the meaning of social work for the first time.

Civilians became acquainted with social work through the extension of its activities into certain new fields. Day nurseries sprang up throughout the country. While some were not operated in a completely desirable fashion, many were expertly run and included in their services the contributions of social caseworkers, who considered problems connected with admission to day nurseries and with the relations between children, nurseries, and parents.

Current Trends

After the Second World War came a period of resettlement and revaluation for social caseworkers. One of the current trends is the continuing movement of workers from the older and more established agencies and organizations which formerly dominated the field to the newer and more experimental areas of social work.

Social casework at the present time is perhaps more aware of its own distinctive contributions to human welfare than at any time in the past. Dependent as it always has been on other fields of knowledge and not always possessing prestige, social casework has still been able to work out some of its major problems as a profession. It is now receiving increased popular recognition. Gone are the days when its right to exist was debated, when many social caseworkers were trying to prove that they were something other than social caseworkers. The laymen's increased awareness of the benefits of social casework has tended to boost morale in the field.

A most promising development is the increased stress on the importance of research. This emphasis has been aided by the increasing number of persons undertaking doctoral programs in the field and by the various intradisciplinary activities of social workers—for example, the intradisciplinary effort to secure more accurate testing of the efficacy of social casework. Furthermore, social caseworkers are recognising the importance of cultural implications for their practice. Thus the past overemphasis on either environment or the personality is rightly giving way to an awareness of the interdependence of these two factors. The contributions of cultural anthropology and social psychology are especially helpful in this connection.

Partly as a result of community concern for juvenile delinquency, social caseworkers have been experimenting recently with newer approaches to those who need their services. They are not always content to accept for service only those who apply. Rather they are interested both in seeking out persons within the community who may be relatively unaware of their own needs and in giving social casework assistance to persons who fall under the authority of the community—for example, those committed to an institution by a court.

Social casework is increasingly aware of the need for further strength. In part this will come about through measures which will permit and encourage more qualified personnel. It will be helped by improving the standards both of practice and of salaries, and by maintaining a watchful eye for newer, useful knowledge being developed in allied fields.

The Practice of Social Casework

Social casework is essentially a generic process; it features certain common elements which can be applied in a number of situations. It is practiced usually within agencies, which are established by legislative action (government agencies) or by the joint efforts of private citizens (voluntary agencies). Initially, social casework was practiced in relatively few types of agencies and institutions. But through the years it has been increasingly utilised in newer settings so that today there are many agencies, institutions, and organizations which find the contributions of social caseworkers valuable. It would be impossible to list all of these, but a number can be mentioned to give an idea of the wide scope of the field: hospitals, clinics, courts, industry, military organizations, family welfare agencies both government (federal, state, and local) and voluntary, the American Red Cross, travelers' aid societies, immigrant agencies, child welfare agencies, institutions for the aged, for criminals and delinquents, for dependent and handicapped children, foster home agencies, day nurseries and schools, adoption agencies, child guidance clinics; mental-hygiene organizations, health organizations, and others.

The importance of the situations in which social casework is practiced varies, as does the volume of services supplied. In a book such as this, which intends to introduce the beginning student to social work, there is no possibility of giving detailed attention to each of the agencies, institutions, and organizations using casework methods. It should be borne in mind that social casework is a generic process modified by the manner in which it is practiced by specific agencies.

Social Work Helps Groups

Social Group Work

That branch of social work which helps individuals in their relations to certain groups is called *social group work*. It embraces educational and recreational activities conducted in leisure time with the assistance of a leader; its effects relate to group behaviour and even to the broader community and its values. Group work is often spoken of as "character building" in its effect, and in this sense it is rather closely related to the aims of social casework. To a considerable measure, the character building results of social group work refer to the over-all contribution of the process to the strengthening of wholesome living for individuals within the community, and to the nature of the activities in which such groups engage.

Group work is based on the fact that all human beings have basic, common needs, including some which can be satisfied through group association. Not all forms of group association, however, will satisfy these needs. Some, in fact, tend to thwart them. In the recent decades especially, through increased industrialism, urbanism, and secularism, some of the means (such as the church, the family) by which individuals were able to satisfy their group needs have lost much of their prestige or influence. In the face of such developments, social group work fulfills a significant function. It promises an even greater contribution to human affairs in the future.

Methods Vary

The method of social group work is somewhat different from that of social casework, though both are concerned with the development of better human relations. Social casework is primarily responsible for treatment. It recognises conditions in many instances both within and outside the individual which need remedying.[2] Social group work, however, is perhaps more positively oriented. It is responsible for the constructive use made by individuals of group experience, but it is also employed extensively to help people to develop more socially acceptable and socially desirable values and abandon socially unacceptable behaviour. Social group work, therefore, is not primarily therapeutic, except in a very broad sense.

In the application of his knowledge to the social group work situation, the professional worker uses a wide variety of methods depending on the nature of the group he is dealing with. Each group, according to the principles of social group work, has the right to determine its own activities as long as certain general but fundamental conditions are not violated. This recognition of the particular group's activity means that theoretically there can be almost as many means of attaining the goals of group work as there are groups. Actually, the activities which have instrumental purposes for the group worker include the following, among others: arts and crafts, dramatics, music, dancing, games, sports, pottery making photography, nature study, woodwork, sewing, public affairs, home management, nursing, first aid, prenatal and postnatal care, sex information and discussion of problems of politics, religion, and labor.

The specific methods used in these group activities vary from group to group according to the inherent interests and abilities of the group, the capacity of the group leader, and the materials available.

It is conceivable that the methods successful in one situation might be questionable in another. What one group leader will be able to accomplish with his particular personality and training may work well in one group work situation and not work at all in another. Given the variables in the composition of the group, the personality of the leader, the materials available, and other factors, it is easy to see how great variation exists in practice. Yet there are common elements in group work which can to some degree be distinguished.

Agencies Engaged in Group Work

The nature of the agency engaged in group work generally determines the type of program and the methods to be used for the achievement of its aims. In the earlier period of social group work, most of the programs were supported by voluntary agencies interested in leisure-time and recreational services directed chiefly toward children and youth. But in recent years group work has been extended to other types of agencies, which today often deal with older people as well as children and youth. The settlement houses, Y's, Boy Scouts and Girl Scouts, and other similar agencies and organizations which dominated the field of social group work previously are still prominent today, but there are at the present time many new explorations of the values of group work in religious education, housing, adult education, hospitals, and child-care institutions.

Interaction of Members

No matter how excellent the group leadership may be, the primary benefits from group work are derived from the interaction of the group members themselves. The reliance of the group work process on the interaction of the members is necessary, for it is among them that the goals of social group work mainly rest. The group leader's job is to give direction to group activities and aspirations. He understands the requirements of the group work process in detail. He can be helpful to groups in providing short cuts for the attainment of their purposes. He has a fund of information and wisdom helpful for the successful operation of the group process. It may be possible for a group to achieve its purposes without the assistance of a group leader, but his presence should enable the members to attain their goals more efficiently and more rewardingly. The quality of the relationship between the social group worker and his group is as important as the quality of the relationship between the social caseworker and his client.

Individual Approach

Basic to the methodology of social group work is the individual approach—an approach based on a recognition of the member's stage of growth and his abilities. The individual exists in the social group work situation not merely for the satisfaction of commendable group goals and the meeting of certain community needs but also to gain satisfactions for his basic needs. Group work, in this sense, must be individually oriented. The group leader cannot assume that the sheer participation of a member in a group will satisfy the member's basic needs.

The responsibility for individualisation obviously rests more on the leader than on the members, for often the members are more aware of their problems than the needs implicit in them. Of interest to youth group leaders is Table 18.1, which shows what a poll conducted by Purdue University found to be problems facing the youth of today.

Developments and Trends

Though professional social group work is a relatively recent development, in one form or another group methods have always been used with varying degrees of effectiveness. It is difficult to date the beginnings of modern social group work. Some would put its inception in the latter part of the nineteenth century, and perhaps its rise can be dated back to the use of group methods by city missions or by the social settlements of that period.

In the beginning, social group work agencies frequently stressed their differences. In some cases they championed individual approaches to problems of a general nature without actively joining in co-operative exploration of those problems. With this outlook many forms of social group work came into existence with varying degrees of significance and effectiveness.

TABLE 1

Major Concerns of Participating Youth By Percentages
(Percentages do not Add to 100 Because of Duplications)

Problem	% of Total	% of Boys	% of Girls
"I want people to like me more."	54	47	60
Get stage fright before a group	53	46	59
"What makes people selfish or unkind?"	39	34	45
Worry about little things	35	26	44
Can't help daydreaming	35	29	41
"I" m worried about the next war."	31	31	32
"How can I make the world a better place in which to live?"	30	25	35
"Must always be `on the go'"	29	30	20
"How will the draft affect me?"	29	57	3
Report that they are nervous	27	21	32
Have guilt feelings about things they have done	26	25	27
"Is there something I can do about race prejudice?"	25	20	30

(*Reaching Teen-agers*, New York City Youth Board, Monograph No. 1, February, 1954, p. 12.)

New Outlook

Subsequently, group workers began a more co-ordinated quest for essential and generic conceptions and methods. The development of these ideas and methods was facilitated by a deeper understanding of human behaviour. The increased knowledge of group life available after many years of trial and error, the more pressing needs within the profession for consolidation and improved standards, the development of perspective gained from other fields, and the general tenor of the times—all influenced the nature of group work. Various study groups were formed during the 1930's, and courses and sections were set up at state conferences on social work. By 1936 these were well enough developed to permit the organization at the National Conference on Social Welfare of a national, year-round co-ordinating agency in the field. As a result the National Association for the Study of Group Work was born. Later it became the American Association of Group Workers, which merged with the National Association of Social Workers in 1955.

Growth of Professional Awareness

During recent years the growth of social group work has been steady and notable. Certainly the most significant progress made in the field has been the development of professional awareness by social group workers. A willingness to undertake patient study of the group process is showing some positive results. Professional standards are higher now than ever before; persons without a full educational background feel increasingly the need for supplementary knowledge. Social work schools have recognised the importance of social group work by organizing curriculums which have greatly strengthened the professional leadership in the field. Social workers generally are more alert to the possibilities of group work and in many instances are co-operating with social group work agencies to their mutual benefit.

The spread of the method of group work is another significant trend. As was mentioned earlier, no longer do the older types of agencies dominate the field. The entrance of group work into such fields as religious education, hospitals, and housing holds the promise of a contribution which is essentially unlimited. In each new application of social group work, additional understanding regarding the nature of the activities is achieved.

Rise of Group Therapy

The rise in recent years of various forms of group therapy indicates another trend.[3] The importance of group therapy is today recognised in many types of agencies. For some years it has been utilised in child guidance clinics and now has reached its most mature development in such agencies. But experience gained in recent years indicates that the methods of group therapy can have a much wider application. As such therapy develops, however, it may become a separate specially within social work, somewhat divorced from group work. Social group work, as mentioned previously, is concerned with the development of normal individuals who wish to take part in constructive experiences. Group therapy, or "psychiatric group work," is aimed more toward those persons who cannot utilise the benefits of normal group experience. However, the boundaries between normal and abnormal, as is generally known, are indefinite.

Social Work Helps Communities

Community Welfare Organization

Social work which helps communities is called *community welfare organization.* Community welfare organization, as a basic process of social work, concentrates not so much on the individual and his needs or the group and its growth as upon the larger and more inclusive welfare problems of the whole community. True, it seeks to strengthen the effective accomplishment of casework and group work, but it has other responsibilities as well.

The focus of community welfare organization is on the activities of groups of people. It is distinguished from casework on the grounds that social casework deals with individuals. It differs from group work in that group work deals mainly with the activities of specified groups. Community welfare organization begins when a relationship is established between two or more groups to effect community welfare. For this reason, it has often been called *intergroup work.*

Community welfare organization is only one phase of a broader process usually called *community organization.* Community organization includes a variety of efforts by churches, schools, city planning agencies, and other organizations to improve the community. That aspect of the general process which is restricted to social work objectives is termed community welfare organization.

Need for Community Welfare Organization

Community welfare organization is necessary because there are community problems relating to social welfare. It is also necessary because at many points it is a logical outgrowth of social casework and social group work problems and perspectives. Thus a caseworker may deal with clients who are delinquent, in part, because of the lack of playground facilities. Group work agencies in the neighborhood may be overtaxed and not able to meet the problem adequately. The creation of new facilities would illustrate the way in which community welfare organization carries out operations which casework and group work cannot undertake independently.

Community welfare organization has grown, particularly in recent years. Even when social work itself was not a major enterprise, there was definite need for such a community organization. But within the last few decades social work itself has grown tremendously and the need for community welfare organization has increased at least proportionately.

The rise of government services in unprecedented volume and range has made new responsibilities for social workers in general and especially for community welfare organizers. In many localities there is today a need not only to co-ordinate the activities of the many voluntary social work agencies but also to organize them and the diverse government agencies into a coherent working arrangement. Much has been done to fashion an efficient welfare pattern in many places, but much more remains to be accomplished.

Community Welfare Organization Activities

There is no easy way of defining the activities of community welfare organization. Some of them are especially connected with social work administration; others are performed by caseworkers and group workers and are felt to be more related to their responsibilities than to those of the professional community welfare organizer. Some of the activities which can be identified as specific operations of community welfare organization are the following: co-ordination, joint financing, public relations work, research, planning, and the initiation of services.[4] These activities may involve an individual agency, or they may involve neighborhood councils, councils of social work agencies, state and regional councils of agencies, national agencies, and international agencies.

Community welfare organization in the past was carried on mainly by casework and group work agencies. In the recent decades, however, since the community needs in casework and group work have become extremely complex, agencies have come into existence which are primarily responsible for certain community activities. The trend at present seems to be toward the creation of a more professional operation of these community activities.

Uneven Distribution

Community welfare organization, like the other elements of social work, is presently unevenly distributed. In some cities there are strong community welfare agencies which assist the casework and group work personnel, but in most cities the possibilities of community action have not been realized and developed. In some instances such lack of development is due to the inadequacy of community leadership. Thus a community may see some irritating problems and may vaguely wish to co-operate toward their solution, but may not have anyone available to point the way. In other instances there is a lack of co-ordination of the various activities aimed at community betterment so that the resulting confusion causes frustration.

Position of Organizer

The growth and the quality of such welfare organizations are always dependent on the willingness of citizens to co-operate toward a common objective. Without co-operation the community welfare organizer can achieve neither his goals nor the community's. In this respect such an organizer takes a position in regard to his particular problems that the caseworker and the group worker take toward theirs. All three specialists within social work are dependent mainly on the desire of persons in need to make a self-initiated response to their needs, though the workers may seek to stimulate this response by their co-operative spirit and their willingness to view problems objectively. Further, they must recognise the values that the people hold and set up the aims of community welfare organization in accordance with these values. This attitude, important in the whole of social work, is fundamental to the community welfare organization process.

The community welfare organizer not only contributes his knowledge to his activities but also acts as a catalyst in stimulating and encouraging community action. While it is true that he does not force his opinions on the community (or groups within the community), nevertheless he cannot remain absolutely neutral. He does have attitudes formed on the basis of some reliable evidence, and, being involved in concrete situations, it is inevitable that he will be sharing those sentiments with others. His enthusiasm sets the pace for those he is leading. His willingness to serve the interests of the community leads others to imitate him. The community welfare organizer is not a passive instrument of groups concerned with community action but a practitioner of the art of democratic leadership. In other words, he allows the people to maintain the basic initiative in achieving their aims, but he still acts as participant leader.

Current Trends

At present there are a number of significant trends in community welfare organization. For example, professional workers are increasingly aware that their efforts necessarily fit into a community power structure of which they themselves are not always the masters. Professional efforts, therefore, are often dependent on a struggle or conflict which is as broad as the community itself and includes political, economic, religious, educational, and other forces.

There is evidence that citizen participation in the concerns and projects of community welfare organization is growing. Community welfare organization depends basically on citizen involvement, and the growing interest of laymen in the community gives community workers a hopeful outlook.

In the past, physical planning and social planning in the community have been relatively divorced. Currently they are often conjoined, as is evidenced, for example, in the field of public housing.

Perhaps the most promising development is the larger number of trained workers becoming increasingly available. It is apparent that in time the achievements of this corps of workers will have substantial effects throughout the nation. The number of workers required, however, far exceeds the present supply.

Auxiliary Processes

Social work, then, consists of three basic processes: social casework, social group work, and community welfare organization. Three auxiliary processes are social research, social administration, and social action. These are called auxiliary because they are employed to serve the basic processes; so far as social work is concerned, they do not have an autonomous function. All three assist social casework, social group work, and community welfare organization in achieving their fundamental goals.

Social Research

While it is true that social work in its entirety is allied to both the arts and the sciences, certainly it requires the development of as much scientific exactitude as possible in order that its skills may have a sound base.

Commonly, social workers undertake social research which is directly related to pressing and concrete problems within their immediate range of experience. For example, in Chicago a comparative evaluation of three different systems of case recording in two family agencies was conducted. Social workers are also interested in analysing their effectiveness in contributing to the welfare of those whom they serve, and several studies have been organized, especially of social casework and social group work, to determine the effectiveness of social work. In addition, wide use is being made by social workers of the findings of other researchers in such fields as health, recreation, psychology, and the social sciences.

Social Administration

Social administration, as an auxiliary social work process, aims both at performing specific social services in the community and at reformulating social policy on the basis of the experience of the social agencies. It is true that social administration is closely related to community welfare organization in certain of its activities and aims, yet the two have separate functions. Community welfare organization largely seeks to formulate the aspirations of communities by social education. Social administration seeks to realize the agreed-upon goals through existing services.

Social Action

Social work has always been concerned with social action, which is related to the ultimate objectives of casework, group work, and community welfare organization. An agency which does not have an active interest in community improvement, no matter what its primary tasks may be, is simply not meeting its full responsibility.

Social action is the opposite of individual action. It is engaged in by groups and is directed toward goals deemed desirable for the community. Social action connotes a marked degree of organization on the part of the groups involved in it. For example, there is usually a very conscious selection of objectives and a quite definite organization related to the achievement of the aims.

Social action may seek to modify the environment in ways which will not disturb its fundamental structure. Such actions are generally feasible simple because they meet with weaker resistance from certain elements of the community. But social action may also strive to effect a basic revision of the social and economic organization of the community for the benefit of all. Such actions are obviously difficult since they usually meet with the combined resistance of many elements within the community. It is impossible to say which type of social action is more effective, and the validity of whole philosophies of general action are involved in each. Generally, social action in social work consists of group efforts both to alleviate conditions which make social services necessary and to make positive social gains.

Basic Concepts of Social Work

Social work possesses its own distinctive body of knowledge, evolved over a long period of time. The current general concepts of social work are numerous and cannot be treated here in detail. Some, however, need to be mentioned and commented on briefly.

An Understanding of Individual and Collective Behaviour

Social work rests on the knowledge of human behaviour. For this understanding, it must rely for the most part on the social sciences, but other branches of learning also are of value. Social work looks to sociology to learn the effect of human culture on individual behaviour and the meaning of the individual's participation in his various groups. It turns to psychology to see the nature of mental and behavioural mechanisms and the details of personality make-up. Social work is interested in economics because material considerations of income, employment, and other economic factors influence the lives of persons. It finds that political science illuminates many of the problems of individuals. History has given social work perspective and detailed understanding of the background of current problems. Philosophy challenges social work with its presentation of the relevance of ideas and ideals, and literature enriches the understanding of the social worker. In the physical sciences, biology and related subjects provide the background for many activities of the social worker in matters of physical health. In all, there are few contributions in the arts, social sciences, and physical sciences which are not pertinent to social work. Anything which casts light on human nature—the requirements of social living, the inspiration of the past, the ideas which influence behaviour, and other related concerns—comprises part of the knowledge essential for the modern social worker.

General Background is Essential

To ask the social worker to understand all these fields of knowledge is obviously to ask the impossible. No person can be completely competent in even a subdivision of one of those fields. But the social worker should seek a full understanding of human behaviour and should learn to call on the experts in any field as required. Some subjects will be more important than others, but all have some place in the preparation of the social worker. Because a general background is so necessary for the social worker, it is appropriate that students not seek to specialise too early in their preparation. But try to gain the widest possible knowledge of human behaviour.

Yet eventually specialisation is necessary. Diverse fields of knowledge have made their contribution to social work practice, but there has also been knowledge gained about human behaviour from social work itself. The graduate schools of social work in large part impart the knowledge gained from this experience, as well as from the other fields of learning. They are able to relate this understanding to the specific tasks which are set before the social worker in practice. Beyond the graduate schools of social work lies the world of practice, where success depends on a sound understanding of individual and collective behaviour.

Development of Understanding

Social work rests on sound knowledge, but it does not end there. It is no ivory tower contemplation of human behaviour but, rather, an effort to educate individuals, groups, and communities in the ways in which they may garner strength to meet future as well as current problems. Information of the most reliable kind must be used, but education will include other factors as well. The knowledge of human behaviour which the social worker possesses must be shared with persons in need so that they will be better able to understand themselves and the problems they face. The development of understanding is a basic concept of social work.

The social worker uses his understanding of human behaviour selectively. Insights are given only when they are relevant. The knowledge which the worker conveys is determined by the maturity of the persons involved. Thus there may be many insights occurring to the social worker that are theoretically helpful; however, he must consider not only the problems but the persons as well. If a caseworker, for example, feels that a client has a problem because of his attachment to his mother, he may not be able to speak frankly about it because the client may not yet be prepared to receive any such suggestion.

Reliance on the Initiative of the Individual

The dynamics of the social work process are also based on the concept that the persons concerned should take the initiative in meeting their needs. This view has development out of social workers' actual experience. Earlier, social caseworkers thought that it was possible to direct others in ways to meet their problems, but they discovered that there are a number of factors which make such a supposition false. For one thing, it is now granted that no social caseworker can even pretend to know the "right" solution to every problem. Secondly, the worker realizes, as a result of his experience, that people do not usually like to take advice, and, when they do take advice, it is successful only in so far as it agrees with their preconceived ideas. It is most difficult for an individual to act on advice which runs contrary to his preconceptions of what is proper. Social workers have realized also that to make a decision for another places them under a certain responsibility, for they must assume the blame or praise which the consequences of that decision entail. No social worker wishes to jeopardise his status with his clients or with the public by accepting such responsibility.

These interpretations are essentially negative, and they miss the main point. The chief concern of social workers today is that individuals assume responsibility for themselves, since it is only by this means that people can grow in understanding and effectiveness. If the person is simply told what to do, the chances are that the next time he faces a problem, he will have to be told again. If, however, he tackles the particular problem himself, he will gain insight and practical experience that will stand him in good stead when future problems arise. Not until the person has made a genuine decision about what he wishes to do and how he wishes to do it has he understood the real meaning of growth. From the valuative point of view, the worker, impressed with the inherent dignity of people, does not feel it within his jurisdiction to encroach upon their prerogatives.

Limitations

Of course, there are limitations which the social worker must set on the right of the person to determine his own actions. The worker, as part of an organization (usually called a "social work agency"), must adhere to the terms for service which are set up by his organization. The help he can provide must always be predicated on that condition, and the person in need must abide by such limitations.

Then, too, social workers must limit the individual's use of initiative when such use would seem to work harm on the person himself or on others. Not all persons or groups have sufficient knowledge or emotional development to make their own decisions. We speak about the Plimsoll's mark on a ship—a load-line mark on the sides of vessels which indicates the limit of submergence allowed by law. Psychologically, all individuals and groups have their Plimsoll's mark, indicating the amount of responsibility and decision which they can really manage without running into danger.

Judicious Employment of Resources

Knowledge is perhaps the basic resource for helping people and is for this reason important to the social work process. In proportion as the social worker knows the resources of the community, he will be able to aid people. In casework, for example, a person with tuberculosis may come to an agency which is set up to carry on another specialised activity. Referring him to an agency which could be of help would be a definite service, and such referral requires a knowledge of the community's resources.

The social worker also uses certain resources which his agency makes available, according to its regulations. Thus a club in need of a meeting place may be provided with space by a settlement house.

Social work, then, is based on the judicious employment of

resources. Community facilities in many localities are almost unlimited. The combined resources of the religious, educational, industrial, medical, and political institutions within large cities are immense.

Quality of The Personal Relationship

Practically all that has been suggested in this section comes into focus when it is again realized that social work rests ultimately on the quality of the personal relationship between the worker and the client. This relationship, present in all forms of social work, constitutes the medium through which persons are able to develop themselves by using their knowledge and that presented by the worker. This relationship, in which resources are discovered and explored, increases the possibility that people will come to act on their own initiative.

Recognition of Client's Personality

The importance of the quality of the relationship is shown particularly in casework. In many cases the client will have contradictory feelings about his problem and a worker who makes judgments about the moral implications of the problem or the solutions made by the person in need will be of little help. But if the worker is able to accept the client, his values, his mistakes, his emotional contradictions, and his uncertain solutions with a calm assurance that deeply respects his dignity, there may come about a release of tensions, anxieties, guilt feelings, and fears which hitherto may have immobilised the person. Quite often in social casework the actual problems persons face are hardly more important to them than the feelings accompanying the problems. They may need the services of the social caseworker because none of those who have sought to aid them has accepted them and their problems as they actually are. Of course, it is undesirable—and probably impossible—for the social worker to make the person's problem and values his very own; it is always necessary and important for the worker to maintain professional standards.

While this discussion makes evident the importance of the relationship between the social caseworker and the client, the quality of the personal relationships in group work and in community welfare organization is equally important.

The five basic concepts in social work just discussed separately are in actual practice synthesised. This integration, of course, is not easy to achieve, and probably no one can secure it simply by understanding the components. Skill, developed through practical experience, is required.

Social Work as a Profession

One of the most serious problems in present-day social work is the shortage of adequately trained personnel. This shortage has been persistent and there are few signs to indicate that it will soon be relieved. It threatens the maintenance, nationally, of high social work standards and cripples at many points the advances social work might make.

Historically, social work has been very largely carried on by persons who volunteered their services for philanthropic activities. In many instances these were persons of independent means with considerable leisure time and social conscience. In the past even the operations of public welfare for the most part were dependent on volunteers.

New Understanding of Welfare Rights

Modern social work had its roots in feelings of charity or philanthropy but came in time to a new understanding of what is involved in helping others. It recognised that feelings of superiority or even genuine charity were not sufficient to meet the requirements of people in need. In many instances such attitudes wrought more harm than good. Gradually, social workers based their work more on philosophies contrary to that of philanthropy. They viewed society as a social organizm in which the welfare of the individuals affected the well-being of the whole. They saw that a realiztic application of democratic theory implied that everyone had certain welfare rights. The pursuit of happiness may be somewhat intangible, but it is a powerful sentiment when taken seriously. Calculations indicated, furthermore, that while social work is expensive to a society it is probably not so expensive as the lack of it. In addition, modern knowledge pointed the way to a more adequate understanding of personal and social failure and the means for overcoming them.

Under the impact of these and other factors, social work came to be considered a basic social requirement for successful and efficient social relations. In place of the philanthropist came the social worker.

While it is possible to claim that social work toady is not theoretically based on the spirit of philanthropy, it is not possible to claim that philanthropy has been entirely excluded. There are many persons, even today, who engage in social work from motives similar to if not identical with those of the philanthropist. But more and more, as adequately trained social workers are made available by the graduate schools of social work, the spirit of philanthropy is diminishing and a newer professional spirit is taking its place.

Rise of Schools of Social Work

The change from philanthropy to social work is mirrored in the rise of schools of social work. It was not until there was at least some basic redirection of philanthropy that social work as a subject to be taught in organized schools could come into existence. This occurred chiefly at the turn of the present century with the organization of the New York School of Social Work and other schools devoted to the education of social work personnel. Today there are sixty-two schools of social work, including seven in Canada. The accrediting body is the Council on Social Work Education.

The schools of social work are graduate schools. They are connected with colleges or universities, and they offer two general types of experience: course work and field work. Through these the schools are able to orient their students to the type of understanding required for successful practice and at the same time to provide supervised practical experience in suitable social work agencies. The training, normally leading to a professional master's degree, regularly requires two years of schooling beyond college. In many of the schools there are organized curriculums which prepare specifically for social casework, social group work, community welfare organization, social research, social work administration and social action.

Undergraduate preparation for social work is becoming more evident and responsible. The degree of preprofessional specialisation varies from college to college, but many colleges have one or more courses in the subject. These courses serve merely as an introduction to later and more extended study of social work in the graduate schools.

In 1952 the Council on Social Work Education was formed, with authority to speak and act for the profession of social work on all educational matters. The Council evolved from the merger of several organizations which had been concerned with some aspect of social work education. The Council is open to accredited graduate schools of social work, undergraduate departments offering a concentration in subjects related to social work, membership associations of practitioners, government and voluntary national employing agencies, and organizations and individuals having an interest in social work education.

Professional Associations

Prior to the twentieth century, social workers, under whatever name they went, did not enjoy sufficient status or specialisation to encourage significant organization. But with the rise of the various specialised practices of family service, child care, medical service (including mental health), probation and parole, leisure-time activities, fund raising, and so forth, and the increased acceptance by the community of the value of the social workers as a trained humanitarian, professional associations became possible.

In the last five decades a large number of specialised professional associations have been founded, from the National Social Workers' Exchange in 1917 to the Social Work Research Group in 1949. In 1955 the National Association of Social Workers came into existence as a result of three years of planning by the five professional associations and the two membership associations which up to that time had attracted professional social workers. There are presently about 23,000 individual members of the Association and 143 chapters, including one in Hawaii and one in Puerto Rico. Only about one third of the total number of practitioners are members since, in the main, only those social workers who have graduated from accredited schools of social work are eligible for membership.

National associations have been established by social work agencies which have some interest in common—for example, family service, settlements and neighborhood centers, community chests and councils, child welfare and sectarian services. A variety of national associations have been formed to foster interest in such areas of practice as probation and parole, and public welfare. The National Conference on Social Welfare, founded in 1873, exists to promote and share in the discussion of problems and methods identified with the field of social work and related fields. About 5,000 individuals and 1,200 organizations are members of the National Conferences.

Several labor unions are open to social workers. Two unions, the American Federation of Government Employees and the American Federation of State, Country, and Municipal Employees, have among their membership social workers employed in government agencies. Other unions are the United Public Workers of America (which includes public welfare workers), the United Office and Professional Workers of America (which includes workers from voluntary agencies), and the United Social Agency Employees.

Social work, like the other professions, requires a number of significant qualities from its practitioners: formal education, continuous study and growth, self-discipline, and high ethical standards. A good social worker has a warm interest in people of all kinds, faith in human beings, ability to follow projects through, ability to work with people, a cheerful disposition, intelligence, and a broad perspective. The social worker must be a person with superior intellectual equipment, a mature personal and social philosophy, and an ability to use his talents skillfully.

The social worker has an attractive profession. He gains satisfactions from contributing to the general well-being of mankind. He is constantly fascinated with the rich variety of the situations which he is called on to face. Although he will never be rich, he is virtually assured of economic security and an income adequate to a comfortable standard of living. He works in a democratic environment within his agency as well as within the community. As a professional worker he is challenged constantly to grow in knowledge and in effectiveness. Finally, in association with his colleagues the social worker finds himself in stimulating and satisfying relations with others who share his purposes.

Requirements for Positions

At present a degree from an accredited school of social work is the chief requirement for positions in the field. In public welfare an important requirement for many positions is qualification according to a merit system. There is also increasing discussion of the value of registration and certification of social workers on a state basis, similar to the requirement for lawyers and physicians. California passed legislation in 1945 along this line. in California, social workers who meet the requirements are entitled to use the title "Registered Social Worker" (R.S.W.). Indiana has at present a voluntary plan of registration.

Social Work and the Social Sciences

Interrelationships

The student who has been introduced to social work through reading this chapter can already piece together something of the relationships between social work and the larger fields of knowledge which make up the social sciences. Social work is not a branch of any of the sciences. In times past a somewhat special relationship existed between social work and departments of sociology in colleges and universities. In some institutions of higher learning, social work is regarded as a kind of applied sociology, and courses in social work are often taught within departments of sociology. Despite the historic ties between social work and sociology, however, it is apparent today that there is no exclusive relationship between the two. As suggested previously, social work draws its insight and skills from many fields of knowledge and sociology is only one of them. Social work depends on sociological knowledge for its practice but the dependence is not absolute or complete.

Social Work is a Profession

Social work differs from the various social sciences in that it is a profession. The word "profession" connotes skill or artistry. Social work has a definite ameliorative and creative function in society. It uses knowledge to meet human needs; in this sense it is an applied science as well. The augmenting of skill by knowledge is important for social work, but it is not the complete story of the development of professional competence. Knowledge, understanding, and skill—all are parts of the social worker's background.

References

Aptekar, Herbert, *Basic Concepts in Social Case Work* (University of North Carolina Press, Chapel Hill, 1941).

Bisno, Herbert, *The Philosophy of Social Work* (Public Affairs Press, Washington, D.C., 1952).

Cohen, Nathan, *Social Work in the American Tradition* (The Dryden Press, Inc., New York, 1958).

Cuber, John, and Harper, Robert, *Problems of American Society*, rev. (Henry Holt & Co., Inc., New York, 1951).

Dunham, Arthur, *Community Welfare Organization* (Thomas Y. Crowell Company, New York, 1958).

Fenlason, Anne, *Essentials in Interviewing* (Harper & Brothers, New York, 1952).

Fink, Arthur; Wilson, Everett; and Conover, Merrill, *The Field of Social Work*, 3rd ed. (Henry Holt & Co., Inc., New York, 1955).

Friedlander, Walter, *Introduction to Social Welfare* (Prentice-Hall, Inc., Englewood Cliffs, N.J., 1955).

Friedlander, Walter, ed., *Concepts and Methods of Social Work* (Prentice-Hall, Inc., Englewood Cliffs, N.J., 1958).

Hamilton, Gordon, *Theory and Practice of Social Case Work*, rev. (Columbia University Press, New York, 1951).

Hollis, Ernest, and Taylor, Alice, *Social Work Education in the United States* (Columbia University Press, New York, 1951).

Kasius, Cora, ed., *New Directions in Social Work* (Harper & Brother, New York, 1954).

McCormick, Mary, *Thomistic Philosophy in Social Casework* (Columbia University Press, New York, 1948).

Miles, Arthur, *American Social Work Theory* (Harper & Brothers, New York, 1954).

Proceedings of the National Conference of Social Work (published annually).

Robinson, Virginia, *Changing Psychology in Social Work* (University of North Carolina Press, Chapel Hill, 1930).

Russell, James, ed., *National Policies for Education, Health and Social Services* (Doubleday & Company, Inc., New York, 1955).

Stein, Herman, and Cloward, Richard, *Social Perspectives on Behaviour* (The Free Press, Glencoe, III., 1958).

4

Principles of Social Work

Social work principles are guiding assertions of statements that have come from experience and research. The objectives of social work can be fulfilled only within the framework of principles. Therefore, it seems necessary to deal with the basic principles which are guiding force for social work practice. Konopka has described the following principles of social work common to case work, group work and community organisation: (a) The social worker's goal is to enable clients or group members or groups as a whole to move toward greater independence and capacity for help; (b) The social worker must use the scientific method to prepare for action; fact finding (observation), analysis, and diagnosis in relation to the individual, the group, and the social environment; (c) The social worker must form purposeful relationships: this means a conscious focusing on the needs of his clients, group members, and communities, on their avowed purpose incoming for help; and on the implied—sometimes not fully conscious purpose; (d) The social worker must use himself consciously. This includes self knowledge and discipline in relationship but without the loss of warmth and spontaneity; (e) The social worker must understand the origins of his own value system and be able to handle it in relation to the value system of others; (f) The social worker must accept people as they are, without condemning all their behaviour. This involves deep understanding of his clients or group members as well as knowledge and identification of values regulating human/society; (g) The social worker must allow people to develop at their own pace and to choose their own point of departure without immediately imposing outside demands. However, he has responsibility for stimulating change; and, (h) Because of his infinite respect for the individual every social worker must help each individual to feel that he is an important and unique person who can contribute in some measures to the whole of society or to a part of it.

Clarke described the principles of social work as follows:

(a) All individuals have an 'inner' and an 'outer' life which interact. How people feel about their situation is perhaps more important than the situation.

(b) All behaviour have a history, the theory of determinism in psychic life.

(c) Most of the behaviour is not intellectually but emotionally motivated and is symptomatic of emotional needs.

(d) The family is a unit of interacting personalities and has the most important effects of any institution upon the degree of personality integration.

(e) Treatment of emotional difficulties is facilitated by understanding the history of the onset of the disturbance which may occur in infancy or early childhood.

(f) Treatment of emotional problems can be effective only in case the person who is emotionally disturbed wants it.

(g) Treatment of emotional problems is facilitated by the worker-client professional relationship; clients differ greatly in their capacity to use it.

Principles of Meaningful Relationship

This is the principle which differentiates social work and some other professions like surgery, medicine, law. In these professions a good interpersonal relationship is desirable for the perfection of the service, but it is not necessary for the essence of the service. But in social work, a good relationship is necessary not only for the perfection, but also for the essence, of the service in every setting. The quality of relationship is the corner stone of helping in social work.

The relationship is the medium through which the client is

enabled to state his problem and through which attention can be focussed on reality problems, which may be as full of conflict as emotional problems. Within the democratic frame of reference the professional relationship involves a mutual process of shared responsibilities, recognition of other's rights, acceptance of difference, with the goal, not of isolation, but of socialised attitudes and behaviour stimulating growth through interaction. A good relationship in social work is the professional one—one that serves the purpose (problem-solving) and includes those elements which will assist the purpose and exclude those elements which will not.

There are five ways in which the professional relationship differs from other social relationship. Social relationship are open ended in duration but the professional relationship ends when the problem is solved. The time that is spent with clients emerges from the needs of the clients and the objectives of professional involvement. Clients are seen in institutions or in their homes, they are not invited for tea or dinner. The focus of professional relationships is not mutual, but the client's needs. Wide aspects of client's life and feeling are examined and brought into pay. Rather than mutual, the relationship in social work is the helper and the helped.

Helping relationship is developed in social work by demonstrating the interests in client. Client is perceived as a 'real' person with spontaneity and capacity for responsiveness. He is convinced of the social worker's warmth as an individual, and conveys respect and caring for him. Social worker tries to understand what is happening in his mind. He tries to share the situations on an emotional plane. He helps the client to trust in his objectivity and feel secured as a worthwhile individual.

Principle of Self-Determination

Social responsibility, emotional adjustment and personality development are possible only when the person exercises his freedom of choice and decision. Today, one of the basic convictions of the social work profession is the client's right of self-determination. Under the ethics of the profession, the social worker must learn to accept others' distinct personalities with their own right of self-realisation and self-determination. Social Workers have always considered the client's right of self-determination to be very important, although there has been serious disagreement among social workers as to the interpretation of this principle. But the general opinion is that if this principle is not followed in its spirit, the social work practice will not be effective.

Social work believes that through the experience of the client worker relationship, the client will become mature and thus be able to deal with his life situation better. Obviously, when once the client has experienced thinking through a problem and arriving at a decision,he will become a less dependent individual. Social worker always tries to stimulate the client to think independently and rationally about his own problem situation and arrive at a decision for himself. It is social worker's responsibility to assess each client's ability to understand and analyse the forces operating in his problem situation and, on the basis of such analysis, determines what course of action he would like to follow. If the client wants stems from lack of knowledge, then it becomes the responsibility of the social worker to help the client to change his ideas. The goal and responsibility of the social worker is to help client move away from superstitious beliefs and primitive concepts. Social worker must guide the client to avail the facilities and opportunities available to them. He should not remain inactive and thereby fall to accomplish this task under the guise of misconceived notion of the principle of self-determination.

Social worker, following the principle of self-determination, helps the client see his problem clearly. He makes him acquanited with the resources available to deal with his problem. The client, using his inner resources and the resources of the community, grow in the potential to work out his own problems, to move along at his own speed and in his own way.

Principle of Acceptance

Social work accepts the individual as he is and with all his limitations. Not out of personal friendship but as a quality of life, it offers warmth, acceptance, and understanding, in quiet illustration of quality in human relations that might have values everywhere. Social work believes that acceptance is the crux of all help. It embraces two basic ideas—one negative and one positive. Social worker does not condemn or feel hostile toward a client because his behaviour differs from the approved one. He feels genuine warmth to form a bridge across which help may be given.

Acceptance is essential for the relationship. Except in social work service, the client becomes the subject of various social control mechanisms like legal condemnation, ostracism, avoidance, beletting, nagging by others or by his own conscious. These methods have failed. Therefore, social work offers the new approach of acceptance and it is out of this that a useable relationship grows.

The principle of acceptance implies that social workers must perceive, acknowledge, receive, and establish a relationship with the individual client as he actually is, not as we wish him to be or think he should be. It means that no matter how much the client may have distorted reality, no matter how much our perception of it may differ from him, or how greatly our values may differ from him, we must acknowledge and accept him as he is if we are to help him. This does not mean that we do not hope to effect change in him, but rather that the art of helping, like any other art, depends on accepting the material with which we propose to work as it actually exists, with its limitations as well as its potentialities. This principle could be restated by saying that in social work one begins where the client is and, at every stage in the helping process, relates one self to the client as he is at each given moment.

Principle of Communication

Communication is a two-way process. Most of the problems that give pain are precisely the problems of communication. When the communication is inadequate or insufficient, the problems appear either automatically or because of misunderstanding. There are three ways in which social worker conceives that clients may have problems of communication of feeling (i) The client may be confronted with a difficult practical problem which arouses such strong feeling in him that he is unable to cope effectively with the problem. (ii) The client may have certain feelings of apprehension or diffidence about asking for help. (iii) The client's feelings may be the main problem about which he is asking for help. Social worker always takes the responsibility of letting the communication culminate wholesomely between himself and the needy (individual, group or community). Communication of feeling is not only important to diagnose the problem but most of the maladies which befall a man may be removed by re-establishing full and goal directed communication between the sufferer and the social worker.

Communication is a royal road to the identification of social worker with his client. The function of social worker is principally to create an environment in which the client will feel comfortable in giving expression to his feelings. Client should feel that he can tell his story in his own way and, he may think that he is given due importance. The atmosphere includes the client's trust and confidence in the worker and the worker's acceptance of the client.

Each of the communication for the client depends on his physical comfort but his emotional comfort will be crucial. Some of the elements of emotional comfort are (i) time, (ii) warm, (iii) a focus on the client, (iv) skill to meet particular communication needs. Towle remarks that since we deal with people in time of trouble when they are 'in the midst of emotions that come from the major upheavals in life' it is important that we help them as they talk to us to express their emotions and that we try to understand the meaning which their problems have for them with a two fold purpose; first, that as they give expression to their feelings they may be relieved of pressures and tensions which have made the problem deeply disturbing.... Second, through understanding the person's feeling we, as representatives of an assistance agency, may though by sharing his problem afford each individual relationship which strengthens him.

Principle of Social Functioning

The principle of social functioning has been amply elaborated by Bartlett who thinks that in social work it is frequently used to refer to the functioning of people in their social roles and relationships, with emphasis on their relation to the environment it focuses not on the behaviour of people, but on the exchange between them and their environment... The concept of social functioning involves two sub-concepts—task and coping. Task implies the demands made upon people by various life situations. These demands may pertain to issue of daily living, family life, entry into the world of work or inability to do so, marriage and divorce, illness or financial difficulties and so on. The concept of coping 'emphasises the conscious, cognitive, and rational aspects of behaviour also. In such behaviour there is usually a direct engagement with the situation and coping can then be described as relative mastery of the tasks in the situation. When environmental demands outweigh the coping capacity of the individual he feels helpless and overwhelmed. Poverty, racial discrimination, lack of access to job, and other societal problems subject large segments of the population to stress, anxiety, deprivation, and alienation. Here, of course, major efforts for social change must be directed at environment. The common base of social work consists in a central focus on social functioning, an orientation towards people involved in the situation, use of social work values and the combined body of social work knowledge for working with individuals, group. Social organisations directly and through collaborative action.

Principle of Tuning Behaviour

Man has body, mind and intellect as three instruments of experiences through which life constantly pulsates. Through the physical body he perceives the world of objects; through the mind he experiences the world of feelings and through the intellects he comprehends his world of ideas. These three instruments have their own distinct characteristics in each person. Hence each person has unique personality. There is a need of tuning these instruments regularly so that he may have the proper experience of the world fully. Medical sciences and other sciences have gained the proficiency in tuning up the body and intellect of the human being but our modern society has not developed and popularised the science for tuning the mind. This is the basic drawback in our scientific developments and achievements. This vacuum is fulfilled by social work profession.

When one sees a challenge which is too much for him, he has a natural tendency to run away from facing it but this is not the solution of the problem. Wherever he will go, the same problem in another form will arise and obstruct him with a challenge. At such moments of mental agony, he always discovers a set of defences apparently eloquent and seeing convincing he knows that this action is cowardice; but his own thoughts supply him with weak excuses, slim reasons and false arguments to justify his actions. Thus, he goes through the convulsions of a psychologically broken personality.

It is not on one occasion that he misses the chance in life, fails in attempts and incurs disappointment but after some time every day-to-day problems seem threatening to him. If on that crucial moment he knows how to remake the inner personality whole and strong he could with a newly found confidence meet the problem successfully. He must learn how to unload himself, how to remove these crushing weights of his conscience. He must find a way to liberate his heart from unsuited chains gathered from the past, so that he may feel really free to live courageous life. Social work believes that through the tuning of the behaviour of an individual his problems can be minimised if not wholly solved and he feels and realises a new strength running in his body and mind.

Principle of Social Learning

Social learning is a pre-requisite to the changes that are inevitably involved in problem solving. Change in individual, group or community will depend on their capacity to learn new facts, attitudes and ways of behaving (capacity for social learning). Social learning is an essential part of social work practice whether the change is initiated by social action or individual therapy.

Goldstein identifies six stages of problem solving: (i) need of difficulty felt or observed, (ii) formulating, locating and defining the need or difficulty, (iii) surveying the information required around the need/difficulty, (iv) formulating possible solutions, (v) appraising the consequences of possible solution, (vi) testing, accepting and internalising the solution.

Goldstein suggests that the social learning processes which go with these stages are:

(i) Arousing and focusing attention and concern;
(ii) Organising and evaluating the problem and planning further action;
(iii) Searching for and acquiring new information and perceptions;
(iv) Experimenting with alternative means, behaviours and consequences;
(v) Rehearsing for action; verifying solutions and gains;
(vi) Acting, evaluating, incorporating the gains and (if necessary) reformulating the problem.

The social work contribution at each stage becomes:

1. Assisting the identification of the problem using guidance, raising motivation, evaluating, informing, defining;
2. Assisting the evaluation of the problem; helping to formulate plans, contributing to the assessment of capabilities and resources; promoting motivation, assisting role clarification and evolving commitment;
3. Stimulating an awareness of the salient practical psychological, social and transactional factors;
4. Enhancing problem solving efforts through sustaining, testing, evaluating, guiding and motivating;
5. Assisting the reality testing by providing opportunities for this; evaluating them, reinforcing and confirming the social learning experienced through them;
6. Assisting the reinforcement of the social learning through validating the capabilities of those involved, assisting the

analysis and implications of the outcomes of the process and planning for the termination of the process.

Principle of Confidentiality

Clients have the right of personal information about themselves in their relationship with a social agency during and following the process of obtaining service, a right which may be superseded in exceptional situations. Recognition of this right requires adherence to the following principles:

1. The client should be used as the primary source of information about himself and information sought from him should be limited to that which is essential to provide service.
2. Within the agency information regarding a client should be revealed only to those persons and to the extent necessary to provide service.
3. Other agencies and individuals should be consulted only with the client's consent and within the limits of that consent.
4. Only that information should be recorded and these records maintained that are essential to provide service and the use of records should be determined by agency function and the consent of the client.

It is a tribute to the reputation that social work has that clients frequently assume that they are talking in confidence and do not very often need specific reassurance about this. Confidentiality is essential for diagnosis and treatment. If clients feel that they cannot reveal material they think could be damaging, social worker will never get real picture of the problem. Confidentiality is essential to the development of truth, which is fundamental to our work and professional relationship. It is the base of having therapeutic relationship with the client and an important part of the model social workers offer to the clients. The obligation to keep confidentiality is stated in the professional code of ethics for social workers in these words, "Respect and safeguard to the right of persons served to privacy in their contacts with the agency, and to confidential and responsible use of the information they give.

There are three classes of confidential information: (i) the natural secret that information if disclosed, would defame the person, (ii) the promised secret promise is made not to reveal the facts, (iii) entrusted secret—it implies a contractual agreement which binds him not to reveal the fact. In Social Work confidentiality includes all the three types of secrets.

References

Barr, A.S. and Burton, W. H: *Supervision—Principles and Practices in the Improvement of Instruction.* Appleton Century Croft, New York, 1938, pp. 32-33.

White, Leonard D., "Meaning of Principles", *The Frontiers of Public Administration,* University of Chicago Press, Chicago, 1936, p. 21.

Konopka, Gisela, *Eduard C. Lindman and Social Work Philosophy*, The University of Minnesota Press, Minneapolis, 1958, pp. 193-194.

Hamilton, G., *Theory and Practice of Social Case Work* (second edition), Columbia University Press, New York, 1951, p. 27.

Tilbury, D.E.F., *Case Work in Context: A Basis for Practice*, Pergamon Press, New York, 1977, p. 109.

White, Helen C., Activity in Case Relationship, *The Family*, 14, 208-214, October 1933.

Robinson, Virginia, P: *A Changing Psychology in Social Case Work.* University of North Carolina Press, Chapel Hill, 1930, pp. 115-150.

Kraus, Hertha, The Role of Social Case Work in American Social Work, *Social Case Work* 31:9, Jan, 1950.

Howers, Swithum, "Social Work and Human Problem." *Social Case Work*, 35:190, May 1954.

Perlman, H. H., *Social Case Work*, Chicago University Press, Chicago, 1957, p. 67.

Moffett, J: *Concepts of Case Work Treatment*, 30. Routledge and Kegan Paul Ltd., London, 1968, p. 55.

Towle, Charlotte, *Common Human Needs,* American Association of Social Workers, New York, 1952, p. 9.

Varlett, Harrier M., *The Common Vase of Social Work Practice,* National Association of Social Workers, New York, 1970, p. 104.

Mirza, R. Ahmad, *Social Case Work in Horizons of Social Work*, Jyotsna Publication, Lucknow, 1986, p. 75.

Goldstein, Howard, *Social Work Practice: A Unitary Approach,* University of South Carolina Press, New York, 1973.

Tilbury, D.E.F., *Case Work in Context: A Basis for Practice*, Pergamon Press, New York, 1977, pp. 39-40.

American Association of Social Workers: Principles of Confidentiality in Social Work, AASW, Washington, DC 1946, p. II.

Tilbury, D.E.F., *Case Work in Context, op. cit.* p. 85.

"Code of Ethics", In *Standards for the Professional Practice of Social Work*, AASW, New York, 1951, p. 5.

5

Social Work: Values and Tradition

Every profession of human behaviour has some values and on the basis of these values it achieves its objectives. Social values have significant role as they maintain social equilibrium, unity in behaviour, psychological foundation of life, determination of role and evaluation of social events and problems.

Kohs has divided the values of social work into primary and secondary. He described ten values as the primary values of social work, these are:

(i) The worth and dignity of man.
(ii) The capacity of human nature to achieve full human potential.
(iii) Tolerance of differences.
(iv) Satisfaction of basic human needs.
(v) Liberty.
(vi) Self-direction
(vii) Non-judgmental attitude.
(viii) Construction social cooperation.
(ix) Importance of work and constructive use of leisure.
(x) Protection of one's existence from the dangers caused by man and nature.

Konopka has enumerated only two primary values of social work:

1. Respect for every person and the right of each person to the fullest development of his/her potential.

2. Mutual dependence of individuals and responsibility towards each other according to their abilities.

Friedlander has enumerated four primary values of social work:

1. Conviction of the inherent worth, the integrity and the dignity of the individual.
2. The right to determine himself, what his needs are and how they should be met.
3. Firm belief in equal opportunity for all, limited only by the individual's capacities.
4. Social responsibilities towards himself, his family and his society.

Misra, R. Ahmad has described 12 primary values of social work:

1. Social work believes in the redistribution of economic and political power in more egalitarian manner.
2. Social work believes in the social feasibility of production and in the subordination of production to social purposes.
3. Organized labour makes a positive contribution to community life and should be accepted as constructive rather than a destructive force.
4. Social work believes that economic roles should not be assigned by ascription, or according to status, but by the standard of achievement.
5. Social work believes in removing economic imbalance by plugging the sources of black money, protecting the public sector from the onslaughts of the private sector and taking sincere and honest measures for the establishment of socialistic state.
6. Social work believes in social planning that is organized for the welfare of the great masses of people in a socialist economy.
7. Social work believes in the service state which is oriented

to the well-being of everyone and makes the acceptance of human conservation as the democratic task.

8. Social work believes in distributive values as against aggregate value.
9. Social work believes in social justice.
10. Social work believes in distributive justice which implies that the rewards should commensurate with the distribution made by an individual to society.
11. Social work believes in religious, political and scientific deencapsulation.
12. Social work believes in modernization.

The curriculum study of Council of Social Work Education presents values of social work in a schematic form:

1.	Importance of the individual	—	Interdependence of all individuals at all times.
2.	Consideration for and acceptance of difference	—	Social utilization of and provision for variability
3.	Self-determination right to select own life style	—	Consideration for self-determining needs and desires of others.
4.	Self-help	--	Obligation to assist others in developing or recovering this capacity; non-blaming acceptance when self-help is not possible
5.	Common needs of man	—	Recognition of similarities as well as differences
6.	Acceptance of every person	—	No condoning of behaviour which hurts others.
7.	Right to equal participation	—	Granting participation to others
8.	Right to protection of body and intellect	—	Obligation not to injure or deprive others
9.	Freedom	—	Limits

10. Change-Process-Growth	—	Preservation of the effective; stability; security; social direction through accepted norms.
11. Validated knowledge	—	Intuitive speculation, insight.

Herbert Bisno has distributed social work values over four areas—nature of the individual, the relations between groups, groups and individuals and between groups, functions and methods of social work, social maladjustment and social change.

I. Values Relating to Individual

The dominating concepts in early years of social work development were individualization and the friendly visitors. Individualization was applied not only to the charity organization worker, but showed up in many other areas of social work. The division of the large body's club into small groups, the abandonment of barrack method in homes and hospitals and reformatories, and the creating of new institutions with many small houses instead of one big one, illustrate the present tendency. Individualization was thought essential as it was believed that "healing comes by the touch, that men are saved not in masses, but one by one, and that every one saved must be saved by an individual whose own heart is filled with love, and who is able to communicate to another the grace which he himself has received.

The welfare of the individual has always been a central value of life, the individual has always counted. In the impersonal, anonymous, and competitive culture which dominates our life today, however, the individual has been progressively forgotten. Today individuality lies in economic prestige, and economic prestige is possible for only a fortunate few. He is thus caught in a veritable rat race, a competitive struggle for economic status and social prestige in which both the successful and the failure individuals suffer anxiety and strain. But for the proper development and growth of the society we have to take into account the welfare of the individual and his individuality as first goal. Whether one thinks of social welfare programmes or of society at large, it is clear that ways must be found to balance the needs of the organization with the integrity of the person. Provisions for the effectiveness of the group must be considered along with measures to give play to the creativity of the individual.

Social work is committed, in this evolving scene, to encourage implementation of needs in manner consistent with concern for individual dignity, legal rights, democratic institutions, and that maximum self-realization of people which does not infringe on the rights of others.

Cohen has expressed the values in relation to individual in the following ways:

1. Help the individual, the group, or the community to help himself or itself.
2. Begin where the individual, the group or the community are and work at meaningful place.
3. Focus on the individual, the group or the community as well as on the problem.
4. Take into account the stage of development.
5. Function with flexibility.

American Association of Social Workers identified the following values in connection with the individual:

1. Firm faith in the dignity, worth and creative power of the individual.
2. Complete belief in his right to hold and express his own opinions and to act upon them, so long as by so doing he does not infringe upon the rights of others.
3. Unswerving conviction of the inherent in alienable right of each human being to choose and achieve his own destiny in the framework of a progressive, yet stable, society, on the basis of the different thoughts discussed above we find the following main values in relation to individual:

1. Every individual has his worth.

2. He has every right to get respect.
3. Individual reacts in totality.
4. Internal and external conditions of each individual are different, therefore, their behaviours differ.
5. Individual has right to develop his personality according to his choice.
6. Individualizations is essential for his concrete help.
7. Personal values i.e. thoughts, feelings, beliefs, are important to be studied.
8. Individual has right of self-determination.
9. Individual rests with total environment.

II. Values Relating to Problem

Problems are needs not being adequately or acceptably met by the needs-meeting facilities of our society. An imbalance is apparent in the person's relationship with the world around him. Meaning of the problem has three dimensions: personal, group and cultural meaning—in both objective and subjective terms. It is important to acknowledge these dimensions since problems come not so much because of their severity, but because of the degree of social disturbance created within these dimensions (for example not the 'strength' of the phobia but what it is of; not the mild dementia, but the reactions of family and neighbourhood). It is as much the interactions effects which trouble people as the 'problem' as such.

Problematic situation arises due to many factors, but where psychological factors have a bearing on problem areas (in the client or others) it is often crucial to determine whether these represent a steady state (ongoing behaviour patterns), a reaction for stress, or attributable to a transitional developmental phase (adolescence, climacteric, for example). But it is also important not to think of psychological factors merely as a list of defects contributing to the problems, nor even as a 'list of strengths' which might be utilised in coping with the problem areas (though they are both) but as a complexity in an international situation which will have a bearing on the total social work process.

The interactional impart route can travel through any combination of the above, in either direction, for example, a well individual may belong to a well family, set in well group, but that group is set in a sick society. A well society may have an interactional impact on a sick group, but that group contains well families and well individuals.

Problem should be viewed not only as the effect of a sequence of preceding events and conditions but also as live cause of emerging problems. Like the person in himself, his problem is not merely the product of the past. Because it is making itself felt now, in transactions with other persons and objects, experienced as stress within the persons' physical, psychological, and social system, it is an active factor in shaping the next hours and days of the person's life.... a problem coped with today or set on the way to resolution — raises the person's level of hopefulness in regard to his chances of coping and being satisfied. These explain why helping a person identify and center on some problem that he feels, sees and experiences in its present immediacy may cut into the problem's vicious spiral and offer him incentive to invest further problem-solving effect.

Social work believes in the following values relating to problem:

1. A problem arises when an individual fails to reach his objective through the learned habits and methods. Therefore, social work believes in the changing of the behaviour patterns and methods of approaching the objective.
2. Problem either effects social functioning or is affected by social functioning. Social worker believes in the improvement of or strengthening social functioning of the client.
3. Problem has many side effects and creates many other problems.
4. Problem has multifarious effect on human life.
5. Internal and external factors of the problem not only happen together but may be a cause of one another.
6. Everybody feels problems. The person who solves these problems, does not become 'client.' Therefore, social work

believes that the problem solving capacity may be increased in the individual.

III. Values Relating to Relationship

Relationship is the social worker's responsible and disciplined use of himself in working with an individual or a group. In this relationship, he applies his professional knowledge and skills guided by the ethical principles and by his ability to develop empathy and trust. The psychological understanding of his client as an individual or a group gives him the necessary sensitivity and inventive capacity to make this relationship constructive.

The flesh and blood (in social case work) are in the dynamic relationship between social case worker and the client, child or foster parent; the interplay of personalities through which the individual is assisted the desire and achieve the fullest possible development of his personality.

Within the democratic frame of reference the professional relationship involves a mutual process of shared responsibilities. Recognition of the other's rights, acceptance of difference, with the goal not of isolation, but of socialised attitudes and behaviour stimulating growth through interaction.[34]

Hollis distinguishes two types of relationship the basic and the special; the basic being the warmth, concern, etc. The worker brings all relationships coupled with our confidence in our ability to help and function as worker. This basic relation may have certain similarities in quality with some social relationship; but the special relationship has a particular therapeutic element which we bring to bear in cases here this is needed.

Relationship is the context within which problem solving takes place. It is the catalytic agent in which the under-levels of the personality of unconscious shifts and changes in the sense of trust, the sense of self-worth, the sense of security, and the sense of linkage with other human beings.

Social work believes in the following values in connection with the relationship:

1. The person who comes for help to the agency is accepted by the worker as an individual, not as a 'case.' The relationship is established on this basic assumption.
2. Client is accepted as he is. Social worker does not have subjective feelings about him.
3. The relationship is established in such a way that the feelings of the client are not hurt. He has right of self-expression.
4. The relationship is established on the basis of equality. There is no feeling of subordination in the client.
5. The basis of relationship is love, cooperation, sympathy and help.
6. Through relationship client is stimulated and insight is developed.
7. Relationship is considered positive or therapeutic when communication begins on the emotional and intellectual level between the client and the worker.
8. Social worker uses relationship as a tool for the solution of the psycho-social problems of the client.

IV. Values Relating to Social Agency

Social agencies are instruments of the people. They represent the organized efforts of individuals or group of people to meet specific human needs which arise out of social conditions. They meet specific, recognisable, visible needs that are agreed upon as important for a substantial number of persons. The social agency makes use of professional social work skills in providing programmes designed to meet these needs. Social agencies move intelligently for affecting culture as well as problem solving instruments.

It is primarily to the agency that the client turns for help; the worker is a part of a range of resources offered by the agency (though many of these other resources may be channelled through the worker). It is the agency which determines the focus of the work, and shapes it through resource provision, policy determination, etc., so it is essential that the worker understands it and his position within it.

The nature of the service may be public or voluntary. In a public service, availability is usually to all who come within certain categories. Voluntary agency takes up those obligations it chooses in terms of category and numbers within the category. The setting of agency may be primary or secondary. A primary agency is one with social work adjectives in which social workers have the primary professional place. But in secondary setting of social work agency social work has secondary place. It uses social work skills to deal with the psycho-social problems of clients. Such psycho-social problems may be grouped as:

(i) Problems of causation: Types of problems arise in hospital settings. Patients have psychosomatic complaints. It gives an opportunity for the social worker to work in hospitals.
(ii) Problems of incorporation: There are a number of problems which create hindnces in properly utilising the agency resources. Social worker helps in such situations.
(iii) Problems of discharge on transfer: Social work ensure that the work of the agency is not vitiated.

It is the primary agency which determines for the worker who he helps, in which way, on what conditions, with what resources, and where the worker's help fits in with other help needed by or being given to the client.

The service which the agency offers to its clients influences the worker's acceptance of the client. Since acceptance means perceiving and dealing with the client as he is, the extent to which the client is helped to reveal himself is determined by the service offered by the agency. Case workers conceive of the agency as a social system exhibiting processes that can train or support helping procedures. The agency is more often seen as an object of change or even as an instrument for change.

Use of agency function as an integral part of social work skill offers a "difference" to the client or group who may come to an agency full of his own problems, or need, or intent, and full of projection that the agency will or will not be well disposed and helpful to him.

The agency must have democratic basis of organization and administration, so that the individuals and groups have an opportunity to share in the important affairs of the agency in so far as they are capable.

On the basis of the above discussion we find the following important values in relation to social agency:

1. The nature of social agency is always welfare and humanitarian.
2. The proper use of agency resources may solve the problem. There are a number of agencies for the welfare of the needy but they are ignorant.
3. Social agency is competent in dealing with maladjustment problems.
4. Problem can only be solved with the help of agency through using its service and opportunities.
5. The objectives of the agency are fulfilled through programmes.
6. Effectiveness of the agency is based on the worker's knowledge of human behaviour and power to influence the clients.
7. The agencies which have faith in democratic values, may use social workers services.
8. Social agencies generally help those individuals who voluntarily wish to solve their problems and have desire to become self-dependent.

V. Values Relating to Social Work Practice

(i) Social work believes in scientific knowledge and scientific practice. Since the beginning of society there had probably been some degree of concern for the man in distress. It might have depended on religious, moral, political and economic considerations of the era. Charity, did not, however, become scientific until the late nineteenth century, Scientific philanthropy, derived from earlier European sources, took not in a general climate of optimism which included the belief that science would cure all social evils and lead to unlimited progress. The Charity Organization Movement was introduced in the late 1870 as a means for making alm giving scientific, efficient and preventive. Charity Organization Societies developed and spread rapidly and made social work as their offspring, became the twentieth century heir of he movement's scientific aspirations. To make charity scientific, mary Richmond began her almost regular attendance and frequent contributions to that body. She is credited with laying the foundation for a scientific approach to social work, and achievement marked by the publication of social diagnosis.

(ii) Social work has humanitarian attitude. It offers both social treatment and psychological education depending on human needs. It considers the worth of the individual being a basic value, and believes that the individual should not be sacrificed for the state. Probably the commitment to the objectives of social work had never been better stated than Frankin D. Roosevelt's Four Freedoms: freedom from want, freedom from fear, freedom of speech and freedom to worship. Social work accepts the basic human needs of all children, of all persons, irrespective of class and caste.

(iii) Social work methods believe in democratic behaviour. The purpose of social work is, on one hand, to strengthen the individual and, on the other, to provide for such arrangement in society so that he may receive maximum opportunities to realise all that is best in him. It is in the background of social philosophy of justice, equality and fraternity that the methods of social work have been developed by the practitioners.

(iv) Social work believes in distributive value. A distributive value is one which is to be maximised for each individual, through not necessarily for the society as a whole. Social work believes in social justice. It gives equal opportunity to all to develop ones personality in the way one likes approved by the society. It further gives attention to the under privileged to help them to face the challenges of life. Provisions have been made for reservations in services and education and other facilities to the Scheduled Castes and Tribes. In short, it can be said that social work directs about the necessary conditions for creating social and economic rights.

(v) Social work believes in distributive justice. Social work believes that the rewards should be given on the basis of individual achievement. This belief requires a social structure where there is not exploitation of masses and where there are no parasites to hold the society at random by their unconscionable mechanization, that are devoid of any constructive contribution to society.

(vi) Social work believes not only in the solution of the problems but also in social development. Social work seeks two things for people economic well-being and the deeper source of happiness, that is, self-realization. The aim of social work is.... to remove social injustice, to relieve distress, to prevent suffering and to assist the weaker members of society to rehabilitate themselves and their families and, in short, fight the five giant evils of (i) physical want, (2) disease, (3) ignorance, (4) squalor, (5) idleness. These evils are the great hinderances in the process of social development.

(vii) Social work believes in modernization. It believes to develop those characteristics in man which Alex Inkless has described a modern man, i.e., openness to new experience, readiness for social change, disposition to form or hold opinion on larger number of issues, measure of information, time orientation to the present or the future rather than to the past, efficiency i.e. the belief that man can learn how to exert considerable control over his environment, orientation towards long run planning both in public or private life, calculability or trust i.e., more confidence that this world is calculable and that the people and institutions around him can be relied upon to meet their obligations and become prepared to trust the stranger, valuing of technical skills and take it as the basis of distribution of reward, educational and occupational aspirations, and awareness of and respect for the degnity of others.

(viii) Social work believes that economic objectives can be achieved through social planning. Social planning is a process of land reform reduction of inequality, equitable distribution of income, enlarged welfare and social services between people and regions, more employment, integrated plans and policies. There are three main objectives of social planning, (a) Improvement in economic system, (b) Adjustment on the basis of equality, and (c) social and political changes in time of need.

References

Bisno, Herbert, *The Philosophy of Social Work,* Public Affairs Press, Washington, D.C. 1952.

Blestek, F.P., *The Case Work Relationship,* Loyola University Press, Chicago, 1957, p. 81.

Bonner, Hubert, *Social Psychology,* An Interdisciplinary Approach Eurosia Publishing House, New Delhi, 1975, p. 411.

Friedlander, A.W., *Concepts and Methods of Social Work,* Prentice Hall of India, Ltd., New Delhi 1977, p. 1.

Friedlander, W.A., *(ed.)*: *Concepts and Methods of Social Work,* Prentice Hall, Inc., Englewood Cliffs, N.J., 1958, 17.

Friedlender, A.W., *op. cit.*, pp. 2-6.

Green T.F., *Schools and Communities: A Look Forward,* Harward Educational Review, 39; 1969, pp. 201-212.

Hamilton, G., *Theory and Practice of Social Case Work,* Columbia University Press, New York, 1951, p. 27.

Hodges, George D.D., "The Progress of Compassion" Proceedings; *National Conference of Charities and Corrections, 27th Annual Session,* Topeka, Kans, George H. Ellis, Boston, 1900, p. 10.

Johnson, H.M., *Sociology:* A Systematic Interpretation 1961, p. 49.

Kahn, Alfred J., *op. cit.*, p. 17. Cohen, Nathan E: "Reversing the

Process of Social Disorganization," in Kahn, A.I. (ed.), *op. cit.*, pp. 139-140.

Kahn, Alfred, J., (*ed.*) *Issues in American Social Work,* Columbia University Press, New York, 1959, p. 23.

Kohs, S.C., *The Roots of Social Work,* Association Press, New York, 1966, p. 62.

Kohs, S.C., *The Roots of Social Work,* Association Press, New York, 1966, p. 64.

Konopka, Gisela, Edward C. Lindeman. *Social Work Philosophy,* The University of Minnesota Press, Minneapolis, 1958, p. 178.

Lee, Dorothy, Culture and the Experience of Values, in *New Knowledge of Human Values,* Maslow, A.H. (*ed.*). Harper and Brothers, New York, 1959, p. 165.

Milford Conference Report: *Social Case Work;* Genesis and Specific American Association of Social Workers, New York, 1929, pp. 29-30.

Mukerjee, R.K., *The Frontiers of Social Science (ed.)* B. Singh, Macmillan Company London, 1956, p. 3.

Nee, Robert H., Robert, W. Roberto; *Theories of Social Case Work,* pp. 148-149.

Quoted by Cora Kasius. *New Directions in Social Work,* Harper and Brothers, New York, 1954, p. 40.

Richmond, Mary: *Social Diagnosis,* Russell Sage Foundation, New York, 1917.

Singh, Surendra and Soodan, K.S.: *Horizon of Social Work, op. cit.,* p. 59.

Tulbury, D.E.F., *Case Work in Context — A Basis for Practice,* Pergaman Press, New York, 1977, p. 101.

Wines, Frederick, H., "The Healing Touch" Proceeding' National Conference of Charities and Corrections, 27th Annual Session, *op. cit.,* p. 25.

Youndahl, B.E., "Social Work as a Profession," *Social Work Year Book,* Russell Sage Foundation, New York, 1949, p. 478.

6

Social Work and Social Welfare

The spirit of service or of rendering help to fellow human beings, on which the superstructure of modern social work rests, was well-known in India from very ancient times. It was realised that holding together of human beings in a society was not possible without perpetual give and take and small or big acts of sacrifice. The *Gita* states: "The Prajapati, the Creator, having in the beginning of creation created mankind together with sacrifice stated that by mutual sacrifice and mutual help they would grow, prosper and multiply. This was to be the milch cow. of their desires which yielded all desired object".

The word 'Yajna' is here taken as any social, national or personal activity to which the individual is ready to devote himself entirely in a spirit of service or dedication. Thus, only when people came forward to work in the spirit of co-operation and dedication can a community thrive. Sacrifices were of great importance in the inner and outer life of people in ancient India. Their value has been great in the evolution of the religious and philosophical thought of the Indo-Aryans. In this form of worship the worshipper renounced his claim to things by placing them in the fire. At the end of sacrifice, liberal gifts were made to priests and others sometimes amounting to the whole of the belongings. By these renunciations he became prepared for the greater renunciation afterwards of home and hearth and everything that bound him to things of the earth. It is true that the individual resorted to renunciation for entering into the bliss of self-realisation. This, however, provided him with the opportunity of giving something of his own to others. It was also seen that even after renouncing the world the noble souls did work for the betterment of humanity. The hermitages were the centres of learning where pupils assembled for acquiring knowledge in various branches of arts, science, philosophy and theosophy from high minded teachers.

The vast majority of teachers in ancient India consisted of householders. They regarded it as their duty not to refuse any qualified student even if the latter was not in a position to pay any honorarium owing to his poverty. At times the teachers were expected to arrange for boarding, lodging and clothing of their students if the latter were not in a position to meet the expense. This is borne out by the fact that until recently the 'tol' (school) teachers in Bengal used to make arrangements for feeding (apart from providing lodging facilities) the students in their care even when they were not able to pay the tuition fees.

Again, we find instance of householders regarding it as their duty to offer food to the student who came to their doors for alms. The rule of begging was laid down for the student in order to teach him humility and to realise that it was through the help of the members of the society that he was able to go through the education. All this does indicate the attitudes of members of the ancient Indian society to help their fellow beings to work towards, Kalyan, Mangal or Bhadram which for lack of an appropriate English equivalent may be translated as social welfare. The above mentioned Sanskrit words have a far richer content than the English word welfare or even social welfare. They imply all round 'good.' Ancient seers knew that the body, mind and spirit formed distinguishable aspects of an inseparable unity. Human nature was all of a piece and the unification of the three was the true aim of Mangal or Kalyan (Social welfare). Sound health was necessary for perfect manhood. So was well developed social and economic organisation for human living. But these were not the ends of themselves. The goal of man was to convert narrow individualism controlled by annual impulses of selfishness, lust and greed to self-actualising universalism devoted to good of the whole.

Kathopanishad classifies all actions with reference to their fruits into sections. There are actions which contribute to some immediate passing material gain (preyas) i.e., pleasant while there are others which contribute in the long run to our self-development and self purification (shreyas) i.e. good. That which is good need not necessarily be always pleasant although there are pursuits which are good and also pleasant. A great emphasis was laid on working for the Kalyan of society which implied a well-developed social conscience. Even if a person did not need to work for his personal material benefit, he was expected to work for the good of others. The Gita strongly mentions that the leaders of the society have a special responsibility for the welfare of the people. It is their duty to discharge it.

The discharge of one's duty was regarded as something that led to the Mangal or Kalyan of the doer, too, besides ding good to the person for whose benefit it was rendered. The latter, it is evident, will have some benefit accruing out of the discharge of duty. The benefit may be material or spiritual or both. What happens to the person who discharges the duty? According to Indian thought, this discharge of duty is in the long run beneficial to its author also, because it leads to his self-development and self-purification. Man has in him good and evil qualities and if he fails to develop the higher impulses of charity, mercy, love etc., he lowers his own self—he does not live up to the innate dignity of a human being. The prevalence of this idea can be noted in the day to day life of an Indian, specially the unsophisticated one. If a householder for instance, refuses to give food to a person (Atithi) who arrives at his door-step and asks for the same it is regarded as something Amangal (bad) arising due to lack of self-development and self-purification on the part of the doer. This, at times, has been interpreted in terms of some evil befalling the householder i.e. Tangible harm to himself. Usually people, today , overlook the distinction, between shreyas and preyas and recognise preyas as the true welfare or the only goal of true welfare, while in olden days due emphasis was laid on shreyas.

In the said context, let us examine our traditional pattern of inviting people to attend a function such as wedding which is regarded as a sacred affair. The head of the household in which the wedding is to take place invites his relatives and friends to attend the wedding for blessing the married couple. The blessings are considered to have a spiritual value. The host family is thankful to the guests for giving their blessings and dining in their abode. Guests are, however, not expected to express thanks to the host for inviting them to lunch or dinner. The assembling of guests with all good wishes for the couple, their taking of food in his house and bringing in a happy atmosphere on the occasion have a spiritual meaning for the host. Therefore, he is obliged to the guests for creating this blissful atmosphere. As has been stated above, the concept of Kalyan or welfare in Ancient India was not restricted to the physical or material welfare alone. Hence we find instances of individuals or groups catering to varied needs of fellow human beings, such as, getting wells or ranks dug up in those areas where there was a shortage of these; establishing schools for education of children, dharmashalas, i.e. halting places for travellers, hospital for the sick, temples, monasteries, centres for philosophical discussions for seekers of spiritual knowledge, etc.

In places of pilgrimage, like Mathura, Vrindavan and Kashi still find poor aged people, or poor windows, who in view of the maintainance by richer individuals, sing holy songs in temples or on the bank, holy rivers. The maintenance is not always given in the spirit of giving' just to feed these people but with the idea that by singing religions songs they create an atmosphere of bliss (Kalyan) for people who reside at these places and for themselves. Apart from giving financial assistance to the needy, the State also provided facilities for work to people. Kautilya's *Arthashastra* states "Those women who do not stir out of their houses (anishkasinyah), those whose husbands have gone abroad, and those who are crippled or girls may, when obliged to work for subsistence, be provided with work (spinning out threads) in due courtesy through the medium of mind servants of the weaving establishment[7] Such in establishment was in charge of a superintendent who used to be a State employee.

Kalidasa, the great national poet, has given the criterion of a welfare state as follows:

> *It was only for the welfare of the people that he (king Dilipa) took taxes from the people' as is the case with the sun which draws moisture from the earth only to shower it back thousand-fold in the form of beneficient rain.*

It is not possible to say how far all the ancient kings regarded it their duty to provide for the welfare of their people. However, there is enough evidence from Indian literature to indicate that a good king did try to take genuine interest in the welfare of his subjects (handicapped or otherwise) and that the society expected it of him.

From what has been stated above it seems that many kings on ancient India realised that prevention was better than cure. The emphasis was on enabling normal people to meet the normal contingencies of life, such as, unemployment, death of the breadwinner, sickness etc., and thus on preventing them form falling into distress by seeing that financial assistance, employment and guidance were available when the contigency arose. The State developed work projects to give employment to people and also operated shelter homes, hospitals and relief centres to meet the varied needs of the handicapped. In other words, sensible kings tried to avoid social casualties. Their attempt was not just to pull people out of the swamp but to drain it too. It is evident that many people who today at some stage become the client of a professional social worker would not have needed his help at all had there been a sound provision in the society to help the normal person to meet the contingencies of life.

The ancient Indian society met the said need to a great extent by inculcating a high sense of duty in its members which enabled them to provide various types of (social) services, as a group or as individuals, for the members in distress. For instance, village elders were respective and in complicated family problems or others their advice was sought and accepted. Counselling was available even without the existence of a counselling bureau.

It is difficult to say how many people discharge their duty due to the fear of public opinion or sanctions provided by external codes and how many discharged it due to inner sanctions. Duty is seldom sweet. Only when love greases its wheels that it runs smoothly. Otherwise there is a likelihood of continuous friction. Following an external code without much of an inner sanction is painful, no doubt. But the acuteness of pain is minimised when many others are found to be following the same code. Again in a society where emphasis was laid not on rugged individualism but on fostering individuality (developing an giving expression to potentialities) within the limits of the law and ethical codes, the opinion of the public would serve as a strong deterrent against swerving from the path of well-being of others.

However, it needs to be stated here that Indian life fostered inner sanctions for the discharge of duty. Indian philosophy is not confined to the function of reason and the art of argument. It is not divorced form life. Indian philosophers have presented that man has four-fold aspirations—*Dharma, Artha, Kama* and *Moksha.* To experience a level of consciousness that is beyond the pale of time, space, change and sorrow (*moksha*) is the greatest single aspiration of man. The Indian philosophy has always proclaimed that man is essentially a spiritual being. His physical possessions *(artha)* and physical satisfaction (*kama*) are not the only objects to be sought by him. They have their place and are necessary for the art of human life., Life is not possible without passions, instinctive drives and emotions. *Artha* and *kama* form the physical basis of life. But those two values have to be regulated by *Dharma,* i.e., moral good. *Dharma* is regulative value. It regulates activities towards the attainment of *moksha* which is an end in itself.

Again, one has often heard people commenting as to how in a country like India, where a major emphasis of life from very early stags has been on *Tyag* i.e. renunciation, people could take to individual or group efforts for social welfare. One often hears remarks to the effect that ancient Indians encouraged inactivity and gave religious sanction for the poor and the miserable to remain in the condition and never to improve their lot. This is, however, a wrong interpretation of the ancient ideology. Indian thinkers have emphasised work because they knew that society could not progress without action. Gita says: "As the ignorant man acts from attachment to actin, O Bharata, so should the wise act without attachment, wishing the welfare of the world." So the difference lies in the spirit of action/ "This subtle difference between the activities of the wise and the ignorant may not strike the modern reader as very important unless his attention is directed towards its universal application. It is the anxious desire for the fruits that dissipats the finer and nobler energies in the worker, and condemns his activity to utter failure.

"Mind can function only when it is attached to something. It cannot remain alive and, yet, detached from everything. Detachment of the mind mentioned here is only its `detachment from the false' and this is gained through the process of `attaching itself to the nobler'....

"Attachment becomes a clog or a painful chain on us only when it is extremely egocentric. To the extent we work for larger schemes to bless a vaster section of humanity, to that extent the attachment loses its poison and comes to bless the age. Many poisons serve as medicines in their diluted form, while the same in a concentrated form can bring instantaneous death! The ego and egocentric desires bind and destroy man, but to the extent he can lift his identifications to include and accommodate in it larger sections of the living world, to that extent the attachment gathers an ethical hold, a divine glow and becomes a cure for life's subjective pains."

The voice of Asia has always been one proclaiming that main is essentially a spiritual being. Man's value arises form the fact that a human person is the, highest form of created being having potentialities, faculties and abilities in his very nature in a superior category which are not available to the next highest form of being, the irrational animal. The uniqueness of man consists in his power of reasoning, the faculty of imagination, the gift of speech and power of self-correction. Besides, man has the capacity to develop self-awareness which enables him to judge his own thoughts and action and condemn them, if necessary. He has not been content to be a mere creature. He has dared to be a creator. Man alone can understand and invent concepts like immortality and infinity which no other animal can. His goal according to Indian thought is to manifest the divinity or dignity which is his real nature. Man has hate, malice, fear, selfishness and wickedness in his heart. So has he also love a beauty, goodness and truth, fellow feeling, respect for mankind and passion for realisation of the higher values of life. Both these forces are warring inside to gain control. Man by the exercise of his reason and will needs gradually to conquer the former by the latter. Whatever leads man as an individual or in groups towards, achievement of the real goal promotes *Kalyan* or social welfare. To explain *Kalyan* in Western terms one may say that social welfare has for its scope social functioning of man. Activities that enable man to live up to his dignity as a social being (man in relation to society) by gradual attainment of self-fulfilment, not through narrow in dividualism, but by self-controlled universalism devoted to the good of the whole, form the bases for *Kalyan* or social welfare.

Indian thinkers geared their activities directly or indirectly towards the said goal. Therefore, providing even so called physical services such as building roads, digging up wells, supplying unadulterated food, could come under the orbit of *Kalyan* or social welfare as they met the needs of human beings (every basic physical needs) to enable them to move towards realisation of their real goal in life. The concept of *Kalyan* was not restricted to a particular class, for instance, the poor or a particular handicap, such as, illiteracy, blindness, mental defect and so on. It was for all, rich and poor, high and low.

In ancient India, it would be interesting to note that there were social welfare workers or social workers who were professionals in the sense that they followed essential characteristics of a true profession. An important characteristic is the existence of a recognised code of ethics. This ethical code commits the members of the profession in certain social values above the selfish ones of income prestige and power. A profession expects its members to dedicate themselves seriously to these values and not just to profess them. Let us, for example, take the profession of medicine. Its code of ethics expects the doctor to dedicate himself to saving the life and protecting the patient's health irrespective of all material and personal considerations.

A profession establishes some form of group discipline in support of the values it professes. A doctor who violates the code of ethics of the profession receives the disapproval of fellow doctors. He may be debarred form further practice of medicine by his fellows. Besides, a profession bases its techniques of operation upon principles rather than on the rule of thumb procedures or simple routine skills.

Let us examine our ancient professional social workers against the essential characteristics of a profession. Persons who renounced the world, lived in hermitages and for the *Kalyan* of society imparted higher education to students who came to them, were no less social workers. So were the seers to whom people went for advice regarding various family problems, or Buddhist monks who used to look after the sick in the monasteries for the *Kalyan* of the people.

The above mentioned persons had ethical codes and they dedicated themselves to the *Kalyan* of the society and in the process they moved towards self-realisation (relation of the innate dignity of a human being). Theirs was a selfless service. Besides, their help-giving process was based on superior knowledge regarding human behaviour, working of the mind, control of impulses, ways of controlled involvement, relationship etc. as is evident form works like the Gita, the Yogashastra of Patanjali, various Upanishads and other learned treatises. In the twentieth century social work makes modern use (though on a lower plane) of the old knowledge.

At times the writer has heard the remark that a social worker who does not earn his livelihood by the practice of social work cannot be regarded as a professional social worker. Nothing an be more absurd than this. It is a very narrow view of professional social work. Do we regard a medical graduate practising medicine without charging fees form his patients as a non-medical person? He belongs to the medical profession, all the same, whether he charges fees or not. Also, about professional social workers in ancient India it can be stated that society or individual provided to some extent for the maintenance of such workers. These workers needed the bare wages at least to live in the world and that the society provided.

Over and above the persons who had totally dedicated themselves (full time) to the *Kalyan* of others, there were some who even though they followed occupations like the practice of medicine or teaching or any other vocation for their livelihood, tried to keep in the forefront the *Kalyan* or social welfare of the people to whom they offered their occupation for the good of the society. They also were no less social workers. It was the spirit of *seva* (a special type of dedicated service) to human beings which they brought into their work that gave depth to it in the cause of social welfare. The spirit of *seven* could premeate all areas of work in the service of man and it is not surprising even today in India to hear people name a doctor, a teacher, a clerk or grocer as a social workers so long as he works for promoting the well-being or *Kalyan* of people in one or more separable aspects (physical, mental or spiritual) of the integrated whole, unmindful of any material gain.

Modern social work in India has taken much form the West but it has yet to enrich itself also through indigenous contributions. It is interesting to note that today much talk goes on about the status, salary, cadre of professional social workers but nobody can deny that there is much of vagueness about social welfare itself. One is often lost in social semantics—social welfare, social service, social legislation, social welfare service, social action, social work, etc. Social workers are uncertain about their areas of work. There is at times a childish struggle to grab a field wholesale, be it public health, family planning or industrial relations and to put it within the fold of social work. For what? The aim is to see how many well paid posts can be bagged for social workers. Some-times it is really amusing to hear that "social work has a tremendous contribution to make in the field of public health or family planning" but this "contribution" fizzles out if well paid posts do not come to the share of social workers.

We also see some professional social workers limiting their work to those areas where classical casework, group work and community organisation methods are applicable. Why so? Social work profession had its origin in the challenge to deal with various ills and meeting the needs of people for their welfare, i.e. *Kalyan.* Unfortunately, some of us are expecting social problems to meet our needs. Methods were developed to helping individuals and groups in meeting their needs in a systematic way but, at times, one is shocked to see that technical matters have become major focus of professional interest.

The writer eels that social work in ancient India has much to contribute to present day social work in the country. It is not only that the principles and methods of social work can derive strength from older knowledge, but also the older concept of *Kalyan* can enrich the modern concept of social welfare and widen its scope. In short, as mentioned before *Kalyan* in neither restricted to a particular class of men or does it aim at removal of certain groups of handicaps. It implies well-being of man as a whole—as a unity and not just in parts, physical, mental and spiritual. Modern social welfare can revive the concept of *Kalyan,* i.e. bliss on physical, mental and spiritual plane, as an integrated whole and being it into different professions and trades like medicine, engineering, teaching, agriculture, business industry and so on. In other words, social work has a tremendous scope to develop in settings where the primary area of work is taken up by some other specialities, such as, medicine. Yet to give fullness to the profession of medicine in the area of *Kalyan* of people, social work can join hands with it and enable it to practice in a way that does not overlook the welfare of total man.

The main goal of medical profession is to enable man to have a sound health. The patient may have several obstacles in attaining it and the social worker offers his services to enable him to overcome these obstacles so that he can make the best use of the medical profession. Thus, the social worker can help the medical profession to work effectively for that segment of *Kalyan* (welfare in physical aspects) of people which is its primary goal.

Besides, social work can co-operate with medical profession to see that there are no frictions of parts (body, mind and spirit) in working out the *Kalyan* of patients. For example, over emphasis on maintaining soundness of health may make the patient a hypochondriac or a selfish person trying to grab the best of food and amenities for himself. There comes again the role of the social worker who needs to work with the medical team, the patient and his relatives and others to bring the patient's physical welfare in adjustment with his mental and spiritual well-being in the interest of the individual as well as that of the society. Similarly, social work can join hands with the profession of engineering and enable engineering departments to carry out their work (such as construction of houses, bridges, canals, institutions) keeping in view the *Kalyan* of the man as a whole. The social worker as a member of the team, can keep the engineering personnel informed about the habits, customs, needs of the people who are to be beneficiaries of the services. In some professions, social workers may be used more for orientation of the practitioner in the matters of social living of the beneficiaries while, in others, they may also play an equally important part in enabling beneficiaries to make adequate use of varied professional services for their *Kalyan.*

The practice of social work in inter-professional setting can also give an added impetus to social work to widen its scope. Historically, social work has been closely connected with social reform. Gradually, however, it developed technical services and methods. But, in some places, technical matters have become the major focus of professional interest. Social medicine provides an opportunity to social workers (in medical setting) to bring in a synthesis of social work and social reform. Therapeutics of social medicine is not medial but social and political actions based on medical recommendations. In the context of social medicine, a social worker's practice is not restricted to the readjustment of the life of the patient and his family disturbed or broken by illness; it is also concerned with finding out adequate measures to ameliorate his objective factors in the environment which may stand in the way of the restoration of his health. The social worker now should be able to work towards a synthesis of social work and social reform and bridge the gap that has long existed between the two.

Social workers have another area to cover so far as the question of *Kalyan* people is concerned. This is the work with social casualties, i.e. remedial work. It is not doubt true that our efforts should be geared towards checking the extent of casualties. However, there would be some casualties, not doubt. It has been noticed by the writer that many modern social workers have taken remedial work as the genuine social work field and feel happy in applying their pet techniques of casework and group work to social casualties. These professional social workers, drawing on psychological or psycho-analytical theories developed in the West, use a different language but basically the same techniques which were used in ancient India (perhaps much more refined then) under the names of *Maitri, Karuna, Ahimsa, nishkam karma* and so on. *Kalyan* or social welfare has an important area to reach out to. This is the area of administration. In the administration of service relating to health, education, social security, etc., for normal people, it is essential to understand that if these services are adequately carried out there would be less incidences of social casualties, for they would provide opportunities to people to meet the normal contingencies of life. In the administration of what are today called social services, social workers can bring in the concept of *Kalyan,* i.e. how these services are to be administered for the welfare of the total man and not just his lop-sided development.

All this does imply a need for change of our outlook regarding social work education—change regarding basis of selection of students, levels of training content of training, and spirit of training and practice. Social work in India today is a growing profession and as such it has to enrich itself through knowledge form different fields and different countries. Yet the writer sees something Indian about Indian Social Work.

The very concept of *Kalyan* mentioned before is somewhat distinct from the concept of social welfare in the West. Also in *Kalyan* (social welfare) we find that the emphasis of our thinkers has been on duties and obligations rather than on rights. This may be regarded as the noteworthy feature of the Indian outlook which distinguishes it from its Western counterpart. In his relation to the rest of the society, the individual, according to the Indian scheme, lays stress upon his duties—dharma by which he is to secure his own advancement and thus he may be distinguished from the Westerner who emphasises his rights. Of course, one implies the other, but while right looks to the acquisition of power and comforts for the physical self, the path of duty lies through the discharge of debts which a person owes to all sentient beings. At his very birth an individual is born charged with liabilities as the ancient works declare: whoever sexists, he, in being born, is born as owing a debtor to the gods, to the rishis, to the forefathers and to man. Ancient seers knew that "right" could not always meet the emotional needs of people. For instance, in a particular society the right of the aged father to maintenance by his grown up sons can be established by the law of the country or the rules of the community. But law cannot establish his right to affection. Affection cannot be solicited as a matter of right. Indians carried the sense of social justice not in terms of rights of the individual but in terms of duties of one human being towards another and Indian Social work has to incorporate it in its practice.

Another important requisite for social work or work towards social welfare in ancient India could be seen in the concept of 'being and becoming.' Indian thinkers, as stated earlier, held that man was essentially divine. He was expected to live up to his innate dignity as a human being. It implied living a good moral life. Indians in their heart of hearts have adored a man more for the life he leads than for what he does. They realise that moral excellence does not lie so much in doing good as in being good. Doing good follows form being good. What a person is, sets the limits to what he does. Social work practice does not depend solely upon what the social worker knows or poses to know but on that he is—not on hat he can do but on what he can be. This implies that professional self of the social worker in the Indian context has to mean spiritual self. The social worker in developing his professional self has to live up to his innate dignity as a human being and manifests clear vision, broad-mindedness, cheerful and resolute devotion to a definite high purpose.

Closely linked with the above is the spirit of seva which is something unique that fits in with our philosophy. It is not merely dedication to some work or cause. It is something more. Let us examine the secrets of action. So long as we are alive we cannot be without work or action. Even a person whom we call an idler and say that he does "nothing" is really doing something for he is not dead. It means he is not doing anything good (*bhadram, kama kalyan*) with his activity either for the society or for his family or for himself. So actions vary from man to man. Actin or work can be divided into three categories: A person, working in society (may hold a so called high pot) only for the sake of pay or wages for his own profit, without any consideration for others, is really not much different form an animal. A profiteer indulging in adulteration of food and thereby marring the *Kalyan* (good) of society, ranks the lowest in the field of action even if he be a prime minister or a millionaire owning several cars and palatial buildings. Then there are people who indulge in work with an ideal which they struggle to convert into an actual fact. A person in this category is working not for mere profit or wages. He wants to give shape to his ideal which, he thinks, will be for the welfare of society. So long as the ideal is worked out in society, he is happy. A doctor, a political worker, a teacher or anybody can belong to this category depending on the motivation for work.

There are some people who work in the world, not for profit, not for success but with a feeling of self-fulfilment *kritakrityata* i.e. a sense that they have done the right thing to be done irrespective of the fact whether the society gives recognition to them in their lifetime or even afterwards. There are still some who, apart form deriving a sense of self-fulfilment, also experience a sense of gratefulness to the people or society that gave them the opportunity to unfold their innate dignity as a human being. It is this spirit of work that is known as *seva.* Rightly have our seers remarked *seva dharmah parama ganano yoginama-pyagamyah* i.e. the spirit behind seva is too deep to be understood even by saints. This spirit of *seva* is the code of social work and it gives depth to the concept of "acceptance" in modern social work. In India the term social work borrowed from the West has come to man *samaj seva* and not *samaj* (social) *karya* (work) or the word 'worker' as in social work or village level worker has been translated as *sevak.*

References

Indians realised that without meeting their minimum physical needs for food, clothing and shelter people could not move systematically towards realisation of spiritual needs.

Indian Mythology refers to a Cow which can fulfil the wishes of persons who can satisfy her by their devotion and service.

Swami Chinmayananda, *The Sreemad Bhagwad Gita.* The Chinmaya Publication Trust, Madras, 1961, Vol. I, pp. 252-54.

Swami Chinmavananda, *The Sreemad Bhagawad Geeta.* The Chinmaya Publication Trust, Madras, 1961, Vol., I, p. 272.

Taittiriya Brahmana, VI, 3, 30, 5; *Satapatha Brahmana,* I, 7, 2, 1.

7

Management of Social Work

There are important differences between social work and social service which do not undermine the crucial integration of the two, büt do indicate the need for a different emphasis in their management. Social work is about flexible personal responses to need, but the confusion which has arisen through the growth of a complex hierarchy has frustrated and weakened the quality of that work. This has happened through a process of role confusion, communication difficulty, ambiguous control devices and a diffusion of responsibility.

Social Work or Social Services?

If we wish to consider the impact of structure on social work practice it is first necessary to establish what that practice is. A first impression would be a range of opinions. On the one hand a British Association of Social Workers Working Party Report in 1977 produced an ambitious attempt to define what social workers should do that was so all-embracingly profound that it could offer few practical guidelines.[1] At another extreme. Baroness Wootton, in the latest other thunderous broadsides against social work, urged an end to professional mystique and preferred a role for social workers largely as advice-givers and poor people's accountants.[2] Yet again, a view widespread amongst the masters of local government may be that their social workers are merely employed to carry out instructions! How can we describe the operational activities at client contact level in social services departments? It may be helpful to make an initial distinction between situations: (*i*) where the main emphasis is on a whole view of both client(s) and practitioner as people; and (*ii*) where the main emphasis is on the clients eligibility for certain services, and on the use of standardised procedures and roles to provide those services. Now there are several advantages to this division. First, it echoes a widespread feeling about a difference between social work and social service (and these separate terms now have even more force since the advent of a new form of training which leads not to a social *work,* but to a social *service* qualification); secondly, the distinction avoids the danger of describing activities as more or less 'professional" thirdly, it deliberately does not imply that certain situations, client groups, etc., require social work while others require social service; and finally, it draws attention to the very personal nature of work with clients. After all, whatever the state of modern social services, there is little doubt that many people enter social work with a desire to help other people, rather than to organize services, dispense aid or deliver benefits. If this is a false assumption, then we share it with the Central Council for Education and Training in Social Work, whose booklet welcoming people to a career in social work says great stress on the personal and relationship elements of the job.

The opinion that social work is about helping people, rather than delivering services, and that the social worker's relationship with a client is a personal one, has widespread backing.[4] Such views can be accepted without any implied exclusiveness, without feeling obliged to assert a strict demarcation between help and service, or to see a personal relationship as existing solely on a one-to-one basis, Indeed, a social worker needs a panoramic viewpoint in order to be effective in identifying, with the client, the focus of interaction. Phelan, who has argued so eloquently for recognition of the whole needs of handicapped people, captures some of the essence of our argument: In my experience many social services referrals of people with physical handicaps are prone to contain more between the lines than on them. Physical handicap is as long as a piece of string and the snippt which is knotted into a referral once unravelled has to be used like a mountaineering rope to bring the person with the handicap and the social worker to the heart of the matter together. And mountaineering ropes are not to be confused with two-ropes and are not to be used for games of tug-of-war.[5]

It follows from this standpoint that client activities can include either social work or social service or both, but it does not follow that one can be a substitute for the other. J. Copper takes up this point in a discussion of the growth of social services in the 1970s. The argument that these indispensable services replicate family provision, are domestic in character and retain a personal service-giving dimension in does not stand up to a situation in which repairs, renovations and modem equipment are needed if people are to be helped to retain independent living. Their isolation and loneliness, where it exists, calls for a different response —a personal and community response....[6]

Within this context, as an illustration, the organizational problem of social work assistants not actually assisting but rather having their own caseloads, is more open to resolution if it is accepted that they are, albeit without training, combining a personal, social worker response, with their service deliveries.

Similarly the provision of telephones under the Chronically Sick and Disabled Persons Act, 1970, can either stem from a full assessment of the disabled client, as a part of social work, or it can be largely an administrative procedure for eligibility based on the recommendations of an outsider (the general practitioner), as a social service. Our impression is that over recent years the latter method has become more common because it takes less time and is easier to quantify. Depending on the approach favoured, the managerial and administrative requirements will differ. A home help organizer can respond to a referral in terms of social work or social service — if the latter she can probably refer to well-established criteria like the client's frailty, isolation, financial situation and family supports or she may go further and look at the whole person (and perhaps discover other needs). The home help may limit herself to domestic chores, or may find time to relate to the client, sit down for a chat, and move into the approaches of social work.

There is no intention here of passing judgement, but difficulties have arisen from the interaction of social work and social services.

The growth of service provision and its overall dominance in social services departments (social workers form only about a tenth of departmental staff) has, in Cooper's words, 'polarised the specialist versus generic issue, the collective versus the personal issue and the family versus the client group issue'.[7] One outcome has been to open social work to criticism as less tangible and quantifiable, less able to handle large caseloads, and less able to show results than social servicing. Another has been to impose restrictions on the practice of social work, commonly by giving it a low place in priority ratings, or making eligibility for a service the necessary criterion for social work.

Organizational Requirements

Is the distinction between social work and social service sufficient to warrant different structural and managerial settings? Social work needs the kind of flexibility implicit in the concept of a front-line organization derived from the observation that only those staff in direct contact with clients can properly interpret needs, and thus must have the day-to-day freedom to provide a sensitive service. However, as Smith points out, there in a dilemma for the central organization which has to exert some controls.[8] The notion of people helping is potentially limitless; practitioners will need guidance and protection against doing too much or doing the wrong thing. Thus management will need to spell out its position clearly in matters which are of necessary concern to headquarters, such as material aid allocations, policy priorities, boundaries with other departments, and so forth. Within these broad limits the organization will need to acknowledge that people helping people is a fluid, unpredictable matter often of an essentially reactive nature. Stevenson writes of the long road to travel', seeking 'a service in which the deep compassion of many individual workers is contained within, and fostered by, sensitive and efficient organizational structures'.[9]

Social services in their turn, while requiring proper local flexibility, depend heavily on carefully worked out administrative procedures and rules, impersonal and impartial systems for monitoring activity, data collection, etc.—systems which operate efficiently—and transcend individual variations and are thus bureaucratic in the best sense. Using such examples as the registration of play-groups, or adaptations for the handicapped, it is clear that the public have every right to expect that impartial criteria both exist explicitly and are followed. So however closely linked social work and social services may be in meeting overall needs, and this interdependency must not be overlooked, yet they are not the same, they are not often interchangeable, and they need different administrative treatment. The task of managing services which need to be integrated and kept distinct involves different categories of staff within social services departments. The rest of this chapter looks at the attitudes and behaviour of managers, advisers and local team leaders.

Manager

Social services departments, as we argued earlier, grew very quickly from a largely unplanned base. Most managerial positions were (and are) occupied by qualified social workers and this has had a great influence on management style. Whether one can combine the social worker with the manager role is a difficult question. One view comes from Brill, given as he was about to become a director.

> The fallacious thing about management theory is that when you become a director you are not expected to 'waste time' doing social work. This is utter nonsense. I doubt if social workers have much time for a manager who turns his back on the profession.[10]

However an alternative view is suggested by Bamford who argues:

> The truth, I suspect, is that the very qualities which make a good social worker are often the antithesis of those required in management. Talking things through patiently and determinedly is an admirable quality applied to work with clients. Applied indiscriminately to management decisions great and small, it is a recipe for administrative paralysis.[11]

Perhaps, being charitable, it is possible for social services department managers to occupy both roles, but as Newman argues. It is essential to be able to identify the role being occupied at the time and to differentiate from it the other role or roles which the person might occupy at other times or in other circumstances'.[12]

In practice, we suspect that managers have tended to oscillate erratically between what one could consider a conventional management role and that of a sympathetic case adviser or supervisor. Thus it is not uncommon to find local managers of area offices being present at case conferences or co-ordinating meetings along with both a team leader and the social worker whose case is being discussed. In Newman's terms, what role is the manager occupying at that time? His social work background makes it difficult for him not to enter into a discussion about the nature of the client and the social worker's approach to the problem. In extreme cases even senior management may fall into this trap. Although we shall look in detail in the next chapter at non-accidental injury it is worth referring here to a decision made in one social services department that no child in care who had been injured could be returned home, even for weekends, without the approval of the director; apparently it could take as long as six weeks for such a decision to be made. The instruction was subsequently replaced by one allowing a middle tier manager to make this decision. The impact on the practitioner is evident—frustration, delay, unnecessary paper-work, contradictory advice, modified and re-modified assessments. The lengthening of the decision-making chain can reach ridiculous proportions, especially where major issues are involved. For example in an informal enquiry involving one of the authors, staff at various levels in a social services department were asked to indicate how many levels in the hierarchy took part in making certain child care decisions, such as place of safety orders, applications for the discharge of supervision orders, care proceedings proposals, and parental rights resolutions.[13] The results were alarming. First, the degree of confusion (not just at basic grade level) was very striking, particularly when staff were asked who actually made the final decisions. Secondly, when aggregated for all staff and for all child care decisions it emerged that at least four tiers in the department were recorded as involved in 70 per cent of the interactions recorded in the study. Decision-making was perceived as being widely dispersed, though concentrated on the committee (32 per cent) and management (18 per cent in headquarters, 16 per cent by the area officer). At the front line decisions were taken by team leaders (15 per cent) and social workers (6 per cent) only in a minority of situations.

The question of practitioner autonomy further highlights the uncertain, uneven style of social services department management. We will argue below that this style has not always done as well as it should in setting clear guidelines for practitioners. At this point it is enough to record that there is at basic grade level a degree of task discretion as described by Hughes.[14] He suggests that the exercise of discretion over a broad range of services is a major part of social work. Clearly practitioners do have a lot of day-to-day discretion, but it is possible that this happens less because senior management believe it right in principle, than because they lack time to exercise controls thus autonomy may arise by default but be likely to be withdrawn or reduced at the whim of management. The most formal expression of this tendency is seen in the fact that out-of-office-hours standby teams are allowed enormous discretion to deal with emergencies.

The role of the local area manager is obviously crucial to social work practitioners. It is not uncommon to see the job descriptions of such staff including, in some form or other, the statement that they are accountable for social work in their area. This is potentially dangerous for it could equally apply to a team leader and to a social worker covering a patch. In reality the area officer is accountable for running a setting (the local office) which enables others to be responsible for actual work with clients. This is an important distinction, yet it is still common for area officers to feel no impediment, from time to time, to getting heavily involved in individual case matters. This kind of role confusion even on basic job descriptions has bedevilled social services; it is reflected too in the plethora of job titles which reveal little consensus in organization design.

This muddled thinking persists at the highest level. In a journal interview in 1978, Herbert, Director of Avon County Social Services Department and president-elect of the Association of Directors of Social Services, was attempting to illustrate accountability differences between the National Health Service and local authority social services. In doing so he said: 'The social services director is actually responsible for the day to day work that goes on in the department.'[15] Does this make any practical sense? Does it mean that in a well-run department with tolerable work pressures, good support and supervision, if a qualified experienced social worker, for example, embezzles money from the local blind group club, that his director will spring forward to shoulder responsibility? Herbert may object to this as a silly example but it does surely point out the organizational naivety of his bland statement; it also reflects the rather nostalgic, well-meaning yearning of many social services managers to retain a contract with direct client work.

If it is the task of a manager to create the setting for work this also implies laying down guidelines, and making out boundaries. Managers have not found the task easy; partly this is understandable, given their lack of training, the great expansion of the work and the uncertainty of the public about what tasks they desire social services departments to undertake. It is observed in social work that much personal freedom is sought by individual practitioners, but they also want clear guidance from above—a point noted in the National Institute for Social Work study of Southampton Social Services Department,[16] and echoed in Parsloe and Hill's research.[17]

The work areas of homelessness (although it ceased to be a social services department responsibility in December 1977) and financial assistance are useful examples for examining whether managers have supported their practitioners through clear policy statements. That these areas are important is confirmed by the Stevenson and Parsloe study (they figured low as work desired but high as work actually experienced).[18] Through the 1970s the reluctance of many housing authorities to take over responsibility for homelessness greatly irked social work: practitioners who spent fruitless hours offering their skills to clients who primarily wanted a roof over their heads. Although the Association of Directors of Social Services added their weight to government.; recommendations, in individual departments the actual problem of crying to distinguish between social need and housing need (and responding accordingly) largely fell on the shoulders of practitioners. Even after December 1977 some laggard housing authorities still refused fully to accept their responsibilities and were not always pressed hard enough by individual social services department managements. What this meant at ground level was that practitioners faced with desperate families had to make very painful individual decisions: if they refused help they could be accused of being uncaring, whereas if they accepted responsibility and sought accommodation for their clients they were making it easier for another department to avoid its proper duties.

Financial instance to clients has, from its origins in Section I of the Children and Young Persons Act, 1963, grown into an area of major expenditure and concern for those staff who implement it. Research by Hill and Long documents the dramatic growth of such expenditure from £66, 600 in 1965-6 to £43 million in 1976-7.[19] What is especially relevant for our purposes is the detailed study of six selected social service department which revealed very wide variations in criteria and procedures used in making and withholding payments to clients, and the nature and size of payments made. These variations could not apparently be explained solely in terms of population differences and client demand. A central difficulty has been the absence of clear policy guidelines for practitioners, and the subsequent occurrence of frequent conflicts, particularly in relationships with Department of Health and Social Security supplementary benefits offices. Many practitioners have come to believe, with real cynicism, that it suits the government to allow the most 'difficult' families to be sustained discreetly by social services rather than run the risk of unpopularity by improving the supplementary benefits system. The whole matter is delicate, politically, and social workers have a right to expect clear support and direction from their managers. Yet as the evidence suggests, the financial props provided to families under the provisions of the 1963 Act have continued to grow chaotically and various authors have expressed strong concern about the risks both to social workers and their clients.[20]

In truth, the kind of discretion we have mentioned has tended to produce a very stressful, erratic and subjective policy at the service delivery front. Thus individual families had to hope that they could catch the sympathy of their social worker, make a fuss, or even look heavenwards for winter rains, darkness and snow to get the bill paid and the lights switched on again. There is much confusion as to whether financial aiding is part of the social work task, obscurity about agency objectives, and resentment amongst social workers at the way the whole matter is handled.

We have concentrated on the issues of homelessness and financial assistance to clients as distinct areas in which to criticise managerial effectiveness. Overall this same uncertainty has left social workers with a lack of clarity about the boundaries of their work. While the expansion of services increased the budgets, and with it the status of of social services departments, it imposed serious pressures on social workers to exercise discretion, without creating an appropriate setting for this behaviour within the managerial system. Social workers can make effective use of discretionary powers, provided there are clear guidelines and a willingness on the part of managers to stop interfering, often inconsistently and negatively, in individual instances. Utting, with experience as a director, suggests that 'Management emerges from the age of expansion with its confidence substantially diminished. It is ironic that the age that bid management be fruitful and multiply was simultaneously arranging the decay of formal authority.' Later on he adds that to managers falls the "main task of bonding the organization; a new craft of management must develop from its present state of simple adaptation to painful reality'.

Advisers, Consultants and Others

Social services departments employ many people who slot into the middle and upper tiers of the hierarchy as what we might call staff officers. That is to say, staff appointed to help managers by focusing on particular aspects of work. We feel that, from the practitioner's viewpoint, the creation of advisory posts has been a significant factor in enlarging the hierarchy. The reasons for the appointment of advisers and development staff are, historically, quite understandable. The establishment of social services departments drew many able staff into senior positions; the loss of pre-1971 specialist skills needed to be made up in other ways because, as events proved, basic grade staff at that time were unable to offer an adequate level of training and experience. In addition new duties were seen to require monitoring and co-ordinating, and it was felt to be sensible to man the front line with general purpose workers, so that specialists could concentrate on their specialisms. In the main these were sensible developments, an attempt to make the best use of scarce resources. In organizational terms these posts have certain features. First, they have officially offered higher salaries than field work; secondly, they have usually been located away from local offices and establishments; thirdly, they have tended to group together in hierarchical terms, as subsystems; finally, and most importantly, they have often acquired a supervisory or quasi-managerial authority.

Advice needs to be readily available to those seeking it. To this extent most advisory posts within social services departments have not been too successful. Stevenson, Strachan and Hallet, in their review of specialists working outside teams, gain an overall impression that they are not used with any great enthusiasm or regularity. If this is typical, it follows that this group of staff will have been inclined to develop their role in other directions, such as in monitoring, co-ordinating and, in limited circumstances, supervising. Our observation is that staff of this kind have tended to co-ordinate front-line practitioners rather than co-operate with them, overseeing rather than participating in their activities. Bills criticises the habit of appointing 'development' officers, whose purpose and job definitions may be far from explicit. Thus we can find situations where local social work staff, faced with a visit from a senior adviser or consultant, have spent frantic last minutes dredging up 'interesting' material to consult about.

In theoretical terms a staff officer has certain authority to require work to be done, follow it up and report back the findings to line management. In practice other things have happened. First, most advisory and development staff soon discovered that, as they were isolated from local practice, they could only work through local staff. Thus, the appointment of a specialist officer, instead of easing local pressures, often had the opposite effect; local staff came under pressure to join departmental groups as local representatives for a special area of work but under the chairmanship of an adviser. The specialist adviser, who had probably ceased to practise on appointment to the job, increasingly took on an administrative role, setting up meetings, devising new procedures, stimulating new channels of communication. Secondly, the lack of skill at practitioner level in the early 1970s caused concern and encouraged tighter controls and inspection channelled through the staff officer advisers. The fact that they enjoyed better salaries than practitioners obviously made it easier to enforce such authority. Unlike basic grade staff, other officers in social services departments have not been bound by national salary scales and in some cases were able to increase their salary by demonstrating increased responsibility.

Although it would be wrong not to acknowledge the important contribution of many staff officers, their actual activities have increasingly been perceived by practitioners as an extension of hierarchical control. The problem has been aggravated by a traditional reluctance in social work to tackle the issue of inspection for quality control. Thus staff have sometimes been appointed ostensively as advisers; only later is it realised that they have a brief to monitor (and to criticise) local social work. Criticism is perfectly legitimate, but because of their distance from fast changing practice, advisers have at times appeared arbitrary and inflexible in their attitudes. Further, when standards at local levels were felt by management to be low, they have sometimes chosen not to improve the conditions of practitioners but rather (because it is hierarchically more palatable) to appoint more advisory staff.

Because advisers do not normally practise social work, their position has increasingly been defined less in terms of their specialist skills and more according to their enhanced position in the hierarchy.

This is what one could term 'radiation of function', whereby an officer, simply because he occupies a senior position, is given fresh tasks in fields where he may not be especially skilled. For example in one social services department four senior headquarters staff who were originally appointed to oversee specific areas of work — child care, hospital work, disability, and adoption and fostering — have had their roles changed and now have a general responsibility for overseeing work in geographical areas. In another department a headquarters principal officer concerned with hospital social work (a staff officer role) later on acquired a co-ordinating role over home help activities. Whatever the individual qualities of such officers we believe that there are serious organizational consequences to such apparently casual changes. This radiation of function is further encouraged because managers who have use of staff officers tend, when they are busy, to delegate not only work but also authority. As a result staff officers may enter the managerial line because staff below them find increasingly that the route to a manager is via a staff officer.

When discussing managers we argued that the lack of clarity in their interaction with the front one caused confusion. With supervisory or managerial advisers the result is the same. There is confusion for social workers who find themselves looking up at a multiplicity of controlling strings, and confusion for local line managers about the division between their own and the advisers' responsibilities.

Local Team Leaders

The relationship between team leader and practitioner is a crucial and distinctive feature of social work. It has traditionally been based on a close professional relationship designed to develop the whole personality of the practitioner. However, our own experience suggests that the team leader role has suffered from many of the confusions which apply to managers and advisers; the role has seen an increase in administration and management rather than supervision, and a decline in consultation based on genuine skill. As with other senior staff, team leaders have had to deal with practitioners who lacked experience and training and who needed close consultation;

yet at the same time the pressures of referrals on local offices have led to much informal, often erratic delegation. At times practitioners have experienced a great deal of day-today autonomy; at others they have found restrictions on such activities as writing letters, contacting legal staff of the local authority, negotiating with other agencies, and using discretion over resources. Interestingly that most criticism of the hierarchy by practitioners seems to exclude team leaders (the Stevenson and Parsloe research indicates this); however, there are inadequacies in the relationship which, in our view, encourage overdependence and ultimately restrict the professional development of individual social workers. Thus while practitioners may be only too aware of their accountability, they may be increasingly uncertain about their responsibility. Faced with a barrage of demands from a wide range of staff they may conclude that while at times their supervisors are happy to give them enormous discretion, at others they choose to check and counter-check work. Thus, the team' continues to be extolled as the hub of social work under the mantle of a caring team leader. Yet when the latter is either absent, sick, or present but incompetent, social workers appear to cope remarkably well and find no lack of support and consultation from their peers. If the team were a truly unified system with a clear sense of purpose, method of working and performance feedback, the loss of its leader would be a serious matter.

Notes

1. The British Association of Social Workers (BASW), *The Social Work Task* (BASW, Birmingham, 1977).
2. Baroness Wootton, 'The Social Work Task Today', *Community Care* (4 October 1978), pp. 14-16.
3. Central Council for Education and Training in Social Work (CCETSW), *Introducing Social Work.*
4. A recent illustration is W. Jordan. *Helping in Social Work* (Routledge and Kegan Paul, London, 1979).
5. P. Phelan, 'Last Word', *Social Work Today*, vol. 10, no. 28 (13 March 1979).
6. J. Cooper, 'The Collective and the Personal — A Decade of Tension', *Community Care* (13 December 1978), p. 15.

7. *Ibid.*, p. 15.
8. G. Smith, *Social Work and the Sociology of Organizations,* pp. 37-9.
9. HMSO, *Social Service Teams,* p. 328-
10. K. Brill interviewed in *Community Care* (4 September 1974), p. 25.
11. T. Bamford, *Social Work Today* (31 October 1978).
12. A.D. Newman, *Organization Design,* p. 33.
13. D.M. Cooper *et al.,* 'Child Care Decisions' (1978), unpublished.
14. B. Hughes, 'Discretion is the Better Part of Social Work', *Community Care* (1 February 1979), pp. 20-1.
15. W. Harbert, interviewed in *Health and Social Services Journal* (3 November 1978), pp. 1242-4.
16. Neill *et al.. Social Work Today, vol.* 8, no. 5 (2 November 1976).
17. P. Parsloe and M. Hill in HMSO, *Social Service Teams.* Chapter 8.
18. HMSO, *Social Service Teams,* Appendix II, Table 8.
19. M. Hill and P. Laing, *Money Payments, Social Work and Supplementary Benefits,* Occasional paper no. 1 (School for Advanced Urban Studies, University of Bristol, 1978).
20. W. Jordan, *Poor Parents.* R. Lister and T. Emmett, *Under the Safety Net* (Child Poverty Action Group, London, 1976).

8

Social Work as Profession

Social workers are concerned with the interactions between the individual and society. We now need to return to a consideration of social work as an interstitial profession which serves both the client in need and society at large. This issue is complex in that the individual social worker's function is defined, and the worker's salary paid, by an agency (public or voluntary, traditional or non-traditional) which receives its sanction from and is accountable to the community or to some community group whose members differ from, although they may include, the members of the client system. This point is of fundamental importance since the parameters of the service any particular professional can offer are determined by the parameters of the agency's societal charge. Social workers utilise two types of tools in their work. The first type are the tools of internalized knowledge and skill, which, while they cannot be used up and, in fact, may be increased and sharpened by practice, are costly in that they are what social workers (or any other professional) sell in order to obtain the money they need to maintain their physical existence in society. Most professionals (lawyers, doctors, and so on) sell their services directly to their clients or patients. In the case of social work, however, services to the client are paid for by the community and may be, at least in theory, available to all members of the community, many of whom cannot afford to pay for them themselves. In addition to knowledge and skill, social workers frequently dispense external resources, such as money. Now, money, whether it is used to pay for the knowledge and skill of the worker or for concrete resources, or is given directly to the client, is usually scarce. And money to support social work efforts is not the social worker's property but belongs to some identified community. The community that allocates its scarce resources to the support of social work services wants to assure itself that these resources are used responsibly.

Clients who go to a lawyer for service, or patients who go to a doctor for treatment, may look elsewhere for help if they think the service they receive is not adequate. Thus they express their evaluation of that professional's competence by depriving the professional of income. If professionals want to support themselves and their dependents, they must practice in a way that satisfies the users of the services by which they support themselves. However, since most client systems do not pay the full cost for social work services, their withdrawal in disappointment and disgust from, the inadequate social work practitioner seldom directly penalises that practitioner. Social workers (and their agencies) are thus well protected from their client's evaluations. However, they are open to the evaluation of their supporting community. The supporting community, however, neither pays nor evaluates workers directly. Bather, it gives its money to an organization, usually called an agency, which hires the professional practitioners. It is usually the agency in interaction with its supporting community through certain representative groups which both sets the parameters of practice within which workers must operate and which evaluates their performance within the parameters.

The Bureaucratic Organization

In the modern world most formal organizations are structured in a particular way. This particular type of administrative organization is known as a bureaucracy and has triumphed in modern society because it is thought to operate with an efficiency superior to that of any other form of secondary group social structure thus far devised. The classical criteria for a bureaucracy were originally set forth by Max Weber (1947, pp. 333-334) as follows:

1. *The employees* are personally free and subject to authority

only with respect to their impersonal official [work] obligations.

2. *The employees* are organized in a clearly defined hierarchy of offices.
3. Each office has a clearly defined sphere of competence.
4. The office is filled by a free contractual relationship. (Thus, in principle, each person makes a free selection, or choice, as to whether the person will accept the office and its terms.)
5. Candidates [for offices in the bureaucracy] are selected on the basis of technical qualifications. In the most rational case, this is tested by examination or guaranteed by diplomas certifying technical training, or both. They are appointed, not elected.
6. *The employees*]are remunerated by fixed salaries in money, for the most part with a right to pensions . . .The salary scale is primarily graded according to rank in the hierarchy.
7. The *position* is treated as the sole, or at least the primary, occupation of the incumbent.
8. It constitutes a career. There is a system of "promotion" according to seniority or to achievement, or both. Promotion is dependent on the judgment of superiors.
9. The official works entirely separated from ownership of the means of administration and without appropriation of his position.
10. The worker is subject to strict and systematic discipline and control in the conduct of the office.

Weber (p. 334) says that the Roman Catholic Church, the modern army, and large-scale capitalistic enterprise, along with certain "charitable organization, or any number of other types of private enterprises, servicing ideal or material ends are bureaucratic organizations."

Although bureaucracy is usually seen in terms of pragmatic necessity as the most efficient way to organize any large group of people to get any big job done, inherent in its very being are certain dysfunctional characteristics which vitally affect its operations. Social workers are often forced to conclude that the relationship between bureaucracy and efficiency is complex, questionable, and perhaps, at its worst, inverse.

To quote from a recent book, *Overcoming Mismanagement in the Human Services* (Weissman, 1973, p. vii), bearing on some of the problems of bureaucracy:

> A very unhappy social worker, after receiving a poor evaluation from a supervisor, once wrote: "Social welfare like all Gaul is divided into three parts. The first has until recently been inhabited by the Hierarchae, which may account for the fact that the field has been subject to unsteadiness. The second by the Supervisii, which explains why too many of the most able no longer work with those in need of help. They are in conference. And the last by the Reformae, who believe the populace is anxious to substitute social change for sex."
>
> Had the worker been more dispassionate, this social worker might have pointed out that social welfare is also inhabited by thousands of hard-working, dedicated people who spend their lives under adverse situations with some (if the most unhappy and unlucky people in the world and still manage to do a lot more good than bad.

Wilensky and Lebeaux (1958, p. 243) describe the limitations of social work bureaucracy as follows:

> Along with its gains, efficiency, reliability, precision, fairness—come what many students have called its pathologies: timidity, delay, officiousness, red tape, exaggeration of routine, limited adaptability. The agency as a means, a mechanism —the agency—for carrying out welfare policy becomes an end in itself. Between the altruist with the desire to help and the client with the need lips the machine, with its own "needs." These needs can result in an emphasis on technique and

method, on organizational routines and records, rather than on people and service.

Barbara Lerner (1972, pp. 169-170), a psychologist, is concerned with this last limitation of bureaucracy when she writes:

> Bureaucratic means are intrinsically unsuited to the achievement of ultimate mental health ends because they are standardized means—the whole people of breaking up tasks into component parts and component parts into subcomponents is to standardise procedures—and standardized procedures are rational only if one *is* striving to produce a standard product. ...
>
> Each human being is a unique entity and wants to remain so. People who voluntarily seek treatment may do so because they want to achieve an ultimate end, such as the realization of something like their full share of the universal human potential for adequate psychosocial functioning, but people want to achieve their own unique version of that end in their own unique way....
>
> Thus clients who come seeking aid come as unique individuals seeking aid which is individually tailored to the totality of their needs by a person who is in close enough contact with them to apprehend them and who has the freedom and flexibility to respond to them in a unique way.

Lerner (p. 171) goes on to say that the bureaucratically organized agency is organized around "abstract, standard parts: specific programmes organized around specific problems that are dealt with by specific procedures," rather than around clients as unique personalities or around the concern of practitioners for their clients. She complains that clients are "then defined in terms of the particular problems around which programmes are organized" and are "processed to and through those programmes and subjected to the various procedures and techniques which constitute them" rather than seen in terms of their own goals and expectations.

Listening to Lerner, one becomes aware that the problems of professionals in bureaucracies are not restricted to social work. These problems occur in any organization staffed by personnel who spend a considerable number of years in developing a particular expertise. Weissman (1973, p. viii) points out;

> Professionals share a desire for and expect a large degree of autonomy from organizational control; they want maximum discretion in carrying out their professional activities; free from organizational interference or confining procedures. In addition, professionals tend to look to other professionals to gain some measure of self-esteem, are not likely to be devoted to any one organization, and accept a value system that puts great emphasis on the client's interest.
>
> Bureaucrats are different from professionals. They perform specialized and routine activities under the supervision of a hierarchy of officials. Their loyalty and career are tied up with their organization. Therefore, conflict results when professionals are required to perform like bureaucrats.

We would differ with the conclusion of this last quote and might repeat that famous quotation, "We have met the enemy and they is us." Professionals and bureaucrats are not two different sets of people. There are bureaucrats who are not professionals, but, increasingly in our society, given the advancement of group practices in medicine and law, there are few professionals who are not also bureaucrats. With regard to social work, we need to recognize that bureaucratic forms of organization are useful in social services, not Because society is unmindful of what is wrong with this form, or because society is basically evil, but because there simply are not at this time any feasible, superior organization models that have properties as well suited to carrying out the very complex functions required of social service's involving the cooperative contributions of large numbers of specialized individuals (Pruger, 1978).

For the foreseeable future, individual social workers will find it necessary to relate to a bureaucratic structure as the environment in which they will work. Thus, it will not help either the worker or the client for the worker to see the bureaucracy as something bad that should be condemned at every turn. Rather, it must be understood as a reality—a complex system in which both worker and client are subsystems. Given this important fact of life—we need to learn to work within and to change bureaucracy rather than to simply make ourselves feel good by holding bureaucracy as bad (Pruger, 1978).

Conflicts Between the Bureaucracy and the Professional

Practicing social workers have been confronted with the harsh reality of the conflict between their judgment as to the ideal interventive actions needed to move toward the clients goal and what is possible given the resources and parameters of the agency within which both they and the client are operating. Often the most sensitive and concerned workers find themselves discouraged and angered by the many unavoidable compromises they must make between their clients needs and those of their agency in particular and of society in general. Perhaps some of this "frustration could be avoided, and workers could be more effective in bringing about change in agency functioning, if they understood better the bureaucracy within which they of necessity operate. Actually, social work has been a bureaucratic profession from its very beginning, and social workers employed in agencies are not only professionals but bureaucrats. Thus, while social work has struggled to synthesise bureaucratic and professional norms, it has not always recognized that a profession and a bureaucracy possess a number of norms that are opposed in principle.

Weissman (1973, p. vii) points out that one of the crucial problems of professionals who are working to change the bureaucratic structure is their lack of recognition of the difference between nonprofit and profit-making organizations. "Money serves as an alarm system in private enterprise: Ford sooner or later must respond to the tension caused by lack of Edsel sales." In nonprofit organizations the connection between the product produced and the, revenues are indirect. Thus the alarm system that would bring change is severely flawed. Both professionals and agency executives may prefer to be judged by effort expended rather than by the success or failure of the effort. Weissman (p. 3) says that without an effective accountability system social agencies cannot solve their problems and administration has little need to seriously consider the views and ideas of lower-level staff since it will not be penalized if it does not.

In an earlier chapter, the importance of evaluation was discussed. This has been a long-standing problem in all professions. Who is to evaluate the professional? Against what standard is the professional's work to be judged? The present struggle of the physician against some kind of publicly supported health care is an example of the problem. Physicians have successfully maintained up until now that only they (or, in some cases, a jury of their peers that they pick) can be allowed to judge their work. Incidentally, this stance probably explains the growing number of malpractice suits, since patients are no longer content, when the results of treatment are negative, to accept the professional's judgment that the process of treatment was correct. So, too, in the social work bureaucracy the question of who shall evaluate the effectiveness of the work is a difficult one. Is it to be the worker, the supervisor, the executive, the board, or the general public? We have said that contracted goals are the appropriate outcome. It would follow that we hold goal achievement to be a decision of client and worker, not of the agency.

Weber (1947, pp. 333-334) held that what is central to bureaucracy is specialization and the standardization of tasks and the rational allocation or assignment of these tasks in accordance with an overall plan. Collective tasks may thus be broken down into component tasks which are means to a collective end. Two assumptions underlie such a concept. The first is that there is something approaching a clear, consistent, complete, and generally agreed-upon definition of the ultimate end toward which the organization is working, and the second is that the end is achievable through standardized means (Lerner, 1972, p. 167). When a social agency defines its function it usually states the ends it intends to pursue in general terms. However, these ends are usually expressed in such general terms (for example, "the support of healthy family life") that the extent to which they have been achieved cannot be measured; or the ends are expressed in programmatic terms, such as "crisis intervention," "aftercare programme," "family therapy programme," or "drug programme," which often result in defining the client's problems in terms of programmes rather than of the client's goals. And most of us would agree that we do not have standardized means to apply even if the client could fit within a standardized goal. We are simply not able to say in working with individual human beings, "If this, then that." There are too many variables in the situation of the unique human system. A profession works by applying principles and methods to resolve problems determined by unique client input and professional judgment rather than by employing standardized procedures toward some predetermined goal established by a hierarchical authority.

Another conflict between the bureaucratic structure and the professional is found in the orientation toward authority. The professional regards authority as residing in professional competence; the bureaucrat sees authority as residing in the office held. An important difference is found in the orientation toward the client, in that professionals orient themselves toward serving the best interests of the client while the bureaucrat seeks to serve the best interests of the organization. Professionals usually identify with their professional colleagues. They should find their identification from their professional association. Bureaucrats identify with their particular social stratum within the bureaucratic hierarchy. And lastly, there is a different orientation toward the method of exercising power. "The professional norm is to influence clients and peers by modes which are oriented toward the pole of free exchange while the bureaucratic norm is oriented toward the pole of coercion" supported by the invoking of sanctions.

Types of Bureaucrats

In an empirical study of social work performance in large public agencies, Ralph Morgan (1962, pp. 116-125) identified and developed an anchoring description of four ideal types of role conceptions of social workers in a bureaucratic setting. His work is summarized below:

Functional bureaucrats are professionals "who just happen to be working in a social agency." They seek interaction with and recognition from their professional peers both inside and outside the agency. "Such individuals by their skill, good judgment, and technical efficiency often provide a type of service" that is recognized by the agency as being highly effective. As a result the agency overlooks certain violations of agency norms as the price it must pay for having such a competent professional on its staff.

Service bureaucrats are social workers who are oriented toward helping their clients but who recognize that they are a part of a bureaucracy. They integrate themselves "into the bureaucratic group while maintaining professional peer group ties." While they are still "ambivalent about their identification with their agency, they see in it the best means of attaining their goals of practicing" their profession, and as helping resources rather than as antagonists of their clients and themselves.

The *specialist bureaucrat* is a classification that Morgan says encompasses the largest group of social workers. Tin's worker is interested in reconciling the "bureaucracy to humans and humans to the bureaucracy." Specialist bureaucrats use the rules and regulations of the agency to guide their professional judgments. "While they recognize that agency directives are in general necessary, they also recognize the richness of the human situation that can never be fully encompassed by specific rules and regulations." They see the agency as authorising them to use their professional discretion, to protect the interests both of the agency and of its clients. They realize that the agency is a bureaucracy and therefore heir to all the dysfunctional characteristics of this form of human organization. They usually have the professional "courage to sacrifice bureaucratic norms when they interfere with their professional function." They have successfully, through understanding and professional judgment, adapted in practice to norms which in theory are essentially irreconcilable. In fact, they may see this constantly shifting adaptation as the very stuff of professional life.

The *executive bureaucrat* likes "to manage people, money, and materials.. While functional bureaucrats are oriented toward their profession, service bureaucrats toward those they serve, specialist bureaucrats toward the profession and the bureaucracy, executive bureaucrats seem oriented primarily toward the exercise of power. While executive bureaucrats are innovators and do not consider themselves bound by a rigid application of rules and regulations [in fact, they may be daring bureaucratic infighters and risk takers], they tend not to appreciate innovations by their own subordinates," They lean toward enforcement of bureaucratic norms for others and run a disciplined agency.

Job bureaucrats are people, professional workers, who "have a substantial career investment in the bureaucracy. At the center of their attention is the security of their own career, and they seek to safeguard and advance it through a meticulous application of regulations and adherence to the norms of the organization." Effective job bureaucrats achieve their greatest success in supervisory or administrative positions. While they hold themselves firmly to official policies of the organization, they realize that the other professionals in their sections have a different orientation, and while they tend to supervise closely, they exercise sufficient "selective non-attention" to the less rigid way in which their subordinate professionals operate, that through the proper amount of "social slippage" the social work job gets done. The ineffective job bureaucrat is characterized by a rigid overcompliance with regulations and norms. Directives that originally were issued to accomplish a mission become ends in themselves, and he mission of social work, or even of the agency itself, become secondary considerations.

Agency Bureaucracy and the Worker

No one ever meets a pure type in real life, so perhaps it is understandable that the authors are not willing to put themselves in any one of the classes listed. But we suppose that we could probably be located somewhere between the service bureaucrat and the specialist bureaucrat. We do not believe that a worker who accepts a position as a member of an agency staff and who utilises agency resources, no matter how unsatisfactory they may be, can act as though the worker were a private practitioner or without concern for agency policies and procedures. As a staff member, the worker is bound by the agency policies. If these policies are unacceptable, one must either work to change them, while remaining bound by them, or one must leave the agency and work for change outside it.

The first principle for workers who would give their clients maximum service is to understand the organization for which they work and to know how its structure and function were and are determined. If one is going to be actively involved in change, one needs to know what the possible points of intervention are. Three major factors affect the organization of agencies: their source of support, the source of their sanction or right to operate, and the areas of their concern. Agencies obviously cannot operate without a source of funds. As a rule an agency's funds come either from public tax funds or from private voluntary contributions, although agencies supported primarily by private contributions "may utilise tax funds through various contracts and grants. Any agency's policy and structure, procedures, and flexibility will be determined by the source and adequacy of its funding. As a general rule, the funds are never adequate to the demands that workers wish to meet, so that difficult choices among real needs must usually be made.

The public tax-supported agency will usually operate within legislation and will be dependent on some legislative body (for example, county commissioners) for its broad policy and for the appropriation of public funds for its support. In some cases the board or commission of a public service may be appointed by an elected executive officer (that is, governor). Such agencies are usually administered by individuals who may be required to prove their competence by passing various tests. These administrators will determine procedures and more detailed policy issues within the broad legislation that established and maintains the agency.

Private agencies usually operate under the general policy directives of a board of directors. Such a board has three primary functions: it establishes the right of the agency to carry on its programme and sanctions the agency's activities; it is responsible for the agency's overall policy; and it is responsible for fund raising. Until very recently almost all boards were composed of an elite group of members with little understanding of the realities of the lives of those for whom they developer programmes. Boards almost always operate by consensus. Because the board members of private agencies are volunteers, the members who are constantly on the losing side of an issue soon drop out unless they have a deep commitment. In most situations the board hires the executive of thu agency, and it often happens that the executivesees the job as keeping the board happy on the one hand and running the agency the executives own way on the other. The executive usually controls staff access to the board and the How of information to the board about the agency's work. So the worker's attempts to represent clients and their interests in policy and programme matters are often unheard.

Some social work departments (such as the social service department of a school system, a hospital, a court, and so on) operate as part of a larger host agency. In this situation the financial support and policy-making processes will be determined by those of the host agency, which generally operate under a similar structure.

Agencies have both a function and a programme. The programme is the ways and means that an agency utilises to carry out its function as defined by the community. For the practitioner, this distinction has some importance in that although an agency's function may remain constant, its programme ought to be responsive to the changing needs of the times. Thus an agency whose function is the care and treatment of children may initially have) cared largely for orphaned or dependent children but now may be concerned primarily with delinquent children.

Each agency has an organizational (bureaucratic) structure by which it delegates its responsibilities and tasks and stabilises and systematises its operations. The executive is the primary administrative officer. Officers have direct responsibility for the day-to-day functioning of the agency. Because they are usually responsible for getting the money to run the agency, this responsibility may occupy most of their time and thought. They are responsible for relationships with the board of directors or a public body. They are usually responsible for working with other agencies toward community social work goals and for the public relations functions of the agency.

Below the executive on the organization table of a large agency one may find a bewildering array of division directors, unit supervisors, consultants, and line supervisors. A small agency may have only three levels of hierarchy the executive, the supervisors, and the workers. Line workers are more conscious of their relationship to their direct supervisor—a professional person who is usually held responsible for two functions that at some times and to some people seem contradictory: (1) helping workers to improve their skills both in the interests of getting the present Job done at the best level possible and for the worker's and client's future benefit, and (2) administratively holding workers responsible for doing the job to certain standards and evaluating their performance relative to those standards.

Many articles in social work literature deal with the supervisory process and its problems. Supervisors, like workers, differ, and some may be more interested in their job security and tenure than in the client's needs for service or the worker's need for both support and learning opportunities. All beginning workers can use considerable help in increasing their awareness of themselves and their way of working, and in adding to their fund of knowledge about people, resources, and helping processes. And in a large agency with considerable work pressure and a constant scarcity of resources, all line workers need considerable support of their supervisors in dealing with the constant frustrations of the day-to-day job.

Harry Wasserman (1970) examined the work of professional social workers in a large public agency. He found that structural constraints rather than social work knowledge and skills dictated what the worker was able to offer in the client's life situations. In this instance, 8 of 12 workers studied had left the agency after two years. Wasserman (p. 99) concluded that "the two principal feelings expressed by the 12 new professional social workers during the two year period were frustration and fatigue," and the "they were exhausted by having day after day to face critical human situations with insufficient material, intellectual and emotional resources and support" Certainly supervisors cannot wave a magic wand and undo the effects of structural constraints on the worker's capacity to help, but a supervisor who cares about the worker's capacity to help and the worker's mental health can, through support and the offer of intellectual and emotional resources, make a great deal of difference in what the worker is able to do and in how the worker grows on the job.

Because of the constant strains and problems of the supervisor's job there has been some push in certain agencies to do away with supervision. Perhaps social work could develop a better form than the supervisory process, but one cannot do away with the supervisory function. Doing away with authority relationships does not necessarily change either people or structural constraints or result in more effective work. As long as personal needs, attitudes, and differing levels of commitment and skill are brought to a job, there is a need for leadership. As Weissman (p. 131) points out:

> The planning and management of an organization requires specific expertise.... there is an ongoing need to reconcile the dilemmas and strains of organizational life.... as long as there is concern for the effectiveness of an organization, there will be considerable strain between the needs of the individuals for self-actualization and the needs of organizations for achievement and efficiency.

Somehow these strains need to be reconciled and resolved if clients are to be effectively served. The question concerning the supervisor that is of critical importance for the worker is the supervisor's position on the list of roles that Morgan developed.

Perhaps the primary problem with supervision is not that it is not valuable, or not necessary, but that it has been used in such a way that agencies have avoided consideration of their effectiveness by focusing on the effectiveness of their employees. In most agencies, workers receive yearly evaluations on the anniversary of their joining the staff. Perhaps what is needed are set dates on which both the workers and the agency would be evaluated. In other words the agency needs to look at itself at the same time that it is looking at its workers. As Weissman (p. 58) writes:

> The environment in which the agency operates—physical, social, financial— affects the worker's efforts. To tell workers to refine their skills or work harder in order to be successful is to ignore the impact of environment. The caseload or lack of cooperation from other agencies, not diagnostic or therapeutic skills, may be at fault.
>
> Evaluating individuals at different times during the year solely in terms of their individual therapeutic skills makes it less likely that the agency will have to react as a system to the results of evaluation. The problems of each worker can be viewed idiosyncratically.
>
> . . . Through consultation with experienced workers, agencies should establish the areas of skill needing improvement and the basis upon which to judge improvement—recordings, observations, client queries, and the like. The worker should choose how to get help, whether through conferences with the supervisor, through taking courses, through peer supervision, or through consultation. Letting the worker decide reduces the dependency feelings which develop through forced supervision.

> A degree of arbitrariness will always exist unless an agency has some method of appraising success with clients. Without agency standards of success and an evaluation of the worker's record, workers and supervisors are dependent on secondary data. Case presentation becomes more important than the people treated. The way one writes or speaks about a case becomes more important than the results achieved.

Weissman (p. 59) then goes on to discuss the Accountability of the agency for evaluation of its job. (This is another side of the earlier argument made by the authors about the need for evaluative research and ways of evaluating services.) He says:

> The key to increasing the influence of lower level staff vis-a-vis their superiors lies in a board (or other body) that can hold the agency accountable there is real accountability, the ideas and experience of all levels of staff become valuable, and the incompetence of individuals becomes a matter of serious concern.
>
> If a board discovers that 80 per cent of the agency's clients feel they have not been helped by the agency, the incompetent supervisors have something to worry about.

Client, Bureaucracy and Workers

The procedures of bureaucracy as well as the limitations of policy may be frustrating to both the client and the worker. It is well to recognize that "red tape" was and is developed to assure that people with equal troubles receive equal help and resources. But often it really operates to reduce the client's access to services or to make an already complex situation more difficult and confusing. It is the worker's responsibility to act as the client's broker and advocate in dealing with the policies and procedures of the bureaucracy. These roles have been discussed earlier, but one last word will be added here.

If workers are to help the client cope with the problems of access to services in the most helpful way possible, it is critically important that they know with accuracy and understanding the policies and procedures of their agency and the way they operate. Workers are not always as careful and disciplined as they might be in getting a really workable grasp of this knowledge. *Paperwork* can become a very naughty word in the worker's language, but the capacity to handle paperwork efficiently, accurately, and with concern for deadlines and the client's time, is an absolute requirement of the worker who would be a skilled advocate and broker. The authors have worked in agencies where certain chief clerks made more important decisions about who got what than some 'workers because the clerks had mastered the paper flow and the workers were too impatient to do so. While paperwork can be irritating, the worker needs to understand that it is an attempt to establish procedures by which clients are assured equal service.

One of the authors of this book is old enough to have worked in public welfare before the Social Security Act took effect, when it was the responsibility of the local township to aid people in need of money. At that time paperwork *ins* considerably lighter than it became after the agency was able to secure federal funds if it established certain procedures to assure people equal service and the right of appeal if they felt that they had been capriciously denied. However, at that time people were able to secure aid only if they were able to convince the worker and/or the supervisor that they were "worthy of, aid." Sometimes this meant that they had supported the proper political candidate with the proper enthusiasm. This decision could not be challenged—there; were no procedures to assure this, no paper on which the basis of the decision was recorded. But back to the present.

The worker needs to thoroughly understand, the parameters of the policy of the agency and the authority available for interpretation. A policy is a broad statement. It has to be interpreted by some individual before it can be applied in the interests of another individual. Far too often, a worker will either ask the worker at the next desk what the agency does about such and such or give the supervisor a quick call.

Our position is that the worker starts with what the client and the worker have decided is needed as a resource in the problem solution. Next the worker is responsible for finding out exactly what the written statement of the policy says. Then the worker sits down and thinks long and hard about what that policy actually means and what all the different possible ways to interpret and apply it are. Next the plan made with the client is used to test the various interpretations. The interpretation is selected that will best enable the worker to help the client with what is needed for problem-solving. Workers then write down that interpretation of the policy and the way they would apply it to the client situation. If necessary, this statement may be submitted to the supervisor for approval, but in any case it needs to be made a part of the record of service to the client. Our view is that taking the quick and easy route of asking colleagues or supervisors about policy is not the proper way to perform one's role as an independent professional person; and our experience has been that following that course increases the likelihood of receiving a directive that limits what one can do. Others do not always want to do the hard headwork either, and when one is in doubt about a policy the easier thing is to say no. It is out of this way of functioning—the use of the traditional messages about policy that circulate on the office grapevine—that old patterns get stabilized and become harder and harder to change. By really knowing policy and by utilising creative interpretations of policy, the worker can help keep the agency active as an ever-changing bureaucracy.

Several years ago one of the authors conducted a study to find out (1) whether clients were receiving aid they needed and (2) why or why not. In the agency under study, workers reported great discouragement with the limitations of agency policies and felt that these policies prevented them from really helping their clients. The study revealed that the average client of that agency was receiving less than half of the amount of services and resources to which the client was legally entitled under its policies. In other words, it was not the agency policies that were limiting client access to services, but rather the narrow and traditional way that workers and supervisors were interpreting the policies. In the year following the study, as workers were helped to assume active responsibility for broadly interpreting policy, the aid to their clients more than doubled in cost, yet no one in the agency or on its board reached out to stop this more expensive way of operating. The point being made is that service to the client is not limited to what one does when one sits with the client. Some of the most important work, and sometimes the work that is most difficult and requires the most self-discipline and commitment, is the work involved when the worker takes on the role of broker with the agency's programmes and its bureaucracy. Social-workers are of ten the kind of people who prefer to deal with people rather than with paper—yet dealing with paper is a part of everyone's life in today's world. So workers can often fail the client in real and hurtful ways if they do not have expert skills in dealing with paper. Operating contrary to traditional grapevine interpretations of policy may often involve the worker in uncomfortable confrontations with the agency colleagues and the supervisor. And it is not easy for an individual worker as part of a system to move contrary to the patterns and relationships in the system. However, if workers' interpretations conform to written policy they can usually prevail in the client's interests, which is what social work is all about.

One more word. If policy does not permit adequate service to clients, this needs to be adequately documented. Workers must assume the responsibility of documenting in some detail the problems they see. It may be difficult to open up board structure and policy so clients can make an impact, but it will never happen if workers only "gripe." They must present organized evidence of their position.

Bureaucracy Changing

An article by Edward J. Pawlak on organizational tinkering has been reproduced in this chapter. More important than its title would indicate, it really relates to what is being discussed in this section; the focus is on tactics for "tinkering" with the organizational structures, rules, and policies in order to bring about bureaucratic change. Another author who has written some excellent articles on the social worker's activities within the bureaucratic structure is Robert Pruger

(1973). The authors have burrowed some of Pruger's ideas to combine with their own thoughts in putting together this section.

The authors' first suggestion for change would be to be clear about what needs to be changed, about the difficulties that can be anticipated in bringing about the solution, and about the cost of both the problem and its solution (problem definition, goals, and plan). So often people not experienced in ; the complexity and the balances of the bureaucratic setting will take a drastic step to change the situation and will be completely overwhelmed by the unexpected repercussions that follow. Let us consider, for example, the worker that feels that clients are being poorly served by a policy. Unable to change anything, the worker resigns in anger and frustration. A newspaper reporter hears of the problem and asks the worker about it. Seeing an opportunity to use the power of public opinion and certain of the obvious virtue of the cause, the worker tells the reporter of the problems. However, many people in the community do not see the story as an attempt toward better service. They interpret it as an example of how poorly social workers administer public funds, and a strong community pressure develops to cut the funds of the agency, to set up more stringent rules and regulations for the social workers to follow, and to replace the social work director with a business manager who will see that rules are followed.

The second principle is to determine what factors and forces inside and side the organization are keeping the problem alive. What the worker did not know in this example was that the executive and the board were as deeply concerned as the staff with certain policies but, given the power position of certain people in the community, they had made a decision that any attempt to change things would result in costly backlash. This is not to say that one does not take on an open fight in spite of the threat' of backlash. It is to say that one should know the approximate force of that movement and have decided in advance how it would be met. The "freedom fighters" in the Civil Rights Movement are an example of this. They knew in advance something of the expected response to their activities and they not only seriously considered them, but drilled themselves in advance so they would not be taken unawares by sudden actions of the opposition.

The next point follows logically from the above. One should anticipate the difficulties of the solution. Almost any solution to a social problem brings other problems in its implementation. Be sure that the solution is not worse than the problem and know some ways of dealing with anticipated difficulties of the solution. Find out whether those who have the responsibility of deciding about the problem are simply unaware of it or are strongly invested in present policy or opposed to any movement because a clash of interests and values is involved. And this leads to point four, which is determine where in the organization the responsibility for formal decision-making in respect to the problem lies. Who formally makes the decision and who or what can influence this decision?

Timing one's efforts can be crucial. Agencies are more often open to change (as are individuals) when they are in periods of crisis, for example, when budgets are increasing or decreasing, when there are great decreases or increases in the number of clients served, when their performance reports are being questioned, or when new methods of dealing with the problem are being widely acclaimed.

The process by which change takes place must be understood, and it must be recognized that the initiation of change often requires a different approach than does the implementation of change. We have often seen workers fight a hard and bruising battle for the initiation of change only to lose the war because they were unwilling or unable to be an active part of its implementation. It is the changes in the way things are done that are the test of how the client will be served differently.

Consider whether change can be achieved more effectively in this situation by advocacy strategy, by collaborative strategy, or by both. Advocacy strategy employs an impressive array of tools, including the use of citizen groups, unions, and professional organizations to engage with the practitioner in litigation, picketing, bargaining, building pressure alliances, contriving for crises to occur, bringing sanctions to bear through external authorities, and perhaps by encouraging noncompliance with policy by workers and clients. Collaborative strategy may employ some of the techniques outlined by Patti and Resnick (1972). Here the change agent may provide facts about the nature of the problem, present alternative ways of doing things, try to develop an experimental project that involves different ways of doing things and get permission to implement it, seek to establish a committee to study the situation and make recommendations for change, attempt to improve the working climate of the agency so that individuals feel trusted and safe and thus can look beyond securing their own position to the task to be done, attempt to bring professional values and ethics to bear, use a logical argument to persuade, and point out what is really happening under the present policy. This last approach will require documentation of the results of present policy.

Pruger (1973) deals with the strategic concerns of the "good bureaucrat" in some ways similar to the above discussion and adds some additional factors. We have summarized his material as follows:

1. "One important property of a good bureaucrat is staying power." This means a recognition that things happen slowly in complex organizations but that whatever changes workers have in mind cannot be implemented if they do not stay in and with the organization.
2. "The good bureaucrat must somehow maintain a vitality of action and independence of thought." Organizational life tends to suppress vitality of action and independence of thought. Workers must resist such pressure.
3. "There is always room for insights and tactics that help the individuals preserve and enlarge the discretionary aspect of their activity and, by extension, their sense of personal responsibility."

And, these are tactics the good bureaucrat will employ:

1. "Understand legitimate authority and organizational enforcement." The inescapable degree of generality found in the regulatory policies and codes of the organization allows for considerable autonomy of the individuals if they just recognize it and use it. The organization's power to control is less than many realize, but if the limits of legitimate authority are recognized, the individuals may expand their discretionary limits.
2. "Conserve energy." Change agents should not thrash around and feel discouraged and unappreciated because they do not receive in a large organization the kind of support they receive from their friends. Also, as stated earlier, master the paper flow of the organization. Tills will not only help the client but will also remove from the worker's shoulders the weight of resentment and emotional turmoil one feels as one looks at the uncompleted statistical forms on the desk. Workers should describe what can be changed and work on it rather than spend valuable hours bemoaning what cannot be dealt with.
3. "Acquire a competence needed by the organization."
4. "Don't yield unnecessarily to the requirements of administrative convenience. Keep in mind the difference between that which serves the organizational mission and that which serves the organization." Rules, standards, and directives as to the way things should be done are meant to be means that serve ends. In organizations means tend to become ends so that a worker may be more concerned about turning in the mileage report than the results of the visit to a client. Ends and means should be kept clear.
5. Workers should remember that "The good bureaucrat is not necessarily the most beloved one."

We would like to stress that these skills in changing the bureaucracy or acting as an advocate for client groups involve the following knowledge and abilities. The knowledge of how individual human beings and social systems develop, grow, exist, change, and cope with problems; the knowledge of how Individuals interact within small social systems such as the family or primary groups (knowledge of family development and interaction, knowledge of group process); knowledge of transactions within larger social systems (organizational behaviour); knowledge of common human needs and the way culture affects how these needs are expressed are all critical knowledge bases necessary for effective planning for advocacy and institutional change. In addition, to carry through such plans, the workers will need self-awareness, especially in certain areas such as innate pushes toward the expression of competition and aggression, their own level of anger and the favourite ways of using it; they will need the capacity to use self in a disciplined way within the parameters of the plan; they will need a high level of communication skills and ability to use effectively the various skills.

The Professiona as a System

Social work is a profession, as we discussed earlier. All professions can be viewed as social systems. Because the social work profession is a system within which every social worker functions, whether it is recognized or not, every social worker ought to understand something about it. The profession through society's assignment of its functions, sanctions to some extent the work of all people who call themselves social workers, or who occupy jobs that are classified social work positions.

We identified the six characteristics of a profession. Throughout the text we have discussed the high degree of generalized and specialized knowledge needed by the professional. The value systems underlying social work practice have also been discussed. We certainly have indicated the need for social workers to have a commitment to community and client interests instead of being primarily motivated by self-interest. In this chapter we would like to continue in a more organized way to look at the sixth system of professional practice—the profession, itself, as a social system.

First, we need to consider the fact that the knowledge and skills possessed by professionals give them powerful control over persons and things. It is important to society, which provides the professional the opportunity to secure this power, that it be used primarily in the community interests and that it not be used to advance professionals at the costs of the welfare of those who support their acquisition of such knowledge. Thus, the community usually has some organized way of sanctioning the persons who may claim status and who may practice in the name of the profession. Also, the profession itself, in order to safeguard itself against self-aggrandisement of its members and assure that its function in society is fulfilled, supports the underlying value of community service.

In all professions, the community sanctions the individual's right to practice through some combination of the following elements: (1) completion of a certain prescribed course of education; (2) proving a certain level of competency through an examination process administered by the profession; (3) the licensing and regulation of the practitioner through a license, registration, or certification administered by the state (usually through a board with professionals as members); and (4) employment by an organization authorized by the state to offer certain services. Thus, there exists licensing of teachers and doctors and the registration of nurses. There has been considerable pressure within the social work profession to license social workers. Those who would license social workers usually make the point that such licensing would benefit the client systems by defining standards of service and the competence necessary for practice. It would establish a public accountability that will protect both the client and the practitioner from inconsistent, biased judgment of effectiveness of help offered. It would establish a legal definition of social work and establish levels of social work practice which should operate to protect both the professional and the client. It would give social work status among other professional groups.

Because of the importance of this question to social work (approximately half the states do presently license social work practitioners), a reprint of a very comprehensive article on licensing, which is highly recommended by the authors, has been included with this chapter (see Reading 15-2). Since licensing has come slowly to social work, the National Association of Social Workers attempted some time ago to set some standards through the establishment of a restricted title. The title, "Certified Social Worker," has been registered with the federal government and can be used only by persons certified by the professional association, the National Association of Social Workers. In order to use this title, social workers have to possess an MSW degree (a master's degree in social work), have worked two years in practice following the earning of the MSW under Supervision of another worker who is an ACSW, must be a member in good standing of the NASW, and must pass a professional examination. People who meet these requirements may call themselves a Certified Social Worker and use the letters ACSW (Academy of Certified Social Workers) after their name. The profession recommends that no one engage in private practice who is not a member of the Academy.

All professions are organized into some kind of professional association. These professional organizations serve three purposes: (1) increasing the adequacy of the performance of the individual practitioner; (2) policing the ranks of its membership to insure competent performance of the individual members: and (3) to protect the members' exclusive right to practice their profession. In social work, the professional association is the National Association of Social Workers, a national association operating through regional chapters in each state. It accepts for membership those persons who have a BA degree in social welfare or social work.

The admission of the BA worker to membership in the professional association was followed by the setting up of professional undergraduate courses in social work in universities and the implementation of an accreditation programme of such work by the Council on Social Work Education, the organization that accredits professional social work programmes in higher education.

Social work as an emergent profession has never had complete control of who could call themselves a social worker and who could do the job in the field. Generally, the social agencies were the ones who effectively decided who could be social workers in that the persons they hired to fill social work positions were entitled to call themselves social workers. Thus, the education, knowledge, and skill of agency employees filling social work positions, who were known to the public and clients as social workers, has varied widely. In general, the private agencies that have often served the middle class have generally insisted on MSW degrees for employment, while the public services have required only a BA (or less) degree. In an effort to deal with this, NASW has developed a statement of levels of social work practice complete with professional qualifications for each level.

Today, the National Association of Social Workers has identified six levels of social work practice. There are two levels—*the social service aide* and *the social service technician* that require less than a college degree in social work. To carry the title *"social worker,"* the person should have a bachelor's degree in social work (BSW).

To be a *graduate social worker,* the person needs a master's degree from an accredited professional school in social work. This usually requires two academic years beyond the BA degree, although it may require less time if the person has a BSW degree. To be a *certified social worker,* one must possess a MSW, have two years of practice beyond the degree under careful supervision, and must pass an ACSW examination. To be a *social work fellow,* one must possess a PhD or DSW in social work and have either two years' experience in specialization or have passed the ACSW examination plus two further years of specialized practice.

It has long been held that the requisite knowledge to judge professional performance is available only to those who have themselves been trained in applying such knowledge. The professional knowledge and skill of the professional person is so different from general knowledge and skill that no one outside the profession can judge the professional. This is usually discussed under the rubric of professional autonomy. Thus, every profession has some means of the self-regulation of practice.

Generally, these "shoulds" of professional practice are stated in a formal code of ethics. However, as certain professionals may engage in unethical or incompetent behaviourvior, and as the community becomes more and more dependent on professional knowledge, the community is increasingly demanding that the people served by the profession should have the right to judge professionals by the outcome of their service *as the public perceives it.* They are questioning whether it is possible for the operation to be a success if the patient dies. This stance may well mark some unrealiztic perceptions of the capacity of professionals on the part of the community, but it also marks a realiztic concern with the notion that clients do not have the capacity to know when they have been well served—that only professionals have the ability to judge the outcome of their actions.

Another clement in this notion of autonomy is that professionals are supposed to be self-directing in their work. As used here, autonomy refers to the professional's control of the content and terms of the work. However, autonomy is not a simple criterion of who is to be considered professional—at least most people have never been willing to designate those wives and mothers who run their own households as being professional. This introduces the notion that when we speak of professionals, what we are really talking about is some kind of organized autonomy—not the autonomy of the individual practitioner. Thus, the more that a profession as a profession is able to exercise autonomy, the more it represents, and its members are controlled by, a hierarchy of institutionalized expertise (Friedson, 1970, pp. 71-92). The question of the professionalization of social work has been raised by many authors on the basis that social welfare organizations are usually considered bureaucratic, not professional organizations. Thus, there are professionals operating in organizations that are marked by the fact that authority is that of the administrative office held. This conflicts with the notion that in a profession the authority is that of expertise. This has already been discussed under bureaucracy but it should be noted that perhaps one of the problems of all professions is that the rigidity and conservatism in the professions are also enforced by the concept of autonomy.

Each profession has its own culture. The interactions of social and professional roles required by the professional activities and professional groups generate particular ways of thinking and acting, and a particular language, unique to the profession. This may be called a professional culture. The value system of the profession in interaction with the value system of the bureaucracy is an important part of the culture of social work. A critical aspect of all professional education and inservice training is the attempt to socialise the workers to the agency and profession. By this, it is generally meant the internalization of the values and culture of the profession so that the professional person is constrained to work in certain ways and to take certain positions.

One of the problems in the achievement of greater autonomy of the profession is found in the fact that when agencies hire people *who have less than the recognized professional training,* these workers do not have a well-integrated identification with their profession that will allow them to stand outside bureaucratic expectation. Instead, they tend to be socialized to the culture of the agency rather than the culture of the profession. Thus, they may first see themselves as public welfare employees rather than first identifying themselves as social workers. As these workers often cannot easily go elsewhere and find employment as social workers, they are tied to their position in the agency rather than their identification as a professional.

Sound internalization of professional values is critically important as protection to the client system since in the helping process workers must use themselves and their judgments. There is seldom any way that another can interfere in the process of action to protect the client in advance of the worker's action. Therefore, the only assurance people have that a professional person can be trusted with professional tasks is that the person acts on the basis of deeply internalized feelings and judgments that stem from professional values and knowledge. This value system and the feelings and actions that stem from it become a part of the culture of the profession. The ambiguous position of social work within society in terms of its multiple functions and purposes also contributes greatly to shaping the culture of social work.

Lydia Rapoport (1959) says that "no other profession is as self-examining and critically self-conscious as social work." While she relates some problems of the profession to its youth, she also attributes much stress to the profession's ambiguous position in society and to its multiple purposes and functions. Social work, concerned with the social functioning of people and the adequacy of the social institutions which affect human functioning, "seeks to embrace and implement some principles and values which may be essentially unpopular and uncongenial to the dominant social order." This particular role of the profession, as has been observed, results in its being seen as a minority group that is both tolerated and feared. From this come outright attacks and depreciation by the society that sanctions social work. In addition, the social views of the profession tend to isolate individual workers from other professional groups.

One problem of social work is that the tasks it is expected to perform are unclear and that the responsibilities for which it is held to account are often contradictory. For example, many people expect the social worker to control every expenditure of the welfare client, but at the same time to further independent behaviour on the part of welfare recipients. Both expectations cannot be satisfied—one or the other must be chosen. Social work is supposed to be working to produce social change, but the society of which social work is a part is totally unable to reach agreement as to the kinds of social change it will support.

Rapoport (1959) points out other sources of strain for social workers, some of which have been touched on earlier in this text. Among them are the following;

1. Being constantly confronted with the problems of human need, pain, and injustice;
2. The capacity for self-awareness and self-control required for the purposeful use of the social work relationship, and the need "to harmonise personal capacity and inclination with professional behaviour and values;"
3. The institutional framework within which the social worker practices;

4. The opposing demands for "the maintenance of nearness and distance, of involvement and detachment, of rapport and objectivity;" and
5. The requirement for the tolerance of uncertainty, given our limited knowledge about human development and our difficulty in attempting to utilise what we do know.

Recapitulation

In this chapter we have moved from our focus on the interaction of client and worker for problem-solving to what it means for the worker to be a part of the action system of an agency and a profession. It is critically important for workers to understand the situation in which they work. We have tried to contribute to this understanding through a look at the nature of bureaucracy and professionalism; the conflicts between bureaucracy and professionalism; the worker and the client as operating within the parameters of agency policy; ways to bring about change in a bureaucracy; and the worker as a professional.

A Look Forward

We are now near the end of the text. Readers have two remaining things to look forward to (1) they have one more brief chapter which will try to summarise the text material; and (2) they should be looking forward to working with people and social systems, and perhaps testing whether the material in this book is really helpful in their practice. After all, that is why the authors wrote the text.

Reading 1: **Organizational Tinkering**

Edward J. Pawlak

To thinker means to work at something in an experimental or makeshift way. Although clinicians positions and roles in many social welfare organizations preclude them from pursuing ambitious organizational change, they still may be able to work at change in modest, makeshift ways. And, despite the fact that clinical social work is usually practiced in an organizational and policy context, many clinicians are uninterested in acquiring the knowledge and skills that might facilitate intraorganizational tinkering on behalf of their practice or their clients. Others are overwhelmed, cynical, or disillusioned by their dealings with bureaucracy (Briar, 1968; Gottlieb, 1974, p. 34; Hanlan, 1971; Piliavin, 1968; Podell and Miller, 1974; Specht, 1968, pp. 42-43). Some front-line practitioners, however, have learned to tinker effectively (Hyman and Schreiber, 1974; Maher, 1974; Senna, 1974).

To help clinicians improve their talent in dealing with organizations, this article identifies tactics they can use to tinker with organizational structure, modes of operation, rules, conventions, policy, and programmes. The specific tactics discussed are tinkering with bureaucratic succession and rules, the white paper or position paper, demonstration projects, modification of board composition, bypassing, influencing grant reviews, leaking information, and protest by resignation.

Although the author takes a partisan stand on behalf of clinicians, it does not follow that managers are necessarily the villains. However, some of the tactics identified here are directed toward those administrators who cause clinicians to harbor severe misgivings about the organization.

This article stems not only from the author's observation of and experience with organizational tinkering, but also from the contributions of others who have addressed similar themes (Bennis, 1969; Brager, 1968; Martin, 1971; Patti and Resnick, 1972; Specht, 1968, pp. 42-52; Weissman. 1973, pp. 57-131). It warns clinicians to bear in mind the pitfalls and dilemmas of organizational tinkering—that it takes place in a political climate and in a structure of authority, norms, and sanctions (Epstein, 1968; Green, 1966; Nader, Petkas and Blackwell. 1972; Patti, 1974; Weisband and Franck, 1975).

Bureaucratic Succession

Bureaucratic succession usually refers to a change in leadership at the highest levels of an organization. Here, however, the author uses the broader concept that includes changes in leadership at all levels in the hierarchy. (Gouldner. 1954, pp. 59-104; Levenson, 1961). Bureaucratic succession must be called to the attention of clinicians because it is an opportunity to influence intraorganizational change. For clinicians to exert influence during this phase of organizational transition, it is essential that they understand certain features of organizational life that frequently accompany succession.

Prior to an administrator's departure, organizations usually go into a period of inaction. Most staff members are aware of the lame-duck character of this phase of organizational life, when any major change is avoided until the new administrator takes office. There are, however, ways in which clinicians take advantage of this period. They can, for example, (1) suggest criteria for the selection of a successor, (2) seek membership on the search committee, (3) prepare a position paper for the new administrator, (4) propose a revision in the governance structure to enhance participatory management, (5) organize fellow subordinates to propose changes that had been unacceptable to the outgoing administrator, or (6) propose the formulation of a task force to facilitate transition.

The "first one hundred days" is another critical phase of bureaucratic succession that should be examined for the opportunities it offers. Although new administrators tend to be conservative about implementing changes until they are more familiar with the organization, they still are interested in developing and in making their own mark. This three-month period, therefore, provides opportunities to orient and shape the perceptions of new administrators who, until they acquire their own intelligence about the organization, are both vulnerable and receptive to influence.

The following case illustrates how practitioners can tinker with organizational hierarchy by taking advantage of a resignation.

The resignation of a clinician who had served as director of staff development in a child welfare agency provided the staff with an opportunity to influence the transformation of the position into that of administrative assistant. The agency had recently undergone rapid growth in staff size, resources, and diversity, without an accompanying increase in the administrative staff. Thus, the clinician's resignation became the occasion for examining whether the position should be modified to serve such administrative staff functions as programme development and grant management.

> Bureaucratic succession, therefore, provides an opportunity for an organization to take pause; to examine its mission, structure, policies, practices, accomplishments, and problems; and to decide what it wants to become. It is incumbent upon practitioners to participate in these processes and to take advantage of the structure of influence during that vulnerable phase.

Rules

Rules are features of organizations that, by their nature, invite tinkering. They act as mechanisms of social control and standardization, provide guidelines for decision-making, limit discretion, and structure relationships between persons and units within the organizational structure and between separate organizations (Perrow, 1972, pp. 23-32), There are two types of rules—formal and informal. Formal rules are derived from law or are determined administratively or collectively. Informal rules—which may be as binding as formal ones—are practices that have been routinized so that they have become organizational conventions or traditions, Rules vary in specificity, in their inherent demand for compliance, in the manner in which compliance is monitored, and in their sanctions for a lack of compliance.

Clinicians can tinker with rules either by the kind of interpretations they apply to them or by using their discretion, as is permitted with an ambiguous or general rule. Rules do not necessarily eliminate discretion, but they may eliminate alternatives that might otherwise be considered (Thompson, 1967, p. 120). Gottlieb (1974, p. 8) describes them as follows:

> Rules are not necessarily static. They appear to be a controlling

> force working impersonally and equally, but they vary both in adherence and enforceability and are used variously by staff in their adaptation to the "welfare bind."

Hanlan (1967, p. 93) suggests that "in public welfare there exists an informal system that operates without invoking the formal administrative machinery of rules." The author overheard the director of a community action programme encourage new workers "to err on the side of generosity in determining eligibility for programmes." A vocational rehabilitation counselor reported that he had many teeth fixed by liberally interpreting a rule that provided dental care for only those clients whose appearance and dental problems would otherwise have prevented them from being considered for employment involving public contact. This shows that one can tinker with the manner in which rules are interpreted and enforced.

Another way of tinkering with rules is to avoid what Gottlieb (1974, p. 8) calls "rule interpretations by agents of the system alone." She goes on to report that welfare workers encouraged clients to seek help in interpreting rules enforced by the National Welfare Rights Organization (NWRO). It is generally known that legal-aid clinics have been called on to give a legal interpretation of welfare rules and rules governing commitment to mental hospitals.

A supervisor for public assistance eligibility once reported that a thorough knowledge of all the rules enables the welfare worker to invoke one rule over another in order to help clients get what they need. This observation is supported by Gottlieb (1974, p. 32), who points out that rules allow for exceptions and that many NWRO members know the rules better than the workers and thus can challenge their interpretations. In his study of regulatory agencies, Nader (1972) suggests that rules not only are opportunities for action but are potential obstacles as well and that major effort is frequently required to persuade the agency to follow its own rules.

Another way of dealing with rules is to avoid asking for an interpretation. One agency administrator has suggested that personnel should not routinely ask for rulings and urges them to use their own discretion. He commented: "If you invoke authority, you put me in a position where I must exercise' it. If I make a decision around here, it becomes a rule."

These ways of tinkering with rules suggest that clinicians should examine the function of rules, discern the latitude they are allowed in interpreting them, and exercise discretion. Although the foregoing examples are primarily taken from welfare settings, the principles outlined can be applied to traditional clinical settings.

Indirect Influence

Too often, clinicians rely on the anecdotal or case approach to influence change in an organization. Such an approach is too easily countered by the rejoinder that exceptional cases do not require a change in policy but should be handled as exceptions. The white paper, or position paper, is a much ignored means of tinkering with organizations.

A white paper is a report on a specific subject that emanates from a recent investigation. A position paper is a statement that sets forth a policy or a perspective. The first is usually more carefully reasoned and documented; the second may be argued instead of reasoned. Both white papers and position papers provide opportunities for social documentation and for formulating a compelling case. Such statements strive for logic and are characterized by their use of both quantitative and qualitative data. As the following example shows, by virtue of their character and quality, both position papers and white papers demand a specific response.

> A student social worker wrote a position paper identifying the number of teenage pregnancies, the number of associated medical problems, and the high rate of venereal disease among adolescents. She argued for the redirection of the original planned parenthood proposal from the main office to satellite clinics in public housing developments and schools. The paper was well received and spurred the executive to obtain funding from the housing authority.

Lindblom (1970) has characterized decision-making in organizations as "disjointed incrementalism." Simon (1957) indicates that organizations "satisfice"—that is, they make decisions that are good enough. Uncertainties in the environment, the inability to scan all alternatives, and the unknown utility of a solution or decision all preclude optimal decision-making. If organizations were to try to comprehend all the information and contingencies necessary before making a rational decision, the complexity would be overwhelming. Thus. organizations are reluctant to make changes on a large scale because this could lead to large-scale and unpredictable consequences. Resistance to change, therefore, may often be attributed to structure rather than to a malevolent or unsympathetic administrator. This calls attention to organizational structure and processes, but does not mean that the values and roles of administrators are to be ignored.[1]

Given this perspective of organizational behaviour, clinicians may consider approaching innovation incrementally and on a small scale by first gaining authorization for a demonstration project.[2] A demonstration project may be bounded by the duration of time or the proportion of the budget or staff time that is devoted to it. The problem with demonstration projects is that the people for whom the demonstration is being carried out are not always specified, nor are they always kept abreast of developments. Often there is a failure to articulate the ramifications and consequences of a successful or unsuccessful demonstration. Practitioners must develop a strategy of demonstration— a means of diffusing innovation throughout the organization or into other organizations and of obtaining commitments from the administration when the demonstration is complete. The following is an example of the commitment one social worker obtained.

> A social worker met with a group of suspended or expelled junior high school students after class to discuss their problems. Realizing that she needed to have a chance to intervene directly in their school behaviour, she persuaded the agency supervisor, the principal, and the classroom teacher to develop a pilot project— "the opportunity class"—to be used as a last

> resort before expulsion. When the project was organized, the social worker remained in the classroom for several periods at least two days each week. She handled the acting-out behaviour problems while the teacher continued classroom instruction. Eventually the teacher acquired skill in handling students who were acting out. The class continued without the social worker's presence, and some students returned to a regular classroom while others were expelled.

Agency board committees are typically composed of elected members and the executive director of the agency. In addition, in some agencies, one or two staff members may also serve on the committee or occasionally attend meetings to make reports. One strategy of tinkering with the composition of the committee and the kind of information and influence it receives is to promote the idea that non-board and non-staff members with certain expertise be included on the committee. For example, a psychiatrist and a local expert on group treatment with children might be recruited to join a case services committee in order to provide legitimation to innovations that board members were grudgingly resisting.

Bypassing refers to a process whereby practitioners avoid taking proposals for change or grievances to their immediate superiors but seek instead a hearing or decision from a higher level in the hierarchy. In an enlightened organization, this form of bypassing is acceptable and even encouraged; government workers, in fact, are entitled to it as part of "due process." Bypassing is risky, however, in that it can discredit the judgment of the complainants if the matter is trivial or if it appears that it could have been resolved at a lower level in the hierarchy. Bypassing also places the administration in a vulnerable situation because if the tactic is justified, it reflects poorly on the judgment of the superior and the administrators who hired them. This may lead to questions of non-retention or spur a desired resignation. A successful instance of bypassing is described in the following example:

> When a clinician's complaints concerning the physical plant

> and security of a youth home went unheeded by the director, he demanded to meet with the executive committee of the board. The director admitted that his own sense of urgency differed from that of his staff, but arranged for the meeting. The executive committee approved some of the recommendations for change and authorized that they be implemented as soon as possible.

Agencies often write grant applications for funds to support their programmes. A critical phase of the application process occurs at a public review of the grant application when the funding agency invites comment or a letter of support from the agency or from interested parties. If clinicians are dissatisfied with a particular programme, and if it is an important matter, they can provide the agency issuing the grant with dissenting information, testify at the review of the grant application, or respond from the standpoint of an "expert witness." In any event, the grant-review process may be an opportunity to voice concern about an agency's programme and to influence the advisory group to give conditional approval or disapproval. As is shown in the following example, clinicians may attempt to influence the review process indirectly—by encouraging an expert third party to raise questions about the grant application—or directly.

> A social worker was asked to serve as a technical reviewer for a volunteer programme for young offenders in a regional planning advisory group. The programme was modeled after an existing programme in another part of the state. The documents supporting the application contained a manual that described the role of the volunteer. It suggested that a volunteer should report any violations of parole to the corrections authority but should not reveal tin's action to the offender. In seeming contradiction, it emphasized that the volunteer should be a "friend" of the offender. The social worker informed the advisory group of this provision and of his strenuous objection to it. The director of the programme had failed to read the manual thoroughly and was unaware of the statement. The advisory group approved the programme on the condition that

the volunteer not serve as an informer and demanded that the staff codify the conditions under which it may be morally imperative for the volunteer to reveal the offender's behaviour.

Social workers are often asked and frequently do endorse a programme or a grant application perfunctorily, without having read the proposal. In other instances, programmes and grants are endorsed in spite of strong reservations. Notwithstanding the pressures toward reciprocity that exist among agencies, such exchanges of professional courtesy are questionable.

Social workers should take advantage of requests for endorsement or participation in the grant-review process, particularly if they believe that certain aspects of a proposal or programme are questionable. The desire for professional endorsement also underlies agency efforts to recruit clinicians for board membership or as paid consultants. Refusal of such offers is a way of "making a statement" about a programme.

Radical Tactics

Leaking information, or the covert release of information about an organization, is a tactic that should be used only in grave matters after all other remedies within the organization have been exhausted. The third party to whom the informant gives the information has to verify it and the credibility of the informant, since this person is not willing to put one's character and job on the line. However, until "blowing the whistle" becomes an accepted institutionalized value, and until protections are legislated, it is likely that members of organizations will continue to act like "guerillas in a bureaucracy" (Nader, Petkas, and Black-well, 1972, pp. 15. 2.5-33; Needleman and Needleman, 1974).

Clinicians who anticipate the need to leak information would be well advised to seek counsel, for discovery could result in liability damages. They are obliged to have a thorough, accurate, and verifiable account of the objectionable situation. As the ethics of leaking information have not been well formulated, clinicians need to consider carefully the professional, moral, and legal standards that support such action (Nader, Petkas, and Blackwell. 1972, pp. vii, 1-8,29-30, 22.5-230). One way in which the clinician may choose to attack the problem is shown as follows.

> The clinician in a foregoing example who was concerned about the physical plant and security of a youth home notified the state monitor about the condition of the home. At the next site visit, the monitor raised questions about the residents' access to balconies and the roof and about the staff-client ratio on weekends.

Resignation in protest, or public defection, is another tactic that should be used only when a clinician experiences unbearable misgivings and finds it both morally and professionally imperative to reveal them publicly. The major problem is that the organization has the financial and operational resources to counter the protest, but the employee has none. Also, with few exceptions, resignation in protest has a history of aversive consequences for the protester (Weisband and Franck 1975).

A resignation in protest may also discredit the agency. Therefore, prospective protesters must be prepared to have their observations and conclusions verified and their judgment subjected to public review and scrutiny. In addition, the protester must realize that future employers will wonder whether such history of protestation will continue. An example follows.

> When his concerns went unheeded by the hoard, a clinician resigned in protest. Moreover, he informed the board and the director that he would discourage any professional worker from accepting employment at the agency. He was effective in discouraging local professionals from accepting employment at the agency unless firm commitments were made to modify policies and practices that were detrimental to clients.

The theory of escalation urges protesters to begin by using conventional and formal means to express grievances and influence change. Only after these have been exhausted, and traditional means have encountered failure and resistance, should they engage in a series of escalations to such unconventional or radical forms of protest as boycotting, "palace revolts," picketing, leaking information, and the like. The essential point of this strategy is that protesters should not begin by engaging in the most radical and abrasive strategy. To document the intransigence of the bureaucracy, change must be approached incrementally. If this is not done, the bureaucracy may point to the failure to follow administrative due process. The protester's etiquette and failure to go through channels then become the bone of contention, and the protester becomes the object of protest (Nader, Petkas, and Blackwell, 1972, pp. 16-25; Needleman and Needleman, 1974, pp. 285-289, 335-339; Weisband and Franck, 1975, pp. 55-94).

As a condition of employment and as a professional right and responsibility, clinicians should have the opportunity to bring their insights into the plans and programmes of the organization they work for. Such participation requires that clinicians acquire skill in dealing with organizations. It is hoped that the participation of clinicians in organizational activity will promote responsive service delivery systems and satisfactory work climates.

At the risk of appearing to be a "double agent," the author plans to write a second article to advise administrators on how to cope with the tinkering of clinicians. After all, organizational power—whether in the hands of clinicians or administrators—"must be insecure to some degree if it is to be more responsible" (Nader, Petkas, and Blackwell 1972, p. 15).

Reading 2: Public Regulation of Social Work

David A. Hardcastle

A major contemporary movement in social work's efforts to attain recognition as a full profession is the move toward public regulation. The National Association of Social Workers, for example, has taken strong action to further this objective, as illustrated in the following resolution approved by its 1969 Delegate Assembly:

> *Resolved:* That the various combinations of Chapters, working in concert at a state level, be authorized to pursue licensing of Social Work practice within each state. . . (*NASW News,* 1974, 1975a, 1975b, 1975c, 1976).

The public or legal regulation of a profession occurs when the public, through formal legislation and the regulatory or legal powers of the state, defines and regulates professional behaviour and conduct. Although the regulated profession may be involved in formulating the definitions and in the processes of regulation, it is the mandate and sanction of the state that ultimately defines the profession. Social work currently has some form of public regulation in Arkansas, California, Colorado, Delaware, Idaho, Illinois, Kansas, Kentucky, Louisiana, Maine, Maryland, Michigan, New York, Oklahoma, Puerto Rico, Rhode Island, South Carolina, South Dakota, Utah, and Virginia.

This article analyses the conceptual foundation of legal regulation, and develops a classificatory scheme of legal regulation according to its major variables. It also analyses and classifies existing legal regulations according to the variables:

Professionalism

There is general consensus on the attributes of a profession, and they have been well discussed by Greenwood (1966) and Feldstein (1971), among others. Basically, these attributes are (1) a systematic and defined theory or a system of abstract propositions, (2) defined and specialized skills, (3) a regulatory code of ethics governing conduct, (4) a supportive professional culture or community with normative standards, values, and symbols, (5) professional authority which holds that professional behaviour can only be evaluated by professional peers, and (6) the sanction of the community to exercise such authority.

The second point—defined and specialized skills—should be a basic prerequisite for public regulation of an occupational activity. These skills describe the activity to be regulated. However, they are not sufficient alone to transform an occupation into a profession nor do they provide all the prerequisites for public regulation.

According to Wilensky (1970), two additional elements are necessary for each transformation. The first element is technical expertise based on systematic knowledge and doctrine acquired through formal training. The neophyte practitioner must have this training to gain the formal knowledge and skills and the implicit or tacit knowledge, values, and norms of the craft. It is the latter —the tacit knowledge, values, and norms— that provide the basis for what is commonly referred to as the "art" of social work. The second critical clement is the acquisition of the regulatory norms by the occupational category, which are needed to limit conduct and behaviour. Essential to and inherent in the regulatory norms are the following factors: (1) other professionals, rather than clients or "outsiders," must make judgments of competence and appropriate professional conduct, and (2) service must be the primary motive for the activity. It is the ideal of service or of a "calling," with the practitioner standing above the sordid considerations of the marketplace, that separates the professions from occupations (MacIver, 1966, p. 51: Parsons, 1951, pp. 314-315; 1954, pp. 38-43). Although "service calling" does not exclude other motives, it does place service as the dominant and central motive.

Public or legal regulation of a profession and its activity indicates that the profession has received the sanction and mandate of the public. Wilensky (1970, pp. 489-490) holds that a benchmark of professional development, although not necessarily an integral part of its natural history, is attained when occupations engage in political action to gain the support of public law for the protection of their job territory and their sustaining code of ethics. Legal protection is an expedient of an occupation "on the make." It enhances status, protects jobs, and restricts jobholding to those who meet certain requirements, and protects the public from incompetence—that is, from practice by persons without the requisite technology, tacit knowledge, or normative behaviour (Committee on the Study of Competence, 1968, p. iii).

Public regulation, therefore, implicitly recognizes the authority of peer judgments, in that the regulatory board is generally composed of professional peers; it also provides explicit community sanctions for the exercise of professional authority. But public regulation per se does not establish an occupational activity as a profession. In contemporary society most occupational activities are regulated in some manner, and many are directly regulated through formal statute. Wilensky (1970, pp. 484-187), for example, reports that egg graders are regulated in Indiana, well diggers in Maryland, and horseshoers in Illinois. Friedman (1962, p. 139) reports that, as early as 1938, North Carolina regulated 600 occupational activities ranging from medicine to dealing in scrap tobacco. During its 1974 session, when the Kansas legislature was considering a social work regulation bill, it was also considering a bill to license timber harvesters.

Purposes of Regulation

The NASW 1975 policy statement (p. 15), by action of the Delegate Assembly, sets forth the following four purposes for the public regulation of social work:

1. Establishing a public, legal definition of the profession which recognizes the differential levels of social work practice.
2. Protecting consumer and clientele rights and raising standards of service competence of practitioners in both agency and independent practice.
3. Establishing a public accountability in the delivery of social services based on professional standards rather than inconsistent, private standards of performance, and that protects the practitioner in the performance of social work tasks.
4. Provide a basis for the development and enhancement of the profession within the context of other social institutions and professions.

The public justification for legal regulation is more general and succinct and is made on a twofold basis: the protection of the public and the development and protection of the profession.

It is assumed that the vendor engages in activities so complex that they require knowledge, skill, and technology for judgment beyond that reasonably expected for an independent evaluation by a consumer. The state therefore provides an a priori evaluation for the consumer. It is also assumed that the vendor's behaviour has an irreversible impact on the consumer. If the vendor does not have the requisite knowledge, skills, and technology, the consumer may suffer severe and irreversible harm. However, as the Virginia statute (1975) states, "the potential for harm is recognizable and not remote or dependent on tenuous arguments." A third assumption is the "neighborhood effect" of the activity, in which the impact of the vendor's behaviour clearly extends beyond the vendor and consumer and affects the general public. Examples of neighborhood effect may be found in the area of physical safely, within such fields as architecture, engineering, and public health, and perhaps social planning, community organization, and education.

The development and protection of the profession is inherent in the protection of the public, although distinct from it. Through its regulatory powers, the state can impose entry requirements and standards for maintaining performance. Tests of continued competence and the updating of knowledge and skill can be imposed. Although these standards are designed to protect the public, they also protect the competent professional from the deleterious neighborhood impact of charlatans practicing under the umbrella of the profession.

Less altruistic reasons for an occupational activity to promote legal regulation are imbedded in the potential for protection of the job market that such regulation affords. Depending on the restrictiveness of the entry for requirements, it has the potential of limiting the supply of the service in relation to the demand for the service. Although rational justification for restrictions can be made on the grounds of protecting the public, if they limit supply in relation to demand, the tendency will be to drive prices up. The potential of legal regulation to provide market control to the vendors or practitioners is related to the degree to which the vendors control the regulatory boards. Friedman (1962) cites a 1956 study indicating that 75 per cent of the regulatory boards were controlled by persons who had a direct economic interest in the regulated activity. Indeed, it is generally a hallmark of full professional status when the vendors control the licensing process utilising the regulatory powers of the state.

The potential of public regulation to provide revenue for states cannot be overlooked. Licensing fees and occupational taxes, like the charges for the sale of liquor licenses in certain states, can be a viable source of revenue. The example of North Carolina with its regulations and fee collections for over 600 occupational and economic activities cannot be ignored. In Kansas, 20 per cent of the registration fees of social workers go into the state's general fund while 80 per cent are used to defray the cost of regulation.

Categories of Regulation

Public regulation can be parsimoniously classified into three categories according to the state's use of its regulatory powers to enforce its definitions and regulations to protect the public. These three categories are registration, certification, and licensure.

Registration

This is the state's listing or registry of persons identifying themselves with the activity. Registration provides a self-identified listing of vendors to potential users. The state's utilization of its regulatory powers is limited. There may be specific requirements for registration, such as the possession of certain educational credentials and the payment of fees, but unregistered vendors do not usually draw punitive measures from the state unless they claim registration. It is up to the market—the client, the agency, the payee—to determine the worth of the registered vendor over the unregistered vendor. This form of public regulation exercises the least degree of regulatory power and the least interference with the activity of the marketplace.

Certification

This is the warranting by the state that the persons certified have attained a specified level of knowledge and skills. Like registration, certification does not prohibit uncertified persons from engaging in the behaviour; it merely prevents their use of "certified" or a similar descriptive term with their title. Registration is a requisite of certification. The latter does further in that it requires that the state make a judgment as to the competence of the vendor. Certification thus provides the public with an a priori judgment of the competence of those using a term such as "certified" with their title. The state defines competence and may test for it, but does not enforce its definition of competence over the activity, only over the use of the title. Consumers and vendors have the choice is to whether they wish to use— and meet—the state's definition of competence. The unregulated vendor can engage in the activity of consumers can be found who are within to purchase the service.

Licensure

This is the third and strongest form of legal regulation. It is a mechanism by which the state decrees that persons may not engage in particular economic activities and behaviours except under specific conditions set forth by the authority of the state and under its regulatory powers. Licensure states explicitly the requirements for knowledge and skills, describes how these are to be obtained and demonstrated, and uses the state's regulatory powers to enforce the definition of standards and behaviours. Licensure protects both the title and job activity. It defines the requirements of those who perform the services and limits the activities to those who meet its definition. For example, individuals may use an accountant who is not certified to monitor and record their fiscal affairs or they may use an unregistered architect to design their homes, but their surgery, whether for a fee or free, must be performed by a state-approved practitioner. Licensure combines registration and certification with control (Agostinelli, 1973; Friedman, 1962, pp. 137-161; Hardcastle, 1973: Levy. 1973a; Sheafor. 1973; Weinberger and Weinberger, 1974; Wilensky, 1974, pp. 483-501).

Regulation of Social Work

As mentioned earlier, 19 states and Puerto Rico have some

form of public regulation of social work. The legislation for public regulation in 18 of these states and Puerto Rico, as well as the NASW Model Licensing Act, were analyzed and classified according to their potential for the protection of the public and the development of the profession (National Association of Social Workers, 1973). (Delaware's legislation was passed after the completion of this study and is therefore not included in the analysis. Several other states may also have enacted some legal regulation of social work by the time this article appears.)

Protection of the Public

Each net of public regulation was analyzed in terms of its potential to protect the public. The stronger the potential for public protection, the more likely is public regulation to approach licensure.

Criteria used to examine the legislation for protection of the public aimed to determine whether the legislative acts contained the following:

1. Definitions and specifications of knowledge, skills, and values required for practice.
2. Entry requirements specified in terms of credentials, experience, and examinations.
3. Standards differentiating the knowledge and skills required for the various levels of practice—when these levels of practice are specified, especially if they are arranged in a hierarchy.
4. Utilization of regulatory powers to protect the public definitions and requirements for social work practice.
5. The functional exclusiveness of the definition.
6. Inclusion of the protection of confidentiality.
7. The degree to which "grandfathering" or the waiving of competence examinations for contemporary practitioners is avoided.
8. Requirements for demonstrations of continuing competence,

such as reexaminations for competence and requirements for continuing education.

Two of the criteria may need elaboration. "Utilization of regulatory powers" refers to the degree to which the legislation prohibits unregulated persons from engaging in the activity. In other words, does the statute regulate functions and actions or merely restrict the use of certain titles? True licensure requires functional exclusiveness.

"Grandfathering" refers to the practice of automatically granting to the contemporary practitioner the credentials of the public regulations. Under grandfathering the practitioner meets the requirements for regulation upon applying and paying fees. The degree to which existing practitioners are grandfathered is critical for the protection of the public. If it is assumed that regulation is necessary to protect the public, the need for public protection must relate to current practitioners as well as future practitioners. Grandfathering, however, could allow current practitioners to practice for perhaps 30 to 40 years, untouched by requirements for updating knowledge or for testing of skills.

Certain issues of recertification are related to grandfathering. Without recertification, two tenuous assumptions must be made before any substantial client protection can be inferred: (1) social work knowledge and skills once acquired are mastered for life and (2) the profession is not generating new knowledge or skills so that social work knowledge and skills are static and will not change over the worker's life.

Regulation with extensive grandfathering and without meaningful recertification offers little protection to the client beyond that available without regulation. The current body of professionals and any future group who pass their entry examinations may have an expectancy of approximately 30 to 40 years of practice life. If so, regulation with grandfathering will have an approximate 20-year "half-life"; 20 years will elapse before the profession is half certified if one assumes a constant rate of entry into it and attrition from those leaving it.

Under the same assumptions of entry and attrition without meaningful recertification for any future point beyond 20 years, only half the profession will have had a testing of competence within a 20-year span.

Table 1 summarises the review of the regulations by the foregoing criteria. No state's legal regulations meet the criteria for full licensure. No state uses its regulatory powers to enforce its definition of social work practice for persons regulated by the legislation. Persons in all states may engage in the economic activity and behaviours without being regulated as social workers. However, they cannot claim the regulated title in the performance of the activity.

Development of the Profession

The second area for analysis was the potential for the development of the profession means that the state, not the profession, assumes regulatory control, legislation can contain mechanisms to promote the development of the profession and of competent professionals. Criteria for analysis included the following:

1. Exclusiveness *of claim to professional praxis*
   Exemptions allowed for other professions
   Exemptions allowed for social workers employed under certain auspices
   Title protection
   Protection of functions
   Clear criteria for knowledge, skill, and function for differentiating between levels of social work if levels are used
2. *Recertification requirements for professional growth*
   Periodic examinations of knowledge and skills
   Continuing education including definitions of what is required
3. *Professional authority and autonomy* Composition of the regulatory board and proportion of social work professionals
   Autonomy of the board
   Decision-making power of the board Autonomy of practice and degree of dependence on controls external to the profession

4. *Reciprocity in terms of allowance for interstate transfer of requirements.*

TABLE 1

Classification of the legal regulations of the social work profession in 18 states and Puerto Rico and in the Model Licensing Act of the National Association of Social Workers (NASW)

Classification	States, Puerto Rico, and NASW model
Licensure: Full use of regulatory powers to enforce functional exclusiveness, credentials requirements for entry, examination of knowledge and skills	None
Strong certification: Use of regulatory powers for title protection, credentials requirements for entry, entry examination of knowledge and skills, and at least one other major criterion, such as continuing education, to protect the public	Colorado Idaho Illinois Kansas Kentucky Maryland South Dakota Utah NASW
Weak certification; Use of regulatory powers to protect preface to title, credentials requirements for entry, and entry examination, but no other major criteria to protect the public	California Louisiana Maine New York Okalahoma Virginia
Registration: Use. of regulatory powers to protect preface only, credentials for entry examination, but no entry examination on knowledge or skills and no other major criteria to protect the public	Arkansas Michigan Puerto Rico Rhode Island South Carolina

The criteria under the third category are critical. They determine whether the regulated professional is an autonomous professional or is limited to carrying out practice activity as a professional under the auspices of an agency.

According to Greenwood (1966), Parsons (1951, 1954) and other students of professions, the mark of a profession is strong reliance on peers for professional authority and for judgments of professional competence. The requiring of judgment-making by agency personnel in positions of control within an agency's organizational structure —that is, supervisors—is a professional. Essentially it substitutes bureaucratic and administrative judgments for professional ones. It does not further the profession but promotes the agency and discourages professional functioning independent of bureaucratic systems. Meaningful public regulation should curtail the need for bureaucratic regulation, not enlarge it.

Utilising the major criteria to justify public regulation for the protection of clients and the public and for the development of the profession, it appears that public regulation of social work falls short.

Impact on Protection

No state uses its regulatory powers to define and regulate functional behaviours for the social work profession. In short, licensure does not exist for social work. Only five states protect the unadorned title of "social worker." The remaining states, following the NASW Model Licensing Act, protect the title of social worker only whim prefaced by "registered," "certified," or a similar term. Although 75 per cent of the states require entry examinations, all but three have liberal grandfathering exclusions, exclusions for related professions, or exclusions from regulation allowed to some social workers because of the auspices of their employment. Recertification requirements are limited to payment of fees with the exception of continuing education required by four states and the NASW Model Licensing Act. Although certification can be revoked, this is done for negative behaviour—"thou shalt nots." Recertification does not depend on positive behaviour—"thou shalts."

Eighty per cent of the legal regulations and the NASW Model Licensing Act specify more than one practice level. None specify functional or behavioural differences between the levels. The major differences relate to educational preparation and occasionally to differences in experience and auspices. Private practice as a regulated social work activity is permitted only for the upper levels.

In summary, protection of the public or clients is little improved by the current body of legal regulations over what existed without legal regulation. With the exception of the entry examination, the states, Puerto Rico, and the NASW Model Licensing Act appear to be certifying only that the professional has met baseline educational requirements associated with a specific title.

Impact on the Profession

Again, the contemporary body of legal regulations appears to do little to promote the development of the profession. Almost all states, either specifically or by implication, exclude from regulation "other professions performing similar functions," whether or not these professions are regulated by other statutes. Approximately 40 per cent exclude social workers who are employed under certain auspices. Only five states protect the unadorned title of social worker. Even NASWs Model Licensing Act does not protect it.

Although 80 per cent of the legal regulations specify levels of practice, they do not explicitly mention differentials in knowledge and skills, nor are career ladders present. Movement between levels is generally by meeting the next requirement for academic degrees. Notable exceptions are the requirements of experience for autonomous clinical practice and Michigan's experience continuum.

Registration or certification is generally for life, contingent on the periodic payment of fees. No state monitors the maintenance and upgrading of knowledge and skills, except for the requirement of continuing education in lour states. It appears unlikely that legal regulation will provide motivation for professional development beyond that existing without it.

On the criteria related to professional authority and autonomy, the legal regulations grade higher. All but two states have regulatory boards composed primarily of social workers. The boards are autonomous and have decision-making powers, with the odd exceptions of the regulatory board in Kansas, which is advisory to the Secretary of Social and Rehabilitation Services, and the board recommended in the NASW Model Licensing Act, which would be advisory to a regulatory agency.

When the statutes contain levels of practice, the autonomy of the professional and the profession is a critical factor. Autonomous practice in the multilevel statutes is limited to the upper level of practice. Practitioners at lower levels can engage in the practice activity, but generally only under the auspices and supervision of an agency. The agency supervisor need not be a professional social worker or even a professional. Qualifications required for private practice may include supervision by an appropriately certified social worker. The point is not subtle. The practice of professionals in the field of social work, except for a limited number of elites at the upper level of practice, remains under the control of agencies, that is, under a professional or non-professional control. If this situation is justified on the basis that the lower levels lack the requisite knowledge and skills for autonomous peer-regulated practice, can their status as professionals be simultaneously advocated? This is not an argument against agencies as delivery systems or against administrative supervision and direction. Nor is it an argument against differentiated practice. It is an argument against the inconsistency of requiring by legal regulation that the majority of the activities of the profession be carried on within the confines of an agency in order to be called professional social work practice.

Slightly over half the states allow for reciprocity with states having similar requirements in their legal regulations. To some degree, the free movement of social workers throughout the country may be inhibited because of the lack of reciprocity between the states. However, this restriction probably has a minimal effect since the legal regulations are relatively flaccid.

Conclusions

The existing legal regulations and the provisions of the NASW Model Licensing Act appear to this author to have little potential for the protection of the public, the development of the profession, and greater impact on the profession than exists without legal regulation. The status quo is not significantly altered. According to Briggs (1975, p. 15) the basic difficulty seems to lie in the uncertainty and lack of preciseness in the definitions of knowledge and skills and the inability or unwillingness of those formulating the legal regulations to include and develop meaningful standards.

If those associated with social work are unable or unwilling to define more precisely the basic competence, knowledge, and skills of the profession, the assumption that they can test and differentiate these appears dubious. However, if they can define more precisely the requisite knowledge and skills, yet fail to test and monitor them, fail to exclude the incompetents and persons with less than full professional attributes from professional practice, and neglect to require periodic re-examination, then it is an unethical profession. The profession appears to want the status and protection of public recognition without the costs. The dangers of weak legal regulations are that they may preempt stronger ones in that the weak regulations offer the semblance of public protection and development of the profession without their substance. Social work, as a liberal profession, has the implicit obligation to resist arbitrary and meaningless public regulation as a bogus status-accruing device. Restrictions, even on a limited basis, are contentious if not offset by the strong and obvious potential for protecting the public and developing the profession of social work.

9

Recent Trends in Social Work

Social work as a skilled and paid occupation, for which there is training, is a twentieth-century phenomenon. Concern for human welfare, and the giving of service, has a long history, and is an integral part of Christian and humanistic philosophies. Welfare work has developed through the church, voluntary social services and the Poor Law. To write about changing fashions is therefore to look at the growth of social work over the last few decades, and particularly at the period since 1945. This chapter is in two parts, separating the organizational from the practice context of social work. In the first part the development of social work is traced, noting, prior to 1971, its organizational fragmentation, and the extent to which social workers were employed in non-social work agencies. The Seebohm Report and the moves towards unification are then discussed, with the view to emphasising the growing importance of administrative concerns, and recalling the anticipated virtues of social services departments. The second part considers a few of the dilemmas of social work practice, and draws attention to the potential for conflict between the values of the social worker and the priorities of the administrator.

Social Work Organization

It is not the intention here to write a brief history of social work, but to look at a number of salient points which have led to the establishment of social work in social services departments. The process has not been a direct one. In a rather indistinct way it is possible to see something of a pendulum swing, from large general-purpose agencies to small specialized ones and back again. Another path traces social work from its tentative beginnings as an appendage to wider services through to fragmented independence and then unification.

The Decline and Fall of The Poor Law

In so far as the state had any involvement in welfare work towards the end of the last century, it was to be found in a growing policy of protecting children and the general provisions of the Poor Law. The gradual demolition of the Poor Law spanned several decades until its final demise in paragraph 1 of the 1948 National Assistance Act, and although there was little social work to be siphoned off from it, the decline and discrediting of the only broadly-based public welfare organization during the 1920s and 1930s deprived the growing social work profession of a natural home. The views and pressures expressed in the Minority Report of the 1905-9 Poor Law Commission played a part in this process, and Donnison draws attention to an interesting organizational aspect of the changes. 'In their plan for the break-up of the Poor Law, the Webbs-those inveterate technocrats — proposed a wholesale eviction of laymen ... and their replacement by paid professional and administrative staff.. .' Social work may have been threatened with homelessness, but the basis is set for a new group of employees. Donnison quotes a contemporary critical commentator suggesting that we shall all become 'sheep shepherded by an enormous and apparently irresponsible bureaucracy....'

The Fragmented Growth of Social Work

As Poor Law provisions diminished so new services emerged, narrower in individual scope, though cumulatively broader, and culminating in the intensive developments of the period immediately after 1945. In the earlier period, before and during the Second World War, there was growth in state activity in housing, health and education. In each of these services it was realized that some of the users were in situations needing more than the regular arrangements of the agency. Some tenants of council housing had difficulty keeping up with rent because of a whole range of upsets outside the direct concern of housing. Health and education services found the same difficulty that some of the problems presented to them reflected more than just health or educational issues, and indeed that the health and educational aspects could not be tackled properly without taking wider concerns into account. This, of course, is a highly simplified version of what happened, but it serves to illustrate why the major social services looked around for help with the personal welfare needs of their customers, and finding nothing, began to employ their own staff for the purpose. The result was that much of the early growth of social work took place under the sponsorship and control of other kinds of service organization, with the continuing absence of a unified base.

The Establishment of Social Work Specializations

The picture offered to the Labour Government in 1945 was of personal welfare services either in process of development or well established, under a variety of controlling organizations. Housing and education welfare are examples of the former; hospital social work an example of the latter. Indeed, psychiatric social work was already showing as the elite service of the profession. There is no indication that the government gave any consideration to a unified social work service at that time, or had moved from the preference of the Webbs for specialized services to meet special needs. In any event, housing, health and education kept their welfare workers, the new National Assistance Board employed some of its own, the link between health and social work was extended into community provisions for the mentally ill (under the control of a medical officer of health), and the needs of children, the handicapped and the elderly were met by the introduction of two new local authority departments: Children's and Welfare. This set the pattern for post-war growth of social work organization, fragmented, partly under social work control, partly an appendage to the major social services. The 1960s saw expertise and efficiency on narrow fronts, but also poor co-ordination and large sectors of unmet needs. Crucially from the organizational point of view, social workers were in small clusters, whether running their own system or responsible to a larger agency. Not only was there no opportunity to gain experience of management in agencies of the size of social services departments, but also social work practice reached high standards of effectiveness in small compact organizations.

The Importance of Children's Services

While all these developments were in progress there was widespread sensitivity to the particular needs of children, and looking back it is clear that many welfare initiatives were either in the direct interests of children or an extension of attitudes and provisions which had first been justified in relation to children. Perhaps the most obvious example of this is the emergence of the probation service out of concern for children who were being subjected to the full severity of the penal services.

> Its early origins derived from the discretion in sentencing employed by some of the magistrates in Warwickshire in the 1820s, who, instead of committing a child to prison, might grant him a pardon on condition that he returned to the care of his parent or master to be more carefully supervised by him in the future.

Arrangements tried with children (for example, the use of a probation order instead of a fine or custodial sentence) have regularly been extended to other age groups, and the preoccupation of social work theory with the early formative years of a person's life have found some parallel in policies towards service developments. Organizationally, too, the first local authority social work agencies (children's departments, established in 1948) reflected the emphasis on child care.

The second phase, or, if one is using the pendulum idea, the return swing, starts with the situation in the 1960s. Looking back, this decade is seen as a period of growing self-confidence inside social work ranks, a golden age for some workers, a time when we approached a high quality of performance in narrow sectors of provision. At the time people seemed less aware of the strengths of the services, more bothered by the weaknesses. The important weaknesses were only organizational in part, a recognition of the unevenness of provisions stemming from the administrative fragmentation, the islands of privileged services in an ocean of unattended needs. Centrally, however, the forward-looking focus of the period was on the need for some guiding theme for social work, a relevant sense of direction to draw together the diversity of social work functions into an effective problem-solving profession. The theme was found in the family; the family as the basic unit of society, as the natural network of personal aspirations and dependencies, as the necessary framework for self-sufficiency, as the desired setting of all right-thinking people, and therefore as the appropriate focus for social work services. Social work skills and practices could be equated with the reality of personal needs, the stigmatised nature of client status could be overcome, and social work could come of age, given this acknowledgement of the central place of the family. The Ingleby Report was an early landmark and pressures grew throughout the 1960s. By the time the Seebohm Committee was set up it was clear that a unified focus for social work was closely linked to the issue of whether or not there should be administrative unification. Indeed, these years saw the gradual decline and increasing criticism of the concept of the family as a sufficiently accurate reflection of social circumstances, in proportion to the growing identification of the family as justification for large-scale service organizations.

It is illuminating to look back to the work of the Seebohm Committee and to parliamentary debates leading up to the passage of the Social Services Act, 1970, to see what were the main issues of the time, what objectives the reorganization was intended to attain, and what sort of development was envisaged for social work by the architects of social services departments.

The Seebohm Committee's expectations from a reorganization of the social services are listed in paragraph 111 of the Report. A unified service would meet the overall needs rather than a fragment of the needs of individuals and families; it would provide a clear pattern of responsibility and accountability; it would attract more resources and use them more effectively; it would lead to more and better staff recruitment; it would extend the range and flexibility of provisions; it would improve research potential; and it would offer a shop-window to the public which was both more welcoming and more easy to understand. The Committee saw themselves putting into practical expression the remark of the Ingleby Committee — 'it may be that the long-term solution will be in a re-organization of the various services concerned with the family and their combination into a unified family service'.

The plan to replace a fragmented system by a unified one was the corner stone of the proposals. Unifying the organizational structure was seen as consistent with and in natural sequence to the way social needs were understood at that time. Fragmentation 'clearly militates against the prospect of helping a family or individual with multiple needs through a single social worker or through a close-knit professional team with comprehensive responsibilities'. Neither the Seebohm Committee nor the members of Parliament debating the Local Authority Social Services Bill queried the validity of the family as an adequate unifying factor of personal needs. (Is that why so much social servicing now has to concern itself with the broken family?) Indeed, there is little evidence of any detailed analysis of the assumptions made about family-based needs, whether their scope or nature. 'Its [the Committee's] references to needs, though forceful, are secondary to a discussion of administration ....' It was asserted that a larger organization would offer an improved equation between needs and services, but beyond some specific concern about whether or not certain small agencies should be included (child guidance is an example), the matter was not taken up. There was little investigation of the interlocking span of human needs, the possible relationships between personal needs of a kind traditionally helped by social work, and education, housing, social security or health, although the potential difficulties were taken up in parliamentary debates. Maurice Macmillan commented: 'I think that the ultimate object is to bring health and welfare as close together as possible, at least from the point of view of those they are designed to help—that is, the customer.'

He criticized the Bill for its divisiveness. But this was rejected in the interests of promoting the professional development of personal social service staff. Arguing that a social services department should be obligatory, Shirley Williams said: 'it would be very unwise ... not to make this an obligation, until such time as the personal social services have the status that they feel they rightly deserve to have'.

The crucial arguments for unification were internalized and organizational. Fragmentation was seen as leading to buck-passing, sometimes with a view to getting rid of burdensome clients, and sometimes through disagreement or lack of clarity about the extent of departmental responsibilities. The theme of accountability is a recurring one. 'Placing responsibility for social care on one committee and department would provide a clear and evident system of accountability.' Good co-ordination becomes the anticipated virtue of the new unified agency. Under the old system 'co-ordination between the various agencies is considered deficient, with the result that families and individuals have received less than adequate service and scarce resources have been inefficiently deployed'. 'But an integrated social services department will ease problems of collaboration as the number of separate units involved is reduced, and above all as issues of responsibility are clarified.'

The Seebohm Committee expected social services departments to face an increase in work, because 'the greater simplicity and accessibility of a unified department is likely to expose many needs which have hitherto gone unrecognized or unmet', but it was perhaps the attempt to implement the Chronically Sick and Disabled Persons Act, 1970, which gave an indication of how extensive this would be. The Seebohm Report expected, though was not certain, that more money would be forthcoming:

> ...we cannot be sure, of course, that a unified department will secure a relatively bigger budget, but for at least two reasons it seems justifiable to hope for this. First, within local councils a committee responsible for the whole range of the personal social services would rank as a major committee.

> Second ... a clear demonstration that a more extensive and better service is required on many fronts may in itself exert the necessary pressure for increased public expenditure.

It also had simple faith in the greater efficiency of the larger organization — 'For instance, an organization with a total budget of £100,000 should be able to do more with it than the sum of the achievements of two separate organizations, each with £50,000' — as did parliamentary speakers—'One of the great advantages of the Seebohm system is that it provides for the maximum efficiency and humanity in the use of our resources.' One of the ways in which this greater efficiency would show itself would be in the quantity of work to be undertaken, but improved quality and more adaptability were other factors. Quality was seen particularly as related to staffing: 'a reformed organization should, in part, be Justified by its greater ability to increase the recruitment and training of appropriate staff, and to deploy them better'. Adaptability was anticipated from the increased freedom with which the personal social services could move resources around: 'An integrated social services department will impose fewer boundaries and require less arbitrary classification of problems.'

The arguments of the Seebohm Committee were overwhelming. There were important flaws in the fragmented system, and social services departments would give a better service to more people — easier access, a broad span of services to be obtained with greater convenience and efficiency than before, and a more coherent relationship between people's needs and the organization of the services.

Social Work Practice

The development of social work in the last few decades has, in part, been a quantitative one. Despite restrictions on public spending, the general pattern has been one of an increasing employment (and training) of social workers. Any changes in the practice of social work therefore have to be set in the context of almost continuous pressure to recruit more staff and catch up with basic training. There are several important components of this context. Social workers have not been recruited solely for social work practice; many of the better qualified and more experienced ones have moved into the newly created administrative establishments of social services departments. Teams of frontline staff are frequently made up of new people, a mixture of trained and untrained, although the proportion of qualified staff in social services area teams is increasing, there is a dearth of experience. In short, front-line teams have not had that combination of theoretical preparation and experience which would enable them to play as dominant a part in the late 1970s as their predecessors played in the 1960s, in the development of social work practice.

The pressure on recruitment derives from the need to fill a host of new posts (mostly administrative and advisory) and meet a growing level and range of demand for services. Concern with these pressures, with getting social services departments through their birth pangs and handling new service legislation, has inevitably detracted from closer consideration of the way practice is moving. There has been little room for experiment (at least that which has no primary concern with improving efficiency), and much of the discussion of new ideas has been frustratingly confined to the classroom rather than getting a detailed airing in the agencies.

Within this rather limiting setting it is possible to identify a number of developmental themes. Five will be suggested here and four discussed:

specialist or generalist?
social work or social service?
theoretical platforms
focus of intervention
professionalism, autonomy and accountability

The first four are discussed here, not comprehensively, but in those aspects which impinge on the central theme of social work and bureaucracy.

Specialist or Generalist

Earlier in this chapter we noted how the organization of social work had first taken solid root in a variety of separate agencies, sometimes as autonomous groups, more often within a larger structure. Out of its growing strength and through recognition of the range of its potential had come pressure for organizational merger and unification. Social services departments brought together, with a view to integration, the diversity of practices and specializations that had hitherto characterized social work services. This movement finds a close parallel within social work theory, beginning with a strongly based cluster of specializations and then growing (or is it reacting?) out of narrow boundaries into the idea of general purpose work.

The theoretical justification of each approach is clear and compelling. Much of the criticism of the old Poor Law (in the Minority Report) concerned its lack of sensitivity towards the nature of people's problems, and it came to be felt (e.g. by the Webbs) that a proper response to personal and family need was to analyse it down to its component parts and then provide an expert service to meet each of the parts. By having specialized agencies and staff it would be possible to offer an expertise relevant to each aspect of the need. For the social worker, specialization offered scope for developing a depth of knowledge and experience in a chosen field, which in turn could be translated into a particularly skilled service to the customer. Further, a specialized social worker was in a better position to join a team of allied specialists, and it is in the health care team setting that this view reached its greatest fulfilment. Certainly in the period after the end of the Second World War it was noted that specializations needed to be knitted together to form a coherent whole, but this could be achieved by such devices as the case conference, without any basic restructuring. Some inefficiencies (multi-visiting by social workers of a single client is the commonly stated example) were tolerated, and some clients were passed around from office to office, but this was accepted as an unavoidable snag to what was otherwise a highly competent service. Specialization guaranteed quality.

The case for general purpose social work follows similar lines to that for a general purpose organization. The basis of social work should be its appropriateness to the needs of the client, seeing the client as a whole, not in disconnected segments. Of course there were outer frontiers for social work which would recognise the areas of concern of other services-health, housing, education and income maintenance — but within those frontiers there should be no demarcations. The client would get the best treatment if a single social worker was involved and had a comprehensive picture of what was needed. Further, the concept of the general purpose social worker allowed a desirable move away from a problem-based categorization of society, towards a patch system, the linking of a single worker with a geographically and socially defined community. It has been an important tenet at government level for many years that categorising people by their problems invited stigmatization, whereas a community approach could minimise it: this belief has been widely accepted amongst social workers. Recognition was given to the difficulties of being an expert, all-round social worker, or having knowledge and experience across wide stretches of activity, but it was argued that most circumstances did not require specialist services, and where these were necessary, a specialist adviser could be consulted. This is the Seebohm position — a good basic service, with specialized advisory back-up when needed, and the prospect for the client of a helpful relationship with a single worker.

With the benefit of hindsight it seems that neither of these polar positions is satisfactory, and there has been some move back to specialization. However, it will be argued later that an issue which began with social workers debating ways of giving service, has now been taken over as an administrative concern with more efficient ways of deploying resources and with keeping control over professional staff.

Social Work or Social Service

One of the reasons put forward by senior staff of social services departments as to why social worker cannot take responsibility for such things as their method of practice. is that the task of the departments is only partially a social work one. It involves many other things — residential and day care provisions, home helps, domiciliary services which do not need the efforts of a social worker, and so forth — and the responsibility of management is to take a balanced overview. This is a reasonable argument in the sense that it is important to ensure that national objectives are being met, but it begs some questions. Is it inevitably the task of the administration to take the overview, rather than that of the range of service personnel in the agency? Is administration just another segment of a social services department, with its own sectional interests? Does a concern to meet national objectives necessarily involve interference in professional matters about methods of treatment? What has happened to the vision of a single organization representing, first and foremost, the interest of a unified social work service? Is there any better prospect for effective social work in the context of general social services than in liaison, with, say, health services?

A point being implied here is that whatever the original intentions, social services departments no longer represent unified social work, but exercise control over and denial of many forms of social work. This is illustrated by noting the context of the remaining themes to be discussed in this section. The theoretical platform, or philosophical base, for social work practice, and the way social workers identify the focus for their intervention, have both been and remain of great importance to new social workers contemplating their future. Yet they are issues of limited relevance to agencies who see their staff as employees first and social workers second. Staff of social services departments can hold whatever views they wish, as long as they practise within boundaries set out by the agency. This has tended to undermine philosophies and to limit flexibility of intervention.

Theoretical Platforms

Accepting that we are, therefore, largely going through a classroom exercise, we can note that theoretical platforms have become more varied over the years, and moved more towards a picture of the client as a person within a family, community and environmental setting. Whittaker, for example, has noted the development from psychoanalytic and behavioural concerns which were routinely internalized and segmented, towards the concept of the whole man in existentialism and man in his social context in the adaptation to social work of general systems theory.

Focus of Social Work Intervention

This has had its impact on the focus of social work intervention. Is the client to be seen uniquely and alone, in a small group, or as part of a community programme? In part the identification in social work method of case, group and community work has been to suggest different approaches to meeting a client's needs. For some workers they have been mutually exclusive alternatives, for others a range of interventions which can operate together in the client's interest. However, there is a further dimension to be considered once intervention extends beyond the individual client. Up to that point the limit of treatment objectives is to help the client to adjust to the surrounding community, its laws, conventions and expectations. Beyond it, the focus of intervention can move to the community itself, to trying to provide an environment suited to the individual. Flexibility can be demanded of social institutions as well as of individuals. But whatever the strength of this development within social worker ranks, it has little place as yet in practice. It creates too much complexity, and too many dangers. Can social services departments be flexible enough to allow their social work staff a range of approaches to clients, or will they continue to use control mechanisms such as case allocation procedures to ensure uniformity? Can social services departments accept the possibility that the focus of action and pressure to change may not rest solely on the clients, but could extend to many of the organizations of society, including the social service agencies themselves?

10

Social Work Research

The use of systematic methodological procedures in seeking of knowledge relevant to the goals of social work practice is unquestionable (Greenwood, 1957: 311-320). Though the social work practitioner act scientifically, his profession is yet considered "as art rather than science" (Hollis, 1968: 7). A near split between research and practice is thus generally conceived. The fact, however, is that social work research as an organised scientific endeavor is an established professional activity toward building up a general theory of human behaviour and social functioning involving a coherent system of interventions. An evidence of increasing production of research for social work is provided by a content analysis of selected social work periodical (Weinberger and Tripodi, 1960). A systematic review of 1,894 articles indicated that the relative percentage of research articles increased from 13.8 per cent in 1956-60 to 20.2 per cent in the period from 1961 through 1965 (Tripodi, Fellin and Meyer, 1969 : 10). Need for a scientific methodology and a sophisticated level of theory is now generally accepted in social work. A synthesis of attributes contributed by practitioner, experts and talented teachers "characterises the ideal social were researcher of the future" Polansky, 1971: 1099). Polansky concludes: "The researcher of the future will not be occupied full-time, hot he will be a teacher and expert practitioner as well" (Polansky, 1971: 1099). Social work research facilitates the use and generalisability of systematically arrived at facts and explanations which help solve social problems and enhance human functioning. Mass indicates two purposes of social work research : first, "to achieve a better fit between human needs and welfare goals;" and second, "to increase the likelihood that these goals can be attained".

Dimensions of Social Work Research

A perusal of the literature reveals that research has been regarded as an essential component of social work education. Gordon, in his challenging article, suggested three lines of development which bear upon the role of research and its future: 1) broadening the professional practice of social work beyond the more traditional activities of conducting studies; 2) examining our research tools, the type of research thinking we bring to social work, and whether the latter is getting the profession anywhere either in social work education or practice: and 3) questioning seriously who the social work scientist is going to be, and whether the social work researcher is going to take on this job (Gordon, 1958 : 99-106). Goldstein observed that by providing scientific standards and scientific methods, knowledge of research would make practice more scientific (Goldstein, 1962: 108-112). Shyne signified evaluative studies in assessing the results of services (Shyne, 1963: 22-33). Kitano made an attempt to classify the strength of social work intervention as an independent variable to be controlled in evaluative research (Kitano, 1963: 34-38). Underlining the importance of research, Goldstein presented several how-to techniques to solve practical problems of an agency (Goldstein, 1968: 22-27). Rosenblatt's study of social workers unfolded that relatively few practitioners make use of research findings or rate them as helpful. Determining the value of research for the social work practitioner, Rosenblatt feels strongly that social workers must accept the need to support research (Rosenblatt, 1968 : 53-59).

Programme evaluation has received considerable attention during the recent years. Rossi's and Williams' anthology includes the theory and application of evaluative research ranging from the Head Start studies to the latest income maintenance experiments (Rossi and Williams, 1972: 326). While Chommie and Hudson contend that evaluating programme process leads to the discovery of facts that explain outcomes, make goals specific and improve delivery of services (Chommie and Hudson, 1974: 626-687), Weiss suggests alternative models of programme evaluation (Weiss, 1974: 675-681). Mold's analysis of the War on Poverty, Medicare, and the Family Assistance Plan shows that political factors rather than need or effectiveness influenced their design and their face. Therefore, social workers' role in promoting the wiser and wider use of research, data for determining social policy is suggested (Meld, 1974: 448.455).

There is no dearth of evaluative studies in different areas of social welfare services and methods of intervention.[1] However, the Mullen and Dumpson book is a significant collection of self-evaluative studies (Mullen and Dumpson, 1972). It is a commendable, professional stock-taking exercise. Still remarkable is *Gaeber's* review of this soul-searching collection (Garber, 1973: 109-114). Evaluative research thus seeks to serve a two-fold purpose: externally it is better used in assessing the strengths and weaknesses, gains and losses of various programmes and agencies; and inwardly it is aimed at a professional self-analysis.

Evaluation research is to be distinguished from evaluative research, a term which usually refers to studies concerned with understanding the effects of a particular programme or method of helping (Tripodi et al., 1969: 61). Evaluation methods and their application involve essentially the use of accepted research methodology and evaluative research also follows the same. Such-man made a fine and clear distinction between the two: "In our approach, we make a distinction between 'evaluation' and 'evaluative research'. The former will be used in a general way as referring to the social process of making judgments of worth... 'Evaluative research' on the other hand, will be restricted to the utilisation of scientific research methods and techniques for the purpose of making an evaluation" (Suchman, 1967:7). Evaluative research, which is defined as a "technique limited to the use of experiments or approximations to experiments for assessing programme outcomes" (Tripodi et al., 1970), is emphasised "as a method for studying the effectiveness of such efforts at planned social change" (Suchman, 1967: 8). In other words, it seeks to measure the quantitative value and to assess the qualitative worth of a researchable task. Typically, Stephen Isaac's book. *Handbook in*

Research and Evaluation (Isaac and Michael, 1975), and the book *Social Programme Evaluation* (Tripodi *et al.*, 1971), respectively refer to evaluation methods and evaluative research. Perhaps the most exhaustive and updated account of evaluation research is the Struenig and Guttentag edited book (Struenig and Guttentag, 1975). Social work researchers utilise various models in shaping and operationalising their interventive modalities. Perhaps an objective assessment of human situations and realities is the ethos of all social work research (Mohan, 1973 : 111-114).

Research Levels and Practicum

Research, particularly in social work, is recognised as a graduate and/or post-graduate academic involvement. This is not a wrong assumption because many a prerequisite is required to form the necessary background of a researcher. Gil contends that student involvement in research is a basic ingredient but at the graduate level (Gil, 1968:14-20). The first volume of the Glick Report on Under-graduate Social Work Education for Practice contains theory building as one of the characteristices of the existing undergraduate programmes (Click *et al.*, 1972). The most authentic support for a kind of grass roots research programme flows from Bisno's theoretical framework. His new methodology, subsuming techniques and skills, has five components: adversary, conciliatory, developmental, facultative-instructional, and knowledge development and testing. He defines the last one, knowledge development and testing, as: 'This method might be appropriate for those situations in which the problem is lack of knowledge about a professional matter, including the need 'to evaluate results of programmes. The essential technique would be those involved in theory building and research, including all the methological procedures. Among the professional roles that might be expected to use this method are researchers and methodologists, although persons in various practitioner roles might use this method as well even if to a lesser degree and in less depth" (Bisno, 1969: 11). This proposition is not given the attention and consideration it deserves. This author's contention, which is subject to further evaluation, is that the need for research content cannot be minimised, even in undergraduate programme because social work majors with BSW or equivalent degrees are increasingly being recognised as qualified practitioners. This formulation is based on two major assumptions: first, grass roots research is fundamental in all the relevant areas, let alone social professions ; secondly, knowledge of evaluation methods (including evaluative techniques) and the required skills to use these should be an integral component of social work education in the whole sequence, from undergraduate to post-doctoral levels.

A study of former doctoral students at the University *of* Pittsburgh, undertaken and implemented as a research methods course, reveals a strong motivational background of the students who entered the doctoral programme; in regard to the general employ- ability it is suggested that "research positions will increase as social welfare programmes seek to establish empirical justification for their continued existence" (Sales, 1975: 107). This signifies the relevance of the accountability issue while designing our curricula. As research positions in human services are being occupied by many other professionals and holders of research degrees in disciplines other than social work, the accountability and productability issues merit closer attention.

A practice-oriented approach to theory building is one of the main distinguishing features of social work research. It signifies the paramount role of the practicum or internship as a lab for strengthening a solid research base. There are several models in practice to develop research courses or concentrations in different schools. Some programmes only focus on agency-oriented research.

The Class-Lab-Agency Research Interaction, a model which this author developed,[2] appears to be a useful tool for accomplishing some of the six functions of evaluative research as suggested by Bigman (Bigman, 1961: 99)'. This model, mainly conceptualised for undergraduate level, has special advantage to the agency for it provides "a systematic feedback of information to be used to improve social programmes". This, however, does not transcend the local horizons and suffers a broadbased conceptual orientation.[3] The internship model as developed and utilised by the School of Social

Welfare, Louisiana Stale University, Baton Rouge, Louisiana, is an exemplar. Research is one of the six Specialisations:

"This Specialisation was developed in response to a growing public interest in social welfare accountability and an increasing demand from within the profession itself for more and better empirical research at both the applied level and the basic research level.

"Social welfare research is concerned with the functions of identification and evaluation of social problems and needs, the development and evaluation of service-delivery systems and client-treatment programmes, and the general problem of public welfare agency accountability. Accordingly, the Research curriculum is designed to provide students with a broad background in social science methodology and research techniques; and competency in the areas of research design, data collection, computer processing, data analysis, and research management" (Daste, 1977:5).

The sequence of Research at the LSU School of Social Welfare provides five research options supported by numerous courses.

The LSU School of Social Welfare research options present a model of consequence in a most innovative professional style. The strengths in this sequence are tremendous and these are attributed to the role of faculty leadership. The UWO model, as presented is a modest attempt to establish the school-agency research interaction in a relatively small community. Its three-component interaction, however, signifies a very crucial dimension of the knowledge-guided research somewhat akin to Gordon's (Gordon and Schutz, 1969: 10-12; Dailey, 1975: 25-31) theoretical model. An overemphasis on the learning-by-doing approach has unfortunately sacrificed the cognitive aspects of research which need to be strengthened. A specialisation-oriented programme in conjunction with an internship model for pacticum perhaps provides an innovative model that involves social workers as consumers and producers of research. This research process interlocks school, faculty, students, agency, and community in a dynamic and creative endeavor addressed to the knowing, understanding, and explaining of social realities; and assumes a more sophisticated design at the doctoral level. The doctoral programmes in social work in the United States and abroad have a challenging responsibility to establish the profession on unquestionable scientific bedrock.

References

Dailey, D.M. (1975) "A learning paradigm for the teaching of social work research." *Journal of Education for Social Work* 11,2.

Daste, B. M. (1977) *Intership Manual.* Baton Rouge: School of Social Welfare. Mimeographed.

Gil, D.G. (1968) "Research—a basic ingredient in the study of social policy and social services." *Journal of Education for Social Work* 4, 1.

Glick, L.J., R.L. Baker, and T. L. Briggs, eds. (1972) *Undergraduate Social Work Education for Practice: A Report,* Vol. I and II. Washington, D. C.: U. S. Government Printing Office.

Gordonm W. E. and M. L. Schutz (1969) *Field Instruction Research Project. St.* Louis: George Warren Brown School of Social Work.

Goldstein, H. K. (1968) "Guidelines for obtaining funds for training, services and research." *Social Casework* XLIX, 1.

Greenwood, E. (1957) "Social work research: a decade of reappraisal." *Social Service Review* (September).

Hollis, F. (1968) *A Typology of Casework Treatment.* New York : FSAA.

Isaac, S. and W. B. Michael (1975) *Handbook in Research and Evaluation.* San Diego: Edits Publishers.

Kitano, H. H. L. (1963) "The concept of 'precipitant' in evaluative research." Social *Work* 8, 4.

Mass H. S. (1977) "Research in social work". *Encylopedia of Social Work* 17, II. New York: NASW.

Meld, M. B. (1974) "The politics of evaluation of social programmes." *Social Work* 19, 4.

Mullen, E.J. and J.R. Dumpson, eds. (1972) *Evaluation of Social Intervention.* San Francisco: Jossey-Bass.

Polansky, N. A. (1971) "Research in social work." *Encyclopedia of Social Work* 16, II. New York: NASW.

Roseblatt, A. (1968) "The practitioner's use and evaluation of research." *Social Work* 13, I.

Rossi, P. and W. Williams (1972) *Evaluating Social Programmes : Theory. Practice and Politics*. New York: Seminar Press.

Sales, E. (1975) "The doctoral student experience : a preliminary study." *Journal of Education for Social Work* II, 2.

Suchman, E. A. (1967) *Evaluative Research.* New York: Russell Sage Foundation.

Struenig, E. L. and M. Guttentag, eds. (1975) *Handbook of Evaluation Research.* Beverly Hills: Sage Publications.

11

Social Work and Social Workers

Social work is a very practical activity, in which the personal qualities of the worker may be as important as the knowledge he or she possesses; in which *how* the worker acts and communicates may be as significant as what he or she decides to do; and the success or failure of which can be evaluated from several different perspectives. The same could perhaps be said of a number of different professional or semi-professional activities. Even in medicine or the law, the importance of the political and social context of the transaction between professional and client, and of skill and sensitivity in communication, are coming to be recognised. But social work has perhaps more in common with nursing and teaching than with these 'ancient professions'. Social workers do not command high status, either as possessors of exclusive scientific or legal expertise, nor as independent and autonomous decision-makers. They tend to be employed in large organisations, usually by local authorities, and thus to be answerable, through hierarchies of professional and administrative superiors, to elected committee members. Yet social workers do have to make important decisions that have major effects on people's lives—sometimes in matters of life and death—and often they have to act alone, without the immediate support of their colleagues, or senior members of their organisations. Alternatively, other social workers — especially in residential homes—have to look after groups of people who have been judged too disturbed, disruptive and difficult to remain in their families, neighbourhoods or schools, and for whom other professionals have failed to make satisfactory arrangements. Even though these workers do have the support of each other, they are often isolated from other forms of assistance. Hence, although social workers do not have a great deal of power and status compared with other professions, they do have a good deal of responsibility in some of the most difficult issues which confront modern societies; and the public have (as media publicity of scandals reveals) high expectations of what they should achieve.

Consider the following short examples of the kinds of situations which face social workers every day:

(1) A thirteen year-old girl has been refusing to go to school. She is unhappy at home, where the situation between her parents is tense and violent; but she will not contemplate leaving home voluntarily, and her parents will not support any alternative arrangements for her education. A social worker from the local authority must try to negotiate with the girl, the family and the education authorities to find some solution to the problem of her need both for schooling and for some relief from the family tensions. If the social worker fails, then a decision must be reached, with the education authorities, and with legal advice, about whether to apply to the court for a care order. If such an order is granted, the girl will probably go to an assessment centre. There residential social workers will try to deal with her distress at being removed from home against her will, to get to know her in a strange environment, and to help her plan for her future educational and living arrangements. The first social worker must continue to work with her angry parents, and help retain their links with her, as well as possible. What is the future for this girl?

(2) A man in his thirties is referred to a social worker by a psychiatrist. Previously he has been seen by his general practitioner and by a neurological specialist for a sudden onset of 'blackouts'. The man is a driver by occupation, and cannot work while he has this condition. A number of tests have been done, but none of them have revealed any physical abnormalities. The psychiatrist has prescribed traquillisers, but can offer no further psychotherapy, and the man's condition is not serious enough to warrant hospitalisation.

The man is angry to be referred to a social worker — what can she do that all these eminent doctors and specialists could not achieve? She finds out, after politely enduring his resentful questioning other credentials, that he is still in the emotional aftermath of a painful divorce, and still very strongly attached to his ex-wife and children. However, he is living with a younger woman, who loves him, but whom he says he does not love. The social worker visits to discuss the situation with them, and finds a difficult and tense relationship full of emotional pain on both sides. Can the social worker help both parties plan their future? If she can, will this relieve the man's symptoms?

(3) A young couple come to the social services department for help. The man has just been made redundant, and has used his holiday pay from work to meet a debt. He did not realise that this holiday pay is counted at his income for the next two weeks by supplementary benefits, so he is not entitled to any money from that source. Because he previously had a long period of unemployment, he has not made sufficient National Insurance contributions to qualify for unemployment benefit; nor does he qualify for any redundancy payment. The couple already have rent arrears on their council flat, and a number of other debts. They are under threat of having their electricity and gas disconnected. They have two young children and they are penniless. The social worker must try to help them disentangle their relationships with a number of powerful agencies—the social security department, the housing department and the fuel boards. He must advocate for them, negotiate on their behalf, or advise them on how to claim, appeal or ask for special consideration. He must also decide what material help his own department should offer, and discuss and advocate within his own organisation over any resources which he considers the family should be offered.

(4) A health visitor refers a couple to the social services department. The couple have just had a baby, and the wife has told the health visitor that her husband, who has been twice married before, has been the father of three previous children, all of whom died in suspicious circumstances. Two of these deaths occurred

while he was in the navy, and a third in his home town, 100 miles away. The woman, who is of fairly low intelligence, is vague about the details, and does not seem afraid of her husband, but the health visitor is very anxious. The social worker must make urgent enquiries, both from the naval welfare authorities, and in the man's home town. Eventually the replies he receives are negative; only one child died, and the man was away at sea when this occurred. The social worker has visited with the health visitor during the delay while the enquiries were being made. The man is both intimidating and, in his opinion, potentially violent, even though the child is being well cared for and the wife shows no fear of him. What should the social worker (and his senior) do next? Should they try to discuss things with the couple, call a meeting of all the professionals involved, or withdraw from the case?

(5) The home help organiser of a social services department refers an elderly lady to the social work team. The lady is complaining that her son, in whose flat she is living, is locking her in and stealing her money. The home help who calls seldom sees the son, because he is working away. The social worker calls, and finds that the old lady is very isolated, and her resentment against her son seems irrational. She meets the son, who is concerned about his mother, but can do no more for her because of work commitments. What should the social worker decide to offer? The department has day care facilities which would reduce the old lady's isolation, but might provide only a short-term solution. Alternatively, should she encourage the old lady to get her name down on the waiting list for residential care in an old people's home? How will she react to the suggestion? Will she see it as a further threat, and be resentful, or will she regard it as a welcome opportunity to get some companionship and more physical care?

Dilemmas of Social Work

These examples give some clues as to what sorts of things social workers do, and what special problems their activities raise for them in everyday practice. At one level, these problems are very practical, immediate, and particular to each individual client. What advice does this person need? What resources would help her solve her problems? Whose responsibility should this be? But at another level the problems are much more general, for each of these particular cases raises fundamental issues about the sort of society we are living in, and the role of social work, and of the social services of the 'welfare state'.

This is not surprising when we consider the structural position of social work in modern societies, and particularly in the advanced industrialised countries of the capitalist world. Whereas before the Second World War most social work was either done by volunteers or for voluntary (charitable) organisations, nowadays it is mainly an integral part of the state's social services. But for the most part social work can best be seen as a special *way* of giving certain social services, which it is difficult to give in other ways. This is why, in spite of important differences within structures, policy and administration, social work services tend to concentrate on the same types of human problems in quite contrasting societies.

Since the Second World War, all the major advanced industrialised countries (with the exception of Japan, though even its pattern is becoming somewhat more similar) have developed systems for social security, state provision of housing, health services, and state education. Proportions of national incomes spent on these services vary (for instance, the USA spends much less on state health and housing systems than Western European, British or Scandinavian countries, but more than most on education), but all gave considerable priority to the development of these social services in the 1950s and 1960s, and all in turn have questioned whether this priority could be maintained in the 1970s and 1980s. At the same time, state social work services were created or expanded in all these countries, and although the relationship between the major services and the social work agencies differed considerably in different nations, some common themes are universal. For instance, even where social workers are not directly attached to public welfare agencies which provide financial assistance (as they are, for instance, in the USA, in many continental countries and in Australia and New Zealand), they cannot avoid involvement in the whole business of poor people getting sufficient benefits to live on—by having to advocate or negotiate for them, if not to provide benefits or assess needs. Equally, whether they are attached to education, justice or public welfare departments, or whether they are part of a free-standing social work department (as they are in Britain) they cannot avoid involvement in issues about child neglect and abuse, and about juvenile delinquency and its appropriate 'treatment'. Whether or not they work directly for health departments, and whether or not they have to 'take orders' directly from doctors, they tend to be concerned with issues of child health, disability and handicap and the care of the elderly; and also with the welfare of patients in mental and general hospitals. Whether probation services are separate departments (as they are in England and Wales) or part of the major local authority social work service (as in Scotland), there will be some people with social work training involved in the work of the criminal courts and the divorce courts; and with providing a welfare service in prisons. And whether voluntary agencies continue to play an important role (as they do in many predominantly Catholic countries) or whether the state has a virtual monopoly of social services, the problems of relationships between the state (as represented by the courts and the other major services) and informal, neighbourhood and community organisations, and between the state and its citizens, are of central concern for social workers.

In other words, many of the duties of social workers seem to stem logically and directly from the social and economic structures of modern societies. The major social services represent the commitment of the state to meeting certain needs in a certain way — though there is much dispute between theorists about why exactly this has occurred, and in whose interests these services are provided. Social work in turn tends to be concerned with the kinds of tasks which require detailed and personal attention of a less specialised kind, and with people who, for whatever reason, do not seem to 'get by' on the standard ration of health care, education, housing provision or social security benefits which is available. Either they have special difficulties, or they reject what is offered, or they just do not 'fit in' with the systems that are supposed to meet their needs.

These universal features of social work services in the advanced capitalist countries have led some theorists to argue that social work can only be properly understood as a direct product of the social and economic structures of these nations. Many such theorists have pointed out that as state employees in such societies, most social workers have clear legal duties to keep under control certain sections of the population which are seen as potentially subversive or threatening to the interests of the ruling class. Thus for instance social workers are disproportionately concerned with the poor, the unemployed, the homeless, residents of deprived areas, and other socially disadvantaged groups. Social workers may seem to be offering them help and some limited material assistance, but much of what they do can be seen as keeping them 'in their place'; ensuring that they do not come to expect or demand more than the state is willing to give them, or undermine the smooth functioning of economic and social life. Similarly, social workers are universally involved with such 'deviant' behaviour as child abuse, delinquency, crime and mental illness, which threatens the status quo, and expresses notions of rebellion, unorthodoxy or protest which the ruling class wishes to suppress. Again, while social workers may seem to be softening the impact of traditional ways of dealing with 'deviants'—punishments, removals from the community to special institutions, physical coercions—closer examination reveals that these methods are still widely used, and in some cases even practised by social workers themselves (for instance, punishments, isolations and occasional violence in children's homes). Finally, even services which seem to be unequivocally 'helpful', and almost universally welcomed by their recipients (such as home help services and other forms of domiciliary and day care for the elderly) are revealed as being very strictly rationed, and even where more generously given, as perhaps contributing to the 'legitimation' (i.e. making more politically acceptable) of regimes which consolidate the power of the wealthy and systematically deny the claims of the poor.

These views of social work (which with modifications apply also to most of the other social services), must be taken seriously, and will be examined in the course of this book. They are not confined to academics and radical critics of social work; they correspond with the views and experiences of many social workers who practise, particularly in deprived city areas, in many parts of the capitalist world. It is worth pointing out too that they find an echoing response in the perceptions of social workers in many communist countries, where despite public ownership of the means of production and central economic and social planning, social workers are still disproportionately concerned with the poor and with 'deviants' (though not necessarily with deviant actions of the same kind, or with subversive ideas which are identical), and where also social services are seen as legitimating their political regimes.

Some social workers, indeed, come into social work with precisely these perceptions of the societies in which they live. In Britain, for instance, a strong political motivation and analysis of social problems is one recognisable background to entry into social work, whether at the level of local authority fieldworker, or in the residential sphere. But many other people who enter social work consider their clients' problems from a quite different perspective. Research has suggested that the majority of social work recruits are still primarily motivated by a religious or humanitarian concern for underprivileged or disadvantaged members of society. This motivation might well allow an equally strong perception of clients as 'unfortunates' or even 'victims'; but the overall context or framework in which religious or humanitarian entrants to social work would evaluate actions, feelings and decisions in human relations would be moral rather than political. This apparent clash between the moral and the political dimensions of social work will be one of the themes of this book.

We might also distinguish a third element in the motivation and background of potential social workers. This could be loosely classified as the 'social' — not so much a 'social conscience', which would be nearer to the religious motive, but more a social *awareness.* Such an awareness might include an acknowledgement of the impact of social and psychological factors on *all* human behaviour, a recognition of the importance of the social services as aspects of modem life, and a consciousness of the career opportunities opened up by the expansion of the social work agencies which has occurred in recent years. This 'social' element is less obviously at odds with either of the two other major traditions of social work, but it is distinguishable and important. It might be suggested that it is increasingly common amongst realistic entrants into social work occupations, especially in lower-status, less well-paid posts in residential, day-care and domiciliary services-home helps, care assistants in old people's homes, nursery workers, residential child care workers, and day-care assistants.

It has also been suggested—for instance by Geoffrey Pearson—that this 'social' element tends to predominate in the training that is offered for social work. Colleges and training centres tend to emphasise the 'consensus' elements in social work, and those aspects of the work and the clients' problems which can best be explained in terms of such 'neutral' social sciences as psychology and sociology. It also tends to present the social services in terms of their structure and administration, rather than the moral and political dilemmas which underlie their policies, and social work practice in terms of technical skills which can be learned and applied in any context, irrespective of the practitioner's moral and political views. This tends, it is argued, to present social work as far more scientific and technical than most full-time practitioners feel it to be, and to drain it of the very ethical and political content which has motivated most of its recruits.

Whether or not this is an accurate picture of how British social work courses have been run in the past, it seems unlikely that these underlying issues can be suppressed in the future, as the continued effects of scarce resources and pressing needs make their presence felt in the 1980s. Therefore in this book we have tried to do justice to all three of these elements—the moral, the social and the political—and to see whether they can be reconciled in practice.

Social Work in Britain

It may at this point be helpful to give a very simple and schematic account of British social work agencies and their staffing. This makes no claim to being exhaustive, and makes no allowances for local variations. The system in England and Wales is described—the Scottish system is slightly different.

Local Authority Social Services Departments

These are the largest employers of social work staff, and have responsibility, among other things, for:

1. *Residential and domiciliary services for the elderly and handicapped:* old people's homes, adult training centres, day centres, hostels for the handicapped, home helps, aids and adaptations, etc.
2. *Child care services:* fieldwork, including preventive work with families; investigation of alleged child abuse and neglect; reports to courts on cases concerning children's welfare and children 'beyond control' or 'in need of care and control'; day nurseries and other day-care services; children's homes, assessment centres and 'community schools' for children (mainly delinquents) requiring residential education and training outside the mainstream educational system.
3. *Social work services in general and psychiatric hospitals:* aftercare hostels, day centres.
4. *General welfare responsibilities:* to provide advice and guidance on a range of social problems, especially children, mental illness and handicap, and disability.

Social services departments staff consist mainly of:

1. *Managers, administrators and advisers:* most (but not all) of whom have a professional social work background and/or training. Some of these are found in local offices, many others are concentrated in 'headquarters' buildings and offices.
2. *Field social workers:* most of whom are now professionally trained who are mainly responsible for assessing needs and co-ordinating work with clients living in the community, and with planning and co-ordinating day-care and residential services.

3. *Residential and day-care social workers:* very few of whom are professionally trained, some of whom are predominantly concerned with the emotional care of clients (e.g. residential child care officers in children's homes, assessment centres, community schools and workers in family centres), but many others of whom are predominantly concerned with the physical care of their clients (e.g. care assistants in old people's homes).
4. *Domiciliary workers:* home helps, family aides, mainly involved with practical tasks of care for vulnerable people living in the community.

The Probation Service

This is a separate service in England and Wales, and comes under the Home Office rather than the Department of Health and Social Security. Its main dudes are:

1. Providing reports to the criminal courts, and supervising offenders placed on probation.
2. The co-ordination of community service order schemes, day training centres, residential hostels, and other special facilities for offenders outside the prison system.
3. Prison welfare and after-care, parole supervision.
4. Providing reports for the divorce courts, and supervising children in cases concerning disputed custody or access.

The great majority of mainstream probation officers are professionally trained, though many community service organisers and residential workers are not.

Voluntary Agencies

A large number of specialised voluntary agencies employ social workers in tasks which are broadly similar to those in the state sector. Some of these agencies provide more intensive work with groups already dealt with by the state agencies—for example, the Family Service Units with 'problem families', Barnardo's and the

National Children's Homes with children—but others provide field and residential services for groups notoriously neglected by the state agencies, for example, the Cyrenians with single homeless people. There are also agencies or branches of voluntary organisations which specialise by method, such as group work, 'intermediate treatment' (including short-term, intensive residential work for adolescents) and family therapy (psychotherapy aimed at changing the functioning of whole families by working with them as groups). Finally there are self-help groups and community associations.

This list should make one paradox immediately evident. With the exception of some of the voluntary agencies, most social work organisations are fairly large and hierarchically structured, and most concerned with the direct implementation of state social policies—either through the provision of certain kinds of legally denned services, or through the control of certain legally proscribed behaviour. So there is an inbuilt tension in social work between *the personal* nature of the tasks and the fairly *impersonal* nature of their organisational and legal frameworks. On the one hand, there would be little point in employing social workers, rather than clerks or administrators, to do these tasks unless they had opportunities to assess their clients' individual needs and scope for dealing with them differently, according to their emotional problems; on the other hand, these services cannot be exclusively related to such individual priorities, otherwise their location in these organisations and legal structures would be counter-productive. Is becoming a social worker primarily to be understood in terms of the 'helping', 'caring' or 'therapeutic' content of the job, or according to the official, bureaucratic, legal and even potentially coercive powers and responsibilities it entails?

Helper or Official?

There is no easy answer to this question, and it uncovers a tension which is present in every social worker's daily life. The truth is that—unless they are working in some very protected or specialised comer of the field—social workers neglect either side of their job to their peril.

To be effective, social workers in every branch of the work—fieldwork, day-care, residential work or neighbourhood community work—need to be able to *understand* people's situations, and to *communicate* this understanding. It has often been pointed out that this understanding and communication is in many ways more like an art than a science. While theory and knowledge from the social sciences may help greatly in giving social workers insights into areas of human behaviour and culture with which they have no personal acquaintance, this form of understanding depends considerably on social workers' ability to use their imagination and intuition, and to perceive the common ground between their own feelings and experiences and those of their clients. A flat, prosaic, jargon-ridden response to a client's account of his problems may indicate that the social worker has read some books on the subject, but is unlikely to give the client any real sense *of being understood,* whether his difficulty is a complex and intimate emotional one, or arises from dealing with a large and powerful organisation. To be effective, to make relationships with clients which will allow him to 'get alongside' them, and overcome their fear and mistrust, the social worker usually needs to be able to demonstrate in words, gestures and actions that he has an all-round appreciation of the client's particular circumstances and point of view.

This requires a very disciplined approach to the tasks of listening, formulating ideas, checking perceptions, making plans, consulting with clients about aims and methods, and working towards goals. It means that the social worker has to be able to distinguish accurately between the client's subjective perceptions and feelings and his own, and to see when the former are influencing the latter. It also requires him to be able to recognise in his own (sometimes uncharacteristic or surprising) reactions to clients or to situations, important indications of stresses in the client's world—including danger signals. None of this means that social workers should not be 'emotionally involved' in their work; but it does mean that they should make a particular kind of use of themselves and their feelings in their relationships with their clients; which has to be learnt and constantly improved if good standards of practice are to be reached.

All this implies that social workers need to spend time with each individual client, group or neighbourhood, and take their different and sometimes conflicting needs seriously. It implies that they cannot be effective if they give people 'standard rations' of time and attention, or standard answers to problems. If people were exactly like each other, then there would be little point in a service which offered them personal attention, and which tried to discriminate between their needs. On the other hand, state social work agencies in particular are certainly not there solely to meet individual needs. On the contrary, they are explicitly charged with duties, to require individuals to conform with legally-defined expectations, and to provide services according to politically-defined standards. Thus although the social worker is supposed to take each client seriously as an individual, he is supposed to balance this individual's needs against those of others competing for his attention and the department's resources, or against the conflicting needs of others in his family or neighbourhood who may be adversely affected by his behaviour.

Furthermore, as well as having to implement legal requirements, state social work agencies have to try to discover ways of working which can be shown *generally* to promote the welfare of the community, or bring about results (such as reductions of children in custody, or in admissions to mental hospitals) which are regarded as desirable for clients. This requires having *policies*—approaches to the tasks of assessment and help which reflect past experience and theoretical knowledge, based on research. This in turn means a particular division of labour, and combinations of social workers into teams, and specialisation (by problem focus, area or method) which allow these approaches to be applied. All this tends to cut across a purely individual and *ad hoc* approach, and to reduce social workers' discretion and control over their jobs. It may or may not increase the amount of his work that is official, and where he is representing the agency in ways he would not necessarily choose to represent himself; but it will certainly mean that he cannot pose as being simply a free-wheeling helper or therapist.

What we have said about the discipline of helping and the

constraints of policies and the legal framework should make it clear that social work is certainly not an activity in which people 'do their own thing' or just go around 'being themselves'. It also involves many of the contradictions to be found in other jobs in the public services, and in the private sector. People who come into social work anticipating an atmosphere of freedom and personal emancipation are likely to be shocked and disappointed. There are opportunities for creativity and self-expression, but they have to be made; the satisfactions of the job are subtle and complex, and come from balancing rival claims on time and energy, and overcoming obstacles and constraints. In many ways, social work embodies exaggerated versions of the dilemmas and problems of society at large, and is certainly not an escape from them. It does not, for instance, offer a haven from the fundamental tensions and conflicts between workers and management. Hence the increasing importance of trade unions in social work, which offer support and solidarity on many important issues, but add still further dilemmas—for example over the ethical justification of strikes which affect very vulnerable clients.

For all these reasons, while many social workers are happy, committed and fulfilled people who retain their freshness and enthusiasm after many years of hard work, others are jaded, careworn, depressed and listless. The phenomenon of 'burnout' in social work has only recently received much attention. It consists in a recognisable tendency among workers under prolonged and intense stress to become unable to respond to their work in ways which match their original motivation or learnt skills. Instead they become defeated and defensive, and seem to avoid the difficult and demanding parts of the job, or respond to them in very negative ways. There are many theories about how this may occur, but all agree that it is due to stress. It seems unlikely that this is simple *quantitative* demand on the worker's energies. It is more likely to reflect a difficulty in reconciling competing or conflicting demands, perhaps simultaneously from clients, the agency and the worker's own family.

Several years ago we ran a one-day discussion group for experienced social workers, in which it quickly became apparent that several of the members were 'burnt-out'. They were cynical, critical, and made it clear that this participation was merely a ruse for getting away from the office for a day. We eventually got the group to look at crucial turning points in their lives, and especially their lives as social workers. The 'burnt-out' workers were able to identify quite clearly the moment at which the demands of the job became too much for them. Often they were working with enormous caseloads, covering for sick colleagues; the agency was putting extra stresses on them, and showing no appreciation (they felt) of their efforts; and the final straw was an illness or family problem at home. Their accounts were vivid and moving testimonies of the strains of social work, and the toll if can take on workers. Good intentions, even altruistic zeal, are not enough. A good social worker needs personal resilience, the support of colleagues and superiors, and a satisfying private life, to give of his best over a prolonged period.

The Client's View

So far we have described social work entirely from the point of view of the worker. What about the client's perspective? Research into the opinions of those on the receiving end of social work has only been undertaken fairly recently, and is still patchy. As might be expected the results are very mixed.

On the whole, elderly people are the most appreciative consumers of all the social services. They seem grateful for anything they receive—even from such notoriously unpopular agencies as supplementary benefits—and particularly value practical and material assistance, which enables them to continue to live in their own homes. From this point of view, the domiciliary services provided by local authority social services departments are particularly popular. It is ironical that services for the elderly, which are least likely to be performed by trained social workers, and which the majority of social workers themselves least enjoy providing, are those most appreciated by clients.

By contrast, trained field social workers *most* enjoy work with children and families. But this work includes preventive work (helping families stay intact) and work entails receiving children into care, or removing them compulsorily from their families. It is this last category of work which gives rise to most potential conflict. Nowadays a high proportion of children compulsorily removed from home are taken under Place of Safety Orders—a social worker comes to the house with a compulsory order, signed by a magistrate, and takes the children away with little or no notice, often against strong resistance from the parents. Also, the proportion of children in care whose parents lose their parental rights to the local authority (either through care orders by the courts, or through administrative transfer of these rights under the Children Act) has been rising. This in part reflects a policy by social workers of trying to arrange more permanent substitute care (including adoption) for children in care, which in turn involves excluding more parents from the lives of their children. (Many of these will already have lost contact with their children in care, but a few are being denied access, even if they have kept in touch.) All this has contributed to a good deal of hostility against social workers, particularly by parents who have experienced these conflicts, and by organisations representing, for instance, single parents. Researchers have encountered angry clients who described social workers as 'the Gestapo', and organisations like Gingerbread advise their members to be very wary of approaching social services departments.

For the rest, opinions are very varied. Here is a small sample of views from clients of a number of different agencies, statutory and voluntary:

> *Dissatisfied client, Family Welfare Association:* The welfare lady came to the house one day when my husband was home and there was a big row between us. We got up to it with my husband and he got up to it with me. The welfare lady knew very well what we went through with my husband, but she just sat there and listened, and she never tried to do anything. She just listened and didn't drum any sense into my husband at all.[1]

> *Satisfied client. Family Welfare Association:* The social worker was nice and pleasant and very polite and quiet in his ways. And sort of steady in asking the questions. The second time we went we felt a bit better in myself and the third time we felt even stronger. Each time we was able to tell him more of what happened. We felt as though he was giving me great strength, that we had someone behind me. We felt that if anything went really wrong, that we had him to go to.[2]

Juvenile delinquent: He doesn't do or say much—just soft questions can't understand him most of the time — is like a record player.[3]

Juvenile delinquent: He's all right — like him — he lets you discuss your family problems and your home. He's trying to get money to take us on a holiday but will be all canoeing and that.[4]

Family casework client: We don't know what her job should be, but she's not much help.[5]

Family casework client: She does a lot more than her job. When her time is up, she goes a bit beyond to try to help me, whereas other social workers would just go home.[6]

Social services client: We think if your face fits you're in; we think you've got to give them a hard luck story, cry and go right down as if you are one bag of nerves.[7]

Social services client: We think that before they see to the immigrants they should see to the English people.[8]

Child in care: My brother and we have had more social workers that we can remember. They'd see us once and then disappear for six months, then we'd have a new one. And it's been going on all the time I've been in the home. They've been leaving or they've been going ill. And if that's happening all the time, we don't see how they can help you.[9]

A few weeks ago children from a teenage hostel threatened

with closure personally lobbied councillors from the floor of Solihull Council Chamber and succeeded in overturning its previous decision to close the home.

Wider Views of Social Work

In recent years, British social workers have been heavily criticised by the press, and seem to be held in low public esteem. However, such research as has been done reveals that the bad press which social work has received on some (mainly child care) issues does not reflect overall opinion. Most people think that someone should do most of the things that social workers do. But there is profound disagreement about how they should do them, whether they should be paid for doing them, and if so, whether they should be employed by the state. In this book, we shall try to disentangle some of the origins of these disputes, and look at how British social work has come to take its current shape. Above all, since most of the fiercest disputes are about the role of local authority social workers, we shall consider some of the contradictions of that role.

Many of the disputes at the heart of these matters concern the nature and origins of the social problems and needs that social workers tackle. These problems are near enough to our day-to-day experiences to allow us to have strong opinions on them. In this sense they are small-scale, personal problems of everyday life—commonsense matters, that call forth domestic or parochial resources for their solutions. But in another sense they raise profound political and ideological issues about the nature of society itself, and the role of the state.

For instance, there is general agreement that old people should not be allowed to starve in filth and squalor, but very little about how to prevent this happening, or who should be held responsible if it does. Is it evidence of inadequate state provision, the isolation of modem urban life, or neglectful neighbours and kin? The ways in which public services mesh in with informal neighbourhood and family networks are far more subtle and complex than is commonly imagined. There are enormous gaps in public consciousness of social problems—'no go' areas, where we as private citizens prefer to turn a blind eye, rather than endure the discomfort of having to do something about persistent suffering or injustice. It is only when these spill out, in highly visible forms, that public and political demands for action by the social services are heard.

Child abuse is one clear example of this. There is no real evidence that more children are hurt, neglected or killed nowadays than in any previous era—if anything, statistics suggest that in recent years social services departments have become more effective at the basic task of protecting vulnerable infants. What is clear is that neither before child abuse became a national issue, nor since, have neighbours and kin (who must always have been aware of the problem) been willing to tackle it directly. Before Maria Colwell, hundreds of children must have died in circumstances which raised profound suspicions in their neighbours and extended families, but where such suspicions were suppressed, or somehow 'managed' within these networks. What has changed is not the inability of these networks to prevent such tragedies; it is public awareness that there exists an agency—social services departments—onto which all the guilt, anxiety and responsibility for such a situation can be offloaded. The vast majority of social problems and needs that the public is willing to recognise as such are met by informal neighbourhood resources. But there remain an enormous number of latent problems, half-recognised or ignored, which constitute potential time-bombs in any community. It is these that, once they explode into public consciousness, become the stuff of controversy about the role of local authority social workers.

It is in these situations that cries go up for rapid and decisive action by social workers, and in its absence the strongest criticisms are made. Public consciousness sees no contradiction in allowing lay opinions much weight in such matters, yet expecting social workers to show professional skill and judgement in affairs which laymen (and especially neighbours) carefully avoid. The boundary areas between the family and neighbourhood on the one hand, and social work (and particularly local authority social services departments) on the other, are areas of confusion and dispute. What is at issue is the nature and extent of personal responsibility and responsibility for others in a shared network. In modern British society there are no abosolute standards in these matters. Our society contains innumerable anomalies, anachronisms and contradictions. There are small rural hamlets where social relations have been little affected by the industrial revolution, and inner-city ghettos populated mainly by post-war immigrants. In these very diverse communities, boundaries are drawn at quite different points.

Every referral of an individual or family to a social work agency entails negotiations about these boundaries; a referral to the local social services department entails negotiations with an official representative of the state.

The state has certain expectations of how families should behave towards their dependants, and the circumstances in which their efforts should be supplemented or superseded. These expectations contain elements of flexibility and adaptability to local circumstances, even though many of them are laid down by statute (e.g. child care, mental health and public hygiene legislation). However, they also depend on local resources, and the ideological complexion of the political party in power.

In many rural or suburban communities, incursions by social workers are rare, and mainly concern problems which have been festering for years, but which finally break out of the framework of local neighbourhood management. Yet there are also inner-city areas where it is normal for social workers to be involved with most households; where they come and go without the courtesy of letters or appointments; where their visits are as expected a part of life as those of kin and neighbours; where people consult social workers about day-to-day aspects of their family relationships and their dealings with other arms of officialdom. Such high concentrations of social work tend to correlate with at least one other indicator of a 'social problem area'—high rates of male unemployment, large proportions of single parent families or high rates of juvenile delinquency. In such areas, social work is not a 'last resort', where neighbourhood methods of problem management break down. It is rather part of the apparatus by which the state monitors and controls a proportion of the population—the inner-city poor—whose social role has itself become problematic. With economic stagnation and mass unemployment, a substantial and growing number of people have no obvious contribution to make to the productive process. Such people often live in subsidised and rent-rebated local authority housing, on state benefits, or work in state-assisted job creation schemes. To call them the 'industrial reserve army', (to use Marx's term) is perhaps over-optimistic, since it is unlikely that British industry will require their services again in an age of automation. They might be more accurately described, in the nineteenth-century term, as 'surplus population'. Although they receive disproportionate attention from most official agencies, including the police, it is social workers who give the closest attention to the quality of their personal lives.

This is itself involves as many difficult boundaries as work in more settled and prosperous communities. Social work in such 'problem' neighbourhoods is by no means politically and morally neutral. The state is concerned to define the limits of its help to such people — to ration its resources in such a way as to reinforce personal and family responsibilities. Social work supplements this fixed ration of assistance, and reinforces the need for limits, by imposing rationing of its own, more detailed and personal kind. Similarly, the state is concerned to control the potential threat posed by this section of the population, which has so little obvious stake in the existing social order. Social workers exercise control over such sensitive areas as child care and delinquency, with the power to remove children and adolescents from the most deviant families, and to enforce standards on the rest. Seen in this light, the role of social workers in certain neighbourhoods—and at the time of writing the male unemployment rate amongst blacks in Brixton was 70 per cent, and amongst all males on some Glasgow estates over 60 per cent—is the time-honoured one of public assistance agencies; regulating the poor. Yet most social workers would want to disclaim this restrictive definition of their tasks. They would see social work as inseparably connected with helping, and with doing so in a distinctively personal and caring way. Thus there is an inevitable tension between the expectations of many politicians and much of the ratepaying public, and the aspirations of social workers themselves, with their clients' needs and wishes forming the third side of a problematic triangle.

The Daily Drama

This scenario for state social work with a largely unmotivated or actively resistant clientele has enormous potential for tragicomedy. The social worker is trapped between competing demands, and has often to acknowledge the absurdity of his situation. He may well need a sense of humour to survive. Here are two examples. The first is from an account by a group of residential child care workers of an experimental project in an inner city which attempted to keep (mainly black) teenagers in care within their local community. The project workers struggled not only with the disruptive behaviour of their resident adolescents, but also with the problems of their relationships with 'outsiders', both friendly and hostile. Here is a sample of the workers' diary (the names are of residents unless otherwise stated):

Sunday, 24 November, 1974 . . . approx. 5.00 a.m. front door bell rang. Mandy dumped by a taxi, very drunk or stoned. Collapsed on floor. Paul and we tried to carry her to bed. After about 15 minutes she became more conscious and started screaming, shouting for Icah, her boyfriend who had dumped her out of the taxi as he thought she was going out with the "e Grove" boys. Wanted to go looking for him, claiming he was going to break into a shop and she was going to stop him. Wouldn't let her go. . . .

Tuesday, 3 December, 1974 . . . approx. 10.00 p.m. the 'black mini' with the Ladbroke Grove boys inside pulled up outside. They knocked the door and wanted to come in. Washington said 'no' and a quarrel started. Kipper (staff) happened to be there and said to them that if Washington didn't want them they should go. A bit of a fight broke out between Washington and the black mini boys and Kipper shut the door. One of the black mini boys slung an axe through the frong door, narrowly missing Kipper. Resisted phoning the police immediately. Went down to Washington's bedsit where there were approx. 13 kids, most of whom we recognised as Mandy's friends. Asked them all to leave which they did quickly. The black mini had left a long time ago. Police arrived. Called by a neighbour presumably. We told them briefly what happened but said we didn't want to report it at this point. They left. We then talked with Mandy, Washington and Paul about pros and cons of telling police officially. After a lot of discussion we decided to tell police officially as feeling was that if we didn't they'd just come back and the same thing would happen. Talked about the implications of this to project and residents generally, particularly Mandy. . . . Phoned police and PC Washbourne came down. Quite helpful. . . . Decided to say to police we wouldn't charge, but that police should hold a general description of mini until 10.00 p.m. tomorrow night when we'll contact them and tell them if we want to proceed or not. . . .

Wednesday, 4 December, 1974 . . . Lads from Grove turned up at 8.15 p. m., quite willing to talk about incident—expressed regret and will pay for damage to door. Will bring money round on Saturday morning. Felt it necessary to show goodwill and develop trust. . . .

The second example is from my own experience. In my book *Helping in Social Work,* we gave an account of the following absurd experience, concerning an ageing ex-seaman, ex-prisoner and ex-tramp, Mr Peterson, whom we had helped to settle down nearby:

He used sometimes to come into town to get drunk, and ring up more for the lift home than anything else. One market day he rang when we were home for tea. We said we would meet him in the bus station a few minutes later. We found him leaning against a wall in a busy concourse, bemoaning his fate. 'We can't go on. Bill, we can't take any more. We are better off inside. At least the Governor always gives me a decent job.' He rocked precariously to and from in his nautical garb, like a bosun in a high wind. At this point Jackie, a young woman who was also under my supervision, walked by with her three-year-old daughter. The little girl cetached herself from her mother and started to swing on my leg, shrieking in a high-pitched voice, "Sweeties, Jordan, we want some sweeties.' we suggested to the swaying mariner that we should go into the bus station cafe for a cup of tea, and we staggered off with the little girl still in tow. The cafe was very full, and we jostled a few elbows and sloshed a few cups as we lurched towards the counter. While Mr. Peterson was ordering his refreshment, the little girl kept wailing that she couldn't see the sweeties, so we hoisted her up to give her a better view. Suddenly she was snatched from my grasp by a furious mother (who must have lost track of her in the crowds) indignantly shouting, 'What the hell are you doing with my child?' Fifty heads swivelled and shocked looks bored into me. Drunken sailor and blushing child molester found themselves seats as quickly as possible.

These examples illustrate, in a rather extreme form, the day-to-day stresses that make social work a demanding and exhausting occupation. They also show how it is of the essence of social work that national social problems-unemployment, race relations, delinquency, single parenthood—should find their distillation in a series of personal and moral dilemmas confronting the social worker. The pain, confusion, distress, bitterness and rebellion of his clients, as they struggle against such adverse circumstances, present him with perplexing and potentially paralysing choices between action and inaction.

The aim of this book is not to 'resolve' all these dilemmas and confusions, but to illustrate some of their origins and consequences. The invitation to social work is not to a tranquil haven of serene altruism, but to a fragmented hotchpotch which reflects the hypocrisies, the heroisms and the heartlessnesses of wider society.

References

1. J. E. Mayer and N. Timms, *The Client Speaks: Working Class Impression of Casework,* Routledge & Kegan Paul, 1970, p. 69.
2. *Ibid.,* p. 84.
3. Howard Parker, Maggie Casburn and David Turnbull, *Receiving Juvenile Justice: Adolescents and State Care and Control,* Basil Blackwell, 1981, p. 125.

4, *Ibid.*, p. 124.
5. Eric Sainsbury, Stephen Nixon and David Phillips, *Social Work in Focus: Clients' and Social Workers' Perceptions in Long-Term Social Work,* Routledge & Kegan Paul. 1982, p. 78.
6. *Ibid.*, p. 78.
7. Carole Satyamurti, *Occupational Survival: The Case of the Local Authority Social Worker,* Basil Blackwell, 1981, p. 114.
8. *Ibid.*, p. 115.
9. National Children's Bureau, *'Who Cares?' Young People in Care Speak Out.* NCB Conference. 1975, p. 35.

12

Social Work Education

Social work education for professional in India began in 1936 when a school of social work was set up in Bombay by the House of Tatas, one of the largest private industrial and business enterprises. The main inspiration for its establishment came from America partly because its founding Director was an American and partly because the American system of graduate social work education was the only successful model available as compared to other systems elsewhere in some European societies. For eleven years between 1936 and 1947, this Institute was the only one imparting professional education in social work. In 1946, the second institution was established in Lucknow under the auspices of the Young Women Christian Association (YWCA) with a substantial grant from its counterpart in the United States, and again its founder Director was an American. It was shifted to Delhi and was named Delhi School of Social Work. After nearly two years of experimentation, it started a formal two-year programme of social work training in 1949 and was affiliated as a graduate school to the University of Delhi for the Master of Arts degree. This institution was eventually merged with the university in 1979 and became one of its departments for administrative matters under the Faculty of Social Sciences. In 1950, another institution was started as a Faculty of Social Work under the University of Baroda somewhat on the same general pattern of the American model which was accepted earlier at Bombay and Delhi. During the next decade 1951-60, fourteen more institutions were started in 1971-80. By the end of 1980, thirty institutions were providing social work education and training at the graduate level. It is now reported that the number has grown to fifty or more in the mid-nineties.

An attempt is made here to look at the Indian social work education and describe its main trends, and assesses the extent to which it has moved toward becoming indigenous in its overall philosophy and goals on the one hand and in terms of the level of training, curriculum content, use of study material and methods of working with people on the other. In the mid-eighties, 28 institutions were requested to send copies of their latest bulletins or prospectuses as they are called; twenty-one sent replies providing them or some other related information while seven failed to supply any information despite several repeated reminders. The material collected from the twenty-one institutions constituted the single most important source of the primary data. Four institutions did not send a separate prospectus. The various volumes of the *Indian Journal of Social Work* were also examined. In addition, informal discussions were held with ten prominent social work educators located in Delhi; five of them worked for the two major institutions of social work; three held important positions with the Government of India; and two were heads of national institutes which were involved in the training of para-professionals or in the organization of refresher courses for professionals already working in the public and private social welfare organizations.

As a part of this study, an attempt has also been made to determine the extent of international orientation of the American social work education as reflected through the bulletins of several leading schools of social work, the cross-cultural coverage in the volumes of three professional periodicals for the decade 1980-90, and the published study material of the Council on Social Work Education. Finally, the role of the United Nations and its allied agencies in relation to social work education is examined to assess the effectiveness of their international activities in the promotion of indigenous elements in different societies.

Organization of Social Work Education

Social work education is mainly organized at the master's level because the American model which it copied was primarily at the graduate level till the end of the sixties. Since then institutions for undergraduate social work education in America have multiplied but in India less than a dozen institutions offer the bachelor's degree in social work even today. Just as in America, social work education originated outside the established university educational system in India. The history of the New York School of Social Work in New York and the Tata Institute of Social Sciences in Bombay presents many similarities in this context. However, in both societies, social work institutions had to seek direct or indirect relationship with their respective university systems in course of time not only to standardise their curricula and improve the quality of training, but also to promote greater acceptance and enhance their status in the academic community.

At present, there are about one hundred graduate schools and several hundred undergraduate programmes in America. In India, out of nearly 200 universities which cover about five thousand colleges, only fifteen universities have separate departments of social work, two institutions are deemed to be universities, and all other social work institutions are only affiliated to universities. The pattern of affiliation and management of the twenty-one institutions included in this study varies. Seven institutions are under public management (four others which did not reply); six are Christian Church related, and the rest are under private management. The private management of social work education is a question which has rarely been discussed or debated as yet. The geographical distribution of the existing twenty-eight institutions has been rather uneven as most states in the north-west and north-east had no social work education institution.

Major Components of Social Work Education

The programme of education has basically three components: classroom courses, research project and field work. The courses offered are generally divided into four groups. The first group consists of courses about Indian society, social structure, history and philosophy of social work and social problems; the second group relates to the study of human growth and development; and the third group includes courses on methods of working with people such as social casework, social groupwork, community organization and community development, social welfare administration and social research; and the fourth group is composed of specialized courses usually offered during the second year of training, and students are expected to concentrate on one of them. The curricula are somewhat similar in all schools, and the original pattern as established by the Tata Institute and the Delhi School in the mid-fifties continues to be followed. But both these institutions had modified their curricula considerably in the late sixties and the early seventies. Essentially, the main pattern is what existed in American social work education in the early sixties. While at the Tata Institute, most courses continue to be labelled on the American model, the Delhi School has attempted generic terms as methods of working with people instead of the traditional titles as social casework, social groupwork and community organization. In most other institutions, the traditional terminology is widely followed, and even where new terms have been introduced, the basic teaching material which is primarily American, has remained the same. In addition to the courses, almost all institutions either require or provide opportunities to their students to complete an individual or group research project report based upon some type of field data. Over the years, this requirement has moved from the mandatory level to the optional level especially during the seventies.

Without exception, all institutions fully recognize that field work is an integral part of social work training. The field work programme generally includes concurrent activities, block field placement, study tours and an annual rural camp. During the first year most institutions have observational and unstructured type of field work for about 15 hours a week. The second year field work is somewhat more structured and is usually related to the student's specialized area of interest as chosen at the time of admission. The block field work placement of four to six weeks is generally arranged after the completion of all other formal requirements of training; in two institutions however this is done as a part of the field work during the second year of training. This placement exposes the student to the actual functioning of social welfare agencies and it often leads to his employment as well. In terms of both emphasis and credit given in the total curricula of different institutions, the field work practices do vary considerably. In general, institutions located in the metropolitan cities of Bombay, Delhi and Madras have somewhat stronger field work programmes than others. In Baroda where social work constitutes a separate teaching faculty in the university, field work is given the highest credit to the extent of forty per cent in the total curriculum whereas most other institutions assign ten to twenty per cent credit. In the university system as a whole, the question of giving adequate recognition and credit to the field work proportionate to the time spent by the student has raised a number of problems which fall outside the present discussion. In many institutions especially those established in the seventies and after, field work programmes are somewhat weaker, and in many others, academic courses continue to receive disproportionately higher attention.

Out of the twenty-one institutions covered in this survey, seven have also their own centres or service units for field work training; three did not supply any information while the remaining institutions had no field work centre of their own. The rationale for their establishment is partly based upon the absence of suitable of social welfare agencies and partly because of the non-availability of social work trained supervisors in most field work agencies. Moreover, it has been recognized from time to time that most social welfare agencies cannot relate the use of theoretical knowledge to the social realities in which they normally carry their practice. To overcome these inadequacies, some institutions have therefore justified the establishment and maintenance of service units for providing field work training opportunities to their students. As a matter of fact, the Tata Institute from its very inception has been maintaining a child guidance clinic for the treatment of personality disorders of children. At present, the Institute also runs a special cell in the office of the Police Commissioner to help women in distress; and there are two additional projects, one to develop job skills among the youth in the slums and the other to help a tribal community in solving some of their basic problems of living. The Delhi School also has a child guidance clinic and a rural development project. Similarly several other institutions are involved directly or indirectly in running community centres, children centres or rural development centres where they place their students for field work training. In such cases, faculty members act both as field work instructors as well as supervisors. This arrangement leads to a considerable burden on the faculty who have to assume day-to-day supervision of students. The effectiveness of such training from service projects has never been evaluated as yet.

Specialities in Social Work Education

The fundamental question which Indian social work education is facing today is the same which was asked five decades ago. This relates to its main purpose, objective or goal. In other words, what are students being trained for? Almost every institution of social work education aims at training competent social work personnel for practice in social services and social welfare services. Some institutions even claim that they prepare students for leadership responsibilities in social policy, social planning and social administration; and there are still others which highlight their commitment to social research, scholarly studies and stimulation of public interest in social issues. But it will not be untrue to say that there are no well defined categories of welfare personnel for which social work training is considered essential at the present time even after about sixty years since the establishment of the first institution. There are however two fields of practice, labelled as medical-psychiatric social work, and personnel management-industrial relations-labour welfare, where social work training is given preference. The former reflects wholesale borrowing from the American social work education model while the latter is an indigenous development because the field of labour welfare has remained outside the traditional social work education in America though industrial social work has taken some roots during the past decade in some institutions located in the metropolitan cities.

During the last three decades, two or three Indian social work educators have justified the creation or the specialization known as medical and psychiatric social work in their writings. As a field of practice, medical and psychiatric social work is reported to be practised in not more than a few dozen hospitals and clinics in the entire country. Moreover, the subject of psychiatry still remains an unknown entity outside the metropolitan cities numbering about 10 or 12. In a society where the problems of physical health remain massive as reflected in higher rates of infant mortality, maternal mortality, malnutrition and many other forms of morbidity, the establishment and promotion of medical and psychiatric social work seem rather ironic. The teaching of these subjects requires reorientation towards physical health and mental health education. Moreover, the delivery of medical services on an equitable basis presents yet another serious dilemma which needs more attention of the social work education leadership. The fact that this specialization has been there for so long is no justification for its continued existence. What is needed instead is health education specialization incorporating the themes of family planning and planned parenthood taking into consideration the social realities of public health and overpopulation and the overall quality of life. As a matter of fact, most institutions are ill-equipped to train specializts as medical and psychiatric social workers because their training requires high degree of competence on the part of teachers and adequate availability of community resources and agencies for their practice. But both of these conditions are lacking at this time and perhaps will remain so for a long time to come.

Among the other specializations are included, family and child welfare, correctional administration, community organization and development, tribal welfare and social welfare administration. Most female students are reported to take up family and child welfare and some job opportunities do exist though family social work as it is understood in America is hardly practised except in some agencies in Bombay. There are great potentialities in correctional administration but in actual practice, social work graduates do not receive any special preference for positions in jails, prisons or courts except in one or two states. Even in the field of community organization and community development, social work remains marginal partly because it is primarily in rural communities where community development programmes are functioning and partly because separate institutions exist for the training of rural workers and public administrators. Moreover, community organization in urban areas has not made much headway though some experiments were launched in the early sixties. The contribution of social work in tribal welfare has been very little so far, though the Tata Institute has been fairly active in offering specialized courses in it during the sixties and the seventies. Social welfare administration as a specialized field is reported to be available only at three institutes. Perhaps, the Tata Institute is the only one which has somewhat adequate resources and suitable staff to offer this specialization. Actually, courses on social administration, social policy and social action continue to be the least developed because the main objective of social work education in India as borrowed from America is to train practice-oriented social workers even if there is no market for them.

With regard to the specialization known as labour welfare, personnel management and industrial relations, it should be noted that it happens to be one of the indigenous elements. The original rationale for including this field in social work educational institutions was that the industrial labour was looked upon as an underprivileged group of population which needed special provisions for welfare services in industrial settings through social legislation. Under the Indian Factories Act of 1948 and its various amendments, a beginning was made in this direction and the act required the appointment of labour welfare officers employing two hundred or more workers who were to hold degrees or diplomas in social sciences from any institution recognized by the state government. Both historically and traditionally, the Tata Institute became the initial supplier, and in subsequent years, this specialization emerged as the most important one for which there was a statutory recognition on the one hand and greater job opportunities on the other. From time to time, social work educators and social welfare leaders have raised many questions relating to the application of social work philosophy, concepts and theories to this field of specialization. Moreover, this field itself has kept shifting its emphasis from labour welfare to the activities of personnel management and industrial relations which have come to assume greater importance in the various industrial settings. Again, it was this field of specialization for which a number of separate training institutions were set up outside the social work education. Eventually in 1967, the Tata Institute established an independent master's programme in personnel management and industrial relations. Even at the Delhi School, a generic programme was introduced which reduced the importance of all specializations including the labour welfare. Despite these changes, the specialization of labour welfare, personnel management and industrial relations continues to remain the most dominant field of study in terms of enrollment, prestige and job opportunities, and this also happens to be the specialization where there has been an increasing divorce from the established American philosophy, contents and techniques of social work education during the past decade. Some institutions have even introduced separate diploma or degree courses in this specialization to compete with the specialized institutions of business and industrial management.

How well equipped and effective are social work educational institutions to offer training in the labour welfare specialization has remained a vexing issue all along. Neither the institutions themselves nor their faculty members have made any serious attempt to integrate social work concepts, theories and techniques with it. The Second Review Committee of Social Work Education of the University Grants Commission had recommended its abolition from social work curricula. Most institutions are however hesitant to accept this recommendation because this specialization is the only one for which somewhat clear cut job opportunities exist irrespective of the fact whether social work training is actually applicable to the preparation of students for the various responsibilities called for by the employing industrial settings. Besides, most male applicants who seek out admission to social work training are reported to show preference for this specialization, and the overall public image of social work continues to be associated with the field of labour welfare. However, the Delhi School, which gave up training in formal specializations several years ago claims to have suffered no loss in its enrollment. The debate on the generic versus specialization continues, and it is fair to say that most institutions in actual practice tend to emphasise some form of specialization either at the time of admission of students or in the course of their training during the second year. Moreover, the findings of some studies about the employment of social work graduates have shown that most employers in practice do not maintain any clear distinction between the specializt and the generalist. At the same time, it is noted that most graduates prefer to take up what is available and as more opportunities exist in the specialization of labour, so its effective demand continues to flourish.

Students and the Faculty

Out of the twenty-one institutions covered by this survey, 15 indicated the available number of seats every year; eight institutions admit 20-35 students; four between 40 and 50; and three more than 50. Among the largest institutions in terms of annual enrollment are the Tata Institute with 70 in its social work programme, the Varanasi School 65; and the Delhi School has 55. Almost all other institutions for which actual data was not available have a capacity of 50 or less each. If the average capacity is taken as forty seats per institution and assuming every one admitted completed his or her training successfully, the annual production of graduates was about 1,100 for a society with a population of about 800 million persons in 1991 and where several thousand organizations both public and private are engaged in some form of social welfare activity. Ironic as it may sound even one thousand plus graduates cannot find suitable employment because most of these organizations are small and cannot afford to employ professional workers. As a matter of fact, they have failed to accept the useful role of the professionals as such in carrying out their services. There is not much data available about the background of students who join social work education institutions. The Second Review Committee on Social Work Education did make some observations. It was said that students who were drawn to social work education were reported to be those who did not obtain admission to other professional disciplines. It was further pointed out that dead end jobs, lack of commitment of public and voluntary organizations to the need for trained workers, and the subordination of professional workers to volunteers and non-professional committees were responsible for discouraging many students from coming to social work institutions. In addition, the questions of employment opportunities, salary scales, availability of promotions, and acceptance of the professional ethics raised important issues in the recruitment of students. At this stage of economic development. Economics continues to be the only social science which attracts relatively well-prepared students as compared to other social sciences. During the past two decades, the institutions of business management and administration have also been sought after at an increasing rate.

As regards the faculty, it was found that nine out of the seventeen institutions which furnished the necessary data employed less than ten teachers each; four had ten faculty members each; and four had more than fifteen each; and the Tata ranked at the top employing about thirty for its social work programme. Institutions which had undergraduate training programmes also did not show their faculty separately. Many faculty members held double graduate degrees; almost every institution had at least one faculty member with a Ph.D. degree; one-third of the faculty at the Tatas, in Varanasi nineteen out of 20, in Udaipur one-third, and one-fifth in Delhi had doctoral degrees. No data was available about their field experience. Generally speaking, most faculty members had suitable academic qualifications but little or no worthwhile field experience after their graduation. This is consistent with the cultural setting because the Indian academic community continues to give higher rewards for academic achievements, and direct service experience is generally frowned upon historically. The Tata and the Delhi School were the only institutions where 6 or 7 faculty members held American social work degrees; and three other institutions had at least one faculty member each who was an American-trained social worker. Although the proportion of foreign trained teachers had gone down considerably over the years, the very pattern of organization and the teaching material used in social work institutions are American both in spirit and content. Most of the faculty lacks research orientation and has published very little except some faculty members at the Tata and the Delhi School who have been fairly productive. But, even they have failed to develop and produce teaching material based upon indigenous social, economic and political conditions. Perhaps, faculty development programmes are needed so that selected faculty members could obtain leave from their teaching duties and work in both public and private social welfare organizations functioning at different levels.

Use of American Study Material

Indian social work education has found a readymade body of formulated concepts, theories and techniques from American social work literature. For more than three decades, Indian social work educators and international consultants have admitted the excessive use of American textbooks and case studies, and have recognized the need to develop and introduce indigenous study material. It is unfortunate that little has been accomplished on this front even till today. In this survey, eleven institutions provided lists of the books suggested or recommended for use in the various courses offered by them. The teaching material for the courses relating to human growth and behaviour, social casework, social groupwork, community organization, medical and psychiatric social work, and social research and statistics is exclusively American; and even for courses on social work history, social work philosophy, social structure, social problems and social deviance, most of the publications used are American. As a matter of fact, the dominance of American publications is so striking that one wonders how students could integrate any concept, theory or technique based upon American cultural ideologies with the practice of social work in Indian welfare settings.

Moreover, some of the books used were published before 1960 and most of them related to the 1970s and before. The all-embracing American characteristic pervades not only the study material recommended on the reading lists but it is also reflected in the organization of the education itself. Even these dated books are not available in the open market and have to be read in the libraries of social work institutions. Thus, we find that there is a crying need for indigenous scholarship and indigenous study material based upon Indian social, economic, and political conditions.

Inappropriateness and Irrelevance of the American Model

American social work education is a product of American history and culture which have been dominated by such ideologies as Capitalism, Social Darwinism, the Protestant Ethic and Individualism. These ideologies tend to emphasise the individual's responsibility in shaping his own welfare, and the public responsibility comes in only when the individual fails to make satisfactory adjustment to the established cultural patterns of life. For over one hundred years from 1830 to 1930, voluntary social welfare organizations as originated from the religious charities and charity organization movement accepted major responsibility for varied types of social welfare activities. The traditional ideologies, however, had a serious setback during the Great Depression in the thirties, and since then public responsibility for social welfare services has progressively increased at all levels of government. The expanding conception that has grown in the last sixty years not only includes increasing income maintenance programmes but also a multitude of both public and private services under such broad categories as home health services, daycare services, recreation and leisure time services, family services, services to the elderly, child welfare services, community mental health services, vocational rehabilitation services for disabled persons, alcohol and drug abuse services, social services in schools, social services in medical care systems and social services in the criminal justice system. With the expansion of these activities, both the social work profession and social work education have also witnessed a substantial expansion in the last three decades.

In 1952, when the American Council on Social Work Education was established, the social work educational institutions adopted a curriculum policy statement emphasising a broad generic sequence of study in (1) social services policy and programmes, (2) human growth and behaviour, (3) social work methods of social casework, social groupwork, community organization, social work administration, and social work research, and (4) social work practice or field work. Till the end of the fifties, social work education was primarily limited to the two-year graduate programme. As a result of a comprehensive study of curriculum in 1959, a revised policy statement was accepted in 1962 which led to the development of undergraduate programmes in social work education, the decreasing role of specializations by methods, an increasing emphasis upon the field of practice and incorporation of additional courses on socio-cultural elements, community organization, social administration, social policy, social planning and social research. In 1971, a new curriculum policy was adopted but current educational programmes continue to reflect the dominant influence of the framework set in 1952. Essentially, the curriculum of American social work education is based upon the principles, concepts and theories derived from the fields of psychology, psychiatry, psychoanalysis, psychodrama, group dynamics, and other related branches of psychology. At the same time, it continues to be encircled with the dominant social philosophies of the American culture which give an overriding importance to the casework method of working with people in almost all settings of social work practice. Perhaps, in no society social work has attained as much professional status as in the United States. But even here out of the estimated 600,000 social workers in 1985, most are employed in public organizations and less than 25 per cent of them hold master's degrees in social work. Moreover, most American social workers are engaged in direct-service methods and recent enrollment data supports that this dominant trend is likely to continue in the future.

Most American scholars who have written about international social work have usually highlighted the universal elements of American social work education and not many have ever attempted to examine their application, their acceptance or their effectiveness in South Asian societies. As a matter of fact, two leaders of the team of social work consultants who worked in India in the late fifties who had their training exclusively in social casework had come out for the propagation of social casework in one form or other as an integral part of Indian social work education. It is true that American social work education has spread far and wide beginning from the early fifties and virtually thousands of Asians have been trained in America. A recent survey conducted by this writer about the international and cross-cultural elements of the American social work education as reflected in the courses offered, faculty members' experience in Asian countries, recruitment of Asians on the faculty and the faculty members' publications strikingly reveal that the American social work educational institutions are woefully ill-equipped to offer training to Asians or other foreigners which could be used in their native societies in any meaningful manner. It is not far from the truth that very few American scholars have ever undertaken any research or published any paper on this subject in any leading professional journals. Moreover, not a single research centre of any social work institution has ever undertaken any research concerning the application of social work philosophy, concepts, principles and methods to Asian societies. Actually, only one social work research centre has completed a few studies about comparative social welfare in European societies. Moreover, social work institutions generally do not maintain much contact with other social science departments of their universities which in many instances have specialized centres involved in research about Asian societies. Thus, it will be fair to say that American social work education is highly ethnocentric and its essential elements are inappropriate and irrelevant for India and other developing societies where not only social structures and social problems are different but even human needs, beliefs, myths, values, traditions, goals, roles, aspirations and human behaviour itself are so different that they demand different solutions.

Diffusion of Americanism: Dilemmas and Problems

As stated earlier, the main inspiration for the establishment of formal training in social work in India came from the United States, and Indian institutions borrowed almost the entire framework and pattern of American social work education as given in the curriculum statement of 1952 except the introduction of labour welfare as one of their specializations. Perhaps, the single most important factor which led to further Americanization of Indian social work education was the bilateral agreement of technical assistance and exchange programme in 1956 under which the Council on Social Work Education sent American social work educators as consultants and faculty members to selected Indian schools of social work, and brought Indian social work educators as students and trainees to selected American schools. In addition, two or three American social work educators were sent to India to work as social welfare attaches in the American Embassy who exerted great influence on the direction of Indian social work education. Most American consultants who went to India had very little knowledge and understanding of India's long historical, religious and philosophical traditions which continue to dominate Indian social life. Neither had they any basic informative knowledge about the socio-economic and political goals to which the society had committed itself under its Constitution and the Five Year Plans. Moreover, in terms of their own training and experience, most of them had very little exposure to the cultural-anthropological, sociological and public administrative literature of America or any other society which could have helped them to understand the major problems and issues confronting the Indian society.

Through the efforts of American consultants, however, these schools which had very little or no field work training programme, were assisted to establish some type of field work practice. Some improvements were also carried out in the teaching of courses on social casework and social groupwork. The most important role which these consultants played relates to the organization of some seminars where representatives of different social work institutions were brought together to exchange their views which ultimately led to the formation of an Association of Schools of Social Work in India. This Association has survived for more than three decades and has published reports of several seminars organized by it from time to time. However, in recent years, this Association has lost its enthusisam and vigour, and is on its way to becoming an impotant organization because many member schools are uncooperative in maintaining and improving the quality of social work education. The overall impact of these developments was substantial which took social work education further towards Americanization.

From time to time, the American Council on Social Work Education has held conferences and seminars where both American and foreign social work educators have participated. The most recent one was arranged in New York at the end of the International Conference in 1985. The activities of American social work educators as Fulbright lecturers and researchers in social welfare programmes provided another source of culture contact. The Cleveland International Programme for Youth Leaders and Social Workers, an annual exchange programme sponsored Jointly by the U S State Department and some social voluntary welfare organizations have brought several hundred persons from foreign countries including India for short durations during the past thirty years. Moreover, American social work education institutions specially located in the metropolitan cities of Atlanta, Boston, Cleveland, Chicago, Detroit, Los Angeles, New York, Philadelphia, St. Louis and San Francisco have admitted a number of Indian students for social work training almost every year. Some of them go back and usually take up teaching positions at social work institutions in India while most choose to settle in America after the completion of their training partly because they do not perceive any prospects of employment back home and partly because of the material allurements available in the United States. The flow of Indians to the United States for social work education and for many other social science fields of training has considerably declined in the last ten years because the U S government has imposed stricter restrictions on entry visas in recent years. The Delhi School and the Tata Institute have attracted the majority of American trained social workers for teaching positions in the past.

Role of the United Nations

During the past four decades, the United Nations and its many commissions and allied agencies have also played a role in the dissemination of American social work in other countries. The United Nations brought out five surveys which identified significant developments and trends in the training programmes in social work in different countries. The surveys, specifically the third and the fourth, highlighted the limited applicability of the American model of social work education and pointed out the need for promoting indigenous methods, curricula and study material. In subsequent years, the United Nations Commission in Bangkok took several initiatives dating back to 1964 to promote the development of indigenous teaching material by establishing a working group consisting of well-known social work educators from the South Asian region. Moreover, the Commission also sponsored a training centre in September 1966 which offered social work teachers an opportunity to work together jointly so as to identify the main principles of curriculum on an indigenous basis, to incorporate cultural factors in the practice of social work and to develop teaching material including case studies reflecting socio-economic conditions of the region.

In later years, the United Nations Centre for Social Welfare and Development in Manila held many conferences and seminars involving selected representatives of schools of social work for mutual exchange of views on issues and problems, and for the development of indigenous case records and other teaching material. It is true that based upon the proceedings of these conferences and seminars, several surveys and reports became available stressing the importance of the development of indigenous approaches and study material. But it is unfortunate that neither any concrete plan has been developed to replace the American model nor any specific indigenous study material has been produced during the past two decades. This may be partly attributed to the fact that most of the United Nations publications and personnel tacitly have assumed all along that American social work philosophy is somewhat superior, and that principles and methods of American social work provide the only model which has universal applicability. Perhaps the only exception is the report completed by a Yugoslavian scholar more that three decades ago. At the present time, most of the U N activities concerning social development and social welfare are being initiated and formulated at the Centre for Social Development and Humanitarian Affairs of the Department of International Economic and Social Welfare which continues to be dominated by the American model. Finally, among the other international organizations which have promoted Americanization of global social work education directly or indirectly are the International Association of Schools of Social Work, International Federation of Social Workers and the International Conference of Social Work. It should also be pointed out that many other international non-governmental and voluntary social welfare agencies which are mainly financed and controlled by American social work interests have also been responsible for promoting the influence of American social work directly or indirectly throughout the world. If member nations want indigenous approaches, social work education leadership must come forward from within as the American model remains exclusively casework oriented and lacks social development and social administrative perspectives.

Need for Indigenous Foundations

The need for indigenous elements of social work education in terms of its philosophy, approaches, principles, theories and study material cannot be over-emphasised because working with people, studying social problems and administering social welfare programmes call for indigenous orientation and skills. The foreignness of social work education is so much all-inclusive and pervasive as reflected in its basic organization, curricula and the teaching material that most social work graduates fail to pursue careers in professional social work. Moreover, existing training does not prepare them to assume roles of leadership in the planning, formulation and implementation of social welfare programmes at different levels of practice and administration. If social work has to move toward professionalism in any society and has to become effective, it must have indigenous foundations incorporating dominant cultural philosophies, on the one hand, and projected goals which are being promoted on the other. Recently, based upon his independent study, a young Indian social educator has concluded that "social work education in India has become irrelevant to the needs of Indian society, because what is needed in Indian society is a primarily preventive and macro based social work." Indian social work educators must accept this challenge and forge a new strategy to transform the existing social work education to develop and use indigenous study material. Unless this is done social work as a profession is not likely to establish its roots in society.

13

Role of Leadership

Still at present Indian society is passing through a period of transition and bewilderment. The new social and economic forces generated by the large-scale development plans have shaken up the social structure and are beginning to alter the old values and attitudes as well. The traditional leadership is also undergoing a change and new patterns of leadership are emerging on the scene. In this context, the introduction of community projects, land reforms, decentralised local administration and adult franchise which aim at the reconstruction of society have brought forth the importance of the phenomenon of leadership. Increasingly, it is believed that the success or failure of development plans and indeed of more general ideological aspirations as embodied in our Constitution may well depend upon the type of leadership available in village, town and district level.

Leadership Theories

Among social scientists, the theoretical formulations of leadership concept continue to shift, focussing first upon one aspect and then upon the other, during the past three decades. Early leadership research focussed on the leader himself to the virtual exclusion of other variables. This gradually took the form of a theory, 'the great man theory' of leadership which assumed that leadership could be explained by isolating psychological and physical characteristics or traits, presumed to differentiate the leader from, other members of his group. Some sought unitary leadership trait capable of characterising leaders whenever found; others looked for a constellation of traits constituting general leadership. However, studies guided by this assumption failed to establish the existence of universal leadership traits and no such general list has ever been successfully derived. The inadequacies of the trait approach led some social scientists to search for other variables. The emphasis, therefore, swung away from the leader as an entity complete unto himself, and leadership came to be viewed as a function of the situation. The situationists did not abandon the search for significant personality characteristics, but they attempted to look for them in situations containing common elements. Soon it was realised that no conception of leadership would be complete, unless it considered the structure of group in which the inter-actions among the members had taken place. Leadership was viewed essentially as a set of functions performed by one or many members of the group under various conditions. Research conducted within this orientation did not attempt to find certain universal personality traits; rather it sought to discover what actions were required by groups under varying conditions if they were to achieve their objectives and in what ways different group members took part in these group actions. In fact, the group members were considered a major variable in leadership research.

Cultural Context and Leadership

In essence, each of the three conceptions — the trait approach, the situationist approach, and the group-follower-oriented approach, taken separately, reveals only a part of the total phenomenon. Indeed, it is felt by many researchers that all the three approaches represent different facets of the same social phenomenon and yet they may not provide an adequate theoretical framework for the study of leadership. Anthropological field studies of rural communities in different parts of the world have demonstrated sharp differences in the patterns of leadership. These studies stress that leadership exists with reference to the social organisation of a particular community and is also heavily influenced by the social climate and the system of values prevailing in that community. This suggests that the performance of leadership functions are dependent not only on the type of the task, the character of the group, the qualities of the members of the group and the relations of group members but also on the nature, of the social organisation and the value system of a group within which leadership is to be studied. It is obvious that leadership is a complex social phenomenon and to concentrate on any one approach without taking into account the characteristics of the total culture in which the group exists, is not enough.

Roles of Leadership

This brief historical review of the leadership concept highlights the shifting focus in theoretical orientations from time to time and helps us to define leadership as a role of function played in situations within the context of the culture, to attain a specified goal or goals. The person who performs this role is perceived as a leader by the members of his group and is given influence, prestige, authority and status which he would not have as a member of the group. This view does not limit the leadership concept to formally appointed functionaries; rather it is applicable to the multiplicity of roles which are determined by the inter-play of the personality of the leader in relation to the personality of the followers (group members) and to the characteristics of situations in the social organisation.

Members of the group when performing the leadership functions play many different roles. Various inventories of leadership roles have been suggested by social scientists. As a planner and policy maker, the leader looks ahead and sees the long-range effects of group action after taking stock of the existing problems; the executive action carries out the group policies; the educator's role assists the group to see alternative solutions to different problems and thereby helps in arriving at a consensus; as a spokesman, the leader represents the group in its relations with other groups; as an expert he brings his knowledge and experience; as a protector he provides security against outside aggression and the harmonizer's role calls for the identification of the areas of agreement in the group, and brings cohesion through this agreement.

These different roles are rarely taken continuously by one individual in different situations. It is one that is taken at a time or another. It is true that a person with outstanding characteristics will, undoubtedly, have greater opportunities to assume these roles and will be called upon more frequently than persons without those qualities. One must not, however, forget that the distribution of leadership roles is highly influenced by such factors as the nature of the group, its history and traditions, and the nature of the task itself as mentioned earlier.

Leadership Patterns

The distribution of leadership roles is also closely related to the variations in the established leadership patterns. Such patterns may be in the form of (a) institutional leadership which refers to formal or appointive leaders who by virtue of their positions are expected to carry the leadership roles. The leadership roles associated with the position centime even though the persons occupying the position may change; (b) situational leadership which emerges at a time when institutional leadership proved to be inadequate for providing the constructive guidance necessary to achieve changes in the group or community; another variation would be what is called informal leadership which commands respect and prestige in specific situations; (c) dictatorial or authoritarian leadership which tends to centralise all the functions in one individual and does not seek to evoke the maximum involvement of other members in the group in finding solutions to common problems. This type of leadership usually fails to generate spontaneity of assent and group solidarity. Some research studies have, however, suggested that what is frequently called authoritarian leadership may not be bad or unproductive. There are always certain situations in which members prefer such leadership for advancement in the interest of the total group as at times permissive leadership blocks movements towards the attainment of the group goal/goals; (d) democratic or creative leadership which promotes responsible participation by other group members and reinforces cooperative inter-personal relations within the group. It makes use of those ways that release creativity in group members and encourage cohesiveness in the group.

None of these patterns, however, exist in pure form in the real world. Whereas institutional leadership has informal aspects, informal leadership has formal aspects which characterise the various leadership roles. Again we need to recognise that there is a democratic-authoritarian continuum and that while one may be embedded to democratic leadership, this does not mean that in all situations there is full realisation of individual abilities and needs. A group's acceptance and tolerance of one or another of these patterns of leadership, depends upon the degree of maturity in the processes of democracy which that group represents. Regardless of the pattern of leadership, the nature of leadership involves elements of all the these conceptions in the context of the culture of a group as discussed above. It must, however, be admitted that differences in leadership patterns do produce different results in different situations.

Leadership Effectiveness

All leadership roles are goal oriented. Once leadership role has been performed, it becomes appropriate to raise questions about the effectiveness of such leadership. As the leadership role is determined by the interplay of many variables, the effectiveness also becomes a function of the dynamic inter-relations of the personality (characteristics of the one who exercises leadership role, the personality traits of the members of the group and of the situation within each individual role. Besides, the effectiveness is closely related to the patterns of leadership as well, which in turn are continuously affected by the influences stemming from traditions, charismatic attributes and legal enactments. The very multiplicity of factors which influence the effectiveness of leadership roles makes clear-cut measurement of effectiveness difficult. The shifting and dynamic nature of the leadership role farther complicates the assessment of leadership effectiveness.

Social scientists, however, agree that the effectiveness of any leadership role should always be assessed in relation to the attainment of goal/goals established either by cooperative and collaborative efforts of the leader or by the group members themselves or by legal processes for the betterment of the entire group. The leadership, which facilitates communication within the group, makes for better morale, increases member satisfaction, promotes greater productivity and helps the group to move towards its goals without causing much friction among the group members, is usually understood as effective leadership. This suggests the need for special skills, personality resources and knowledge of the dynamics of leadership on the part of the leader, but undoubtedly, each member of the group contributes to the effectiveness in leadership.

Rural Scene and Leadership

The rural community in North India consists of caste groups and caste factions at the village level. The traditional leadership based on the principle of caste system has been patterned as a hierarchic pyramid with a mass of so-called 'untouchables' at the base and a small stratum of elite at its apex. It has been common for students of Indian rural society to identify two major patterns of leadership—one influenced by hereditary privileges of the caste, wealth, education, family status etc. and represented by such functionaries as 'lambardar', 'mukhia', 'sarpanch' and 'pradhan'; and the other by charismatic attributes resting on devotion to the specific and exceptional sanctity that attracts followers almost irresistibly and represented usually by informal leaders. "While a charisma seldom occurs in its pure form, it is seen in some degree at many levels of human relations in our rural society. Both these patterns are highly conditioned by the caste-contoured social organisation which emphasises authoritarian ways of achieving group goals. As a result thereof, broad-based community leadership is, by and large, absent from the village scene. Essentially, at least till recently, leadership at the village level has been closely related to caste groups, and rigidity of paste loyalty in one form or the other, still remains.

Modern systems of transport, technology, industrialisation, mechanisation and western-type education during the last four decades have certainly brought significant changes in the rural life, and the social structure is changing from a relatively closed system ordained by caste hierarchies to a relatively open system governed by secular law. The influence of technological change has set the process of social change in motion and the traditional leadership has begun to change with a shift from an ascribed status system to an achieved status system. The general weakening of the old system has facilitated the emergence of a new leadership structure and has widened the base of leadership. At the same time the development programmes have offered tremendous opportunities to all individuals —irrespective of their caste identification—to take up leadership roles. This has created a hope that functionally organised leadership will gradually emerge as the community development programme becomes established as the peoples' movement. One must add that despite the introduction of democratic decentralisation programmes, the appointed functionaries of both State and Central Civil Services continue to play the dominant role of leadership in shaping the future of our rural communities.

Urban Elite

Whether it is a rural community or an urban area, public policies are primarily shaped by an elite group consisting of political leaders of major political parties and professional civil servants of the governmental bureaucracy. By virtue of numbers alone, the bureaucracy at all levels of government constitutes a vital force both in the formulation and in the execution of national public policies. Most people have little or nothing to do with the great decisions which affect their living and their communities. It is true that political process in one form or the other does take place at the national, state or local level, and some attempts are made to enlist wider participation from influential groups representing industry, business, social welfare and other interests. But no matter who may be the real wielders of power, most of the decisions on public policy are ultimately made by those who occupy positions of formal authority in the governmental system. The public officials have, therefore, come to play a unique role in shaping the course of future India. The establishment of the National Planning Commission at the Centre and the Planning Cells at the state level provide an excellent example on this behalf. Again every State and in almost all large cities, special Boards, Commissions, and Development Authorities have been set up to cope with some of the major urban problems. Though some formal representation is given to non-official groups and interests, but in actual practice, all such bodies constitute the governmental bureaucracy and not only determine the major policy issues, but also exercise control over day-to-day affairs.

Although there are no formal educational requirements for candidates who seek election in the representative assemblies, they generally do have at least a high school diploma. Perhaps a considerable percentage of elected representatives also holds college degrees. At the other end, almost all public officials must possess college degrees to enter national or state civil service. Of course, public officials are constantly subject to various forces and pressures in varying degrees. Both the professional civil servant and the elected official are considerably influenced by the "Western social, economic and political philosophies. As a matter of fact, the former is more likely to be the product of the Western education than the latter. It is in this context that the need for indigenous orientation is urgently called for. The increasing industrialisation and urbanisation have also swelled the ranks of government employees. The rise in their unionisation is yet another dimension to be taken into consideration. In addition, the unionisation of industrial workers has considerably influenced public policies concerning working conditions, wages and benefits, and housing needs. The organisations of business and industry continue to wield power and influence in spite of public pronouncements to achieve socialistic pattern of society. Thus there are several elements which determine the pattern of leadership roles and power structure. Nevertheless, a stable power hierarchy drawn largely from the dominant political parties, the official and semi-official boards, and the governmental bureaucracy is easily identified at different levels of administration.

Social Research Need

True, the social, economic and political changes of the last three decades have loosened the rigid social structure to a considerable extent and increasingly leadership is cutting across the caste differences. The new forces have reduced the influence of wealth, family status and age as determinants of leadership roles; education has gained significant importance and political identification with the ruling party has also become a dominant factor. Undoubtedly, there is in

Indian villages today a process of socio-economic change from the traditional forms to some other forms about which new knowledge has been acquired in recent years through field studies. However, our knowledge about the urban elite and the functioning of urban local governmental units remains inadequate. There is an urgent need for microcosmic study of urban life by anthropologists, sociologists and political scientists to enable us to form correct perspectives about the changing patterns of urban leadership. The demand for detailed field studies of both traditional and new leadership structures also arises from the fact that the nature of social organisation differs considerably from one region to another in the country. The district administration continues to be of vital importance and, therefore, it requires systematic examination. The prevailing low level of literacy and the continual struggle with basic problems of living have generally prevented the masses to participate in the development and execution of the large-scale programmes of social and economic development. The formal structure of district administration has, therefore, become a pivotal force in both rural and urban communities. The networks of informal structures do exist, however, and exercise some influence on the functioning of the formal structure. "We need to know more about these networks. The knowledge gained from such studies will help the planners of our nation to discover potential leadership, to know the key variables which constitute effective leadership for the implementation of socio-economic programmes including family planning activities and schemes for the promotion of community integration.

14

Social Action and Social Work

Of late, it has become the practice for the Association of Schools of Social Work in India to focus attention on various social trends with respect to their implication for the curriculum. Examples of these are family planning, poverty, weaker sections, rural development and now social action. All these imply a continuing concern to make the curriculum relevant. In effect it may lead to a patch-work quilt instead of an integrated curriculum. The addition or deletion of a subject, to fit in with changing trends, does not constitute curriculum development. Adding social action as a subject and entrusting its teaching to one teacher will result in either social action being seen as an esoteric activity which only a few can do, or, it will create a cynicism on the part of the students who may see into the hypocrisy of the institutional vested interests in perpetuating the old while giving lip-service to the new.

In considering social action in the curriculum for social work education, it should be seen in the context of the whole and not the part. A curriculum is a fabric in which theories, practice, ideas and research are the warp and woof. Unless they are designed to provide an over-all scheme of education, by integration and by examining the implications of the part to the whole, it will show, like a badly woven fabric, loose threads, gaping holes, and a lack of capacity to stand up to use. It is necessary, therefore, to examine the entire thrust of the programme, and then to locate the parts in relation to the whole. Unless the institution is guided by an over-all philosophy, suggestions from ASSWI of additions or subtractions to the curriculum will have no impact. In this context some relevant issues are:

(i) The current Indian situation and the role of professional social work.

(ii) What will constitute an improved socio-economic-political situation and what will be its implications?

(iii) What will need to be done with the client, target and action systems to bring about the change?

(iv) What will be resistances and the problems encountered in undertaking such activities?

(v) What methods/approaches will be required; which methods/approaches are sufficiently developed that can be utilised in the class-room and in field training, and which are yet to develop?

(vi) What are the value/norm considerations, if any, which are likely to affect what we choose to do or not to do?

(vii) How do we monitor the effects of the curriculum on our students and the impact on the field?

(viii) What are the administrative implications in the institution for social work education for such a change?

Is there a Theory?

Utilisation of a theory in the class-room assumes that there are some well explicated theoretical propositions based on phenomena which have been repeatedly observed, or even tested through empirical means, and integrated into a cohesive explanation of the phenomenon (a) under consideration. A review of the literature does not show any theory, or theories of social action, only attempts to develop it based on either the individual experiences of those involved as activists, or by theoreticians identifying the strategies utilised by such persons. Possibly, one can say that some models exist which are themselves based on existing and widely recognised theories such as Marxism. This problem places a limitation on the transmission of ideas since the class-room context assumes that such existing theory becomes the basis for reflection and discussion in the teacher-student interaction.

As stated by Paull,

> There is as yet no accepted conceptual system for organising knowledge about social-change activities. Commonly, there is an ad hoc typology loosely related to objectives (for example, anti-war, civil rights, welfare rights, etc.) but goals and issues are so fluid that there is a tendency to add the criterion of methodology employed by various groups.

There is not even a consensus as to whether social action should always have inherent in it the dynamic of conflict; whether it should always involve the beneficiaries of the action effort, and whether it is underpinned by any basic value orientations. There are several strategies which has been identified, but there is no developed theory to identify the context within which selected strategies may be utilised; whether personal characteristics and predilections of the individual will, ultimately, determine which strategies are most likely to be used; whether there should be any value underpinning in the social action, process or whether attitudinal change (values, beliefs and attitudes) is an essential ingredient before political changes can occur, since people are conditioned by their cultures to retain the status and power arrangements.

These unresolved issues may constitute, therefore, a major problem for the teacher in organising the theory, principles, concepts, and the extrapolation of the models and strategies of social action for teaching in the classroom. Unless we recognise this uncomfortable fact of life for the educator in dealing with. such materials, we may have a very naive approach to the curriculum for social action.

Given these problems, each teacher will end up developing his own approach to the subject (which in itself can be appropriate only when based on an educated decision among choices and alternatives), because he has little organised theory to count on in developing the subject. In formal educational programmes, this is a hasard since the assumptions on which they are based are different from the non-formal. Hence, the problem of what needs to be included, how this subject can be best handled in the curriculum, and which behavioural objectives will need to be achieved have to be dealt with. Further, it calls for an examination of these subject level objectives with, what seem to be the over-all objectives of the total curriculum of the individual institution which adopts social action. The institutional auspices, its convictions (or lack of them), its mission, vision or philosophy, will ultimately affect the curricular choices that are made, and to what extent they are implemented.

What is Available Now?

In an excellent review of the literature on social action, Khinduka and Coughlin point out three broad types of written materials that are available on social action:

(i) Material related to social workers' involvement in influencing social policy through an understanding of the political process.

(ii) Material which is involved with identification of the stages in the action process: researching the problem; planning a .solution; enlisting public support; presenting the proposal to those with authority for adoption; and enforcement or execution of the new policy. Advocacy and using influence, through persuasion, inducements and pressure tactics are implied in such a process.

(iii) Material seeking to understand the nature of social action: the mobilising of group effort towards achieving social objectives by the removal of the offending problem or situation, through advocating a cause or a measure, or a struggle related to status, power and resources.

They also point out that there is no consensus in the literature as to whether the actions should necessarily be within the "legal framework", or can be "illegal", that is, outside the rule of law; whether it is an aspect of the evolutionary process since no institutions can be permanent (Wickenden), or a means of changing history (Paull); whether social action must necessarily be linked to the theory of social conflict (Coser); and its degree of compatibility with the ethical values of the profession.

Another issue which is brought up by Khinduka and Coughlin is that of the scope of social action which we feel pertains to the applicability of what we teach in the classroom to the student's practice. What he learns he must be able to utilise in his work immediately, or in the foreseeable future. The scope, then, of social action should be considered as it has a bearing on what will be useable in a number of situations which the social worker will encounter. They distinguish social action which is at the intermediate or macro level from "a strategy for overhauling an entire social structure" which they regard as revolution and not social action. This is not to underestimate the need for a radical change in the total social structure, but to limit the scope of what is possible within the anticipated level of involvement of the type of student entering social work education. This is a problem of every curriculum, framer. Do we design the curriculum and hope to get a student who fits it, or, do we develop a curriculum in which we appraise the type of learner we are likely to get, and how far he can be behaviourally changed by the learning experience in terms of the development of his knowledge, skills and attitudes? In considering, therefore, social action as an element in the curriculum, we should appraise our students, their socio-economic background, their expectations and aspirations in professional, social work education and practice. It is well to remember, that while the curriculum content and teaching may be in the hands of the curriculum framer and the teacher, it is the student who experiences learning and controls what he gets out of it. Hence, the nature of our student population must be taken into consideration in formulating the syllabus for social action.

Social Action Strategies

There is hardly any consensus on the strategies that are possible and available, and will form the core of social action practice. Generally, the strategies available to social workers may be divided into:

(a) Collaborative
(b) Bargaining, negotiation, advocacy
(c) Conflictual/confrontational

In collaborative strategies, the change in the institution is sought to be brought about through education, persuasion, demonstration, experimentation. One of the premises on which it is based is that all those who have power will not necessarily respond to change only through a conflictual approach. Through the above techniques they can be brought to effect change because, for them, the intended change is either the lesser of the two evils, or, they- have themselves identified the factors which affect the very existence of the institution, or the achievement of its goals; they are disenchanted, or dissatisfied and therefore willing to engage in the change effort though some part of the system may show initial resistance. The discomfort produced acts as a leverage in the change agent's attempts to bring about the change resulting in basic, changes in the structure and functions of the institution and its effects on people. The techniques used are those within the norms of every day behaviour with the difference that they are selectively utilised to bear upon change in the system.

The second set of techniques are based on the premise that one anticipates some resistance to change, and the activity of the change agent may have to be accompanied by tactics which are not persuasive but rather seek to affect change through pressure. These could include techniques of bargaining and negotiation, publicity which leads to discomfort for the target of change, advocacy through the media and attempts to isolate the target group from the opinions of the community at large. The techniques utilised may, to some extent, deviate from the usual interpersonal behaviours, and include methods such as satyagrah, morcha, and other methods of dramatising the situation and developing public opinion.

Lastly, the third set of techniques are based on the premise that in the struggle between those who are pro status quo and those who are pro change, resistance is an aspect of the change effort and, therefore, the dynamic of conflict is inherent in the social action effort. They may include agitational techniques such as protests, demonstrations and civil disobedience.

Khinduka and Coughlin do not agree with the assumption that "social action is a derivative of the conflict theory of society" because conflict assumes annihilation, defeat, subjugation, injury or elimination. In practical terms, in fact, there is some element of conflict but the end result is rarely the total elimination of the "oppressor", or the total elimination of the causal factors in the social situation which negatively affects people.

To quote at some length, Khinduka and Coughlin state:

> Just as the social actionist employs both norm-adhering and norm-violating strategies, his social philosophy and theoretical starting point are neither the "consensus" or "integration" model of society nor the "conflict" or "coercion" model....
>
> The social actionist's world, perhaps, like the world in general, is "Janus-headed", it is composed of both elements. Dahrendorf insists on the complementary nature of these elements. Both models are useful; neither is exclusively valid. In his words: "We cannot conceive of society unless we realise the dialectics of stability and change, integration and conflict, function and motive, force, consensus and coercion. Conflict per se does not necessarily lead to desired social change. Coser has argued both that some conflicts car strengthen an existing system, thus making it more viable, and that internecine conflict among believers in the same cause may destroy their ability to act rather than add to their capability to effect change in the social system at hand. As Cohen says: "The two models are not genuine alternatives: to say that a room is half-full is not to deny that it is half-empty."

It is possible to view the three strategies as overlapping rather than water-tight compartments. While one modality may be selected over another, there might be a subsidiary use of the others. It may be that one sets out with one strategy, and appraisal of the situation might require change to another. The context of the situation, the client system and target group, as well as the goal to be achieved, may determine the selection of the technique. In fact, the confrontational/conflictual model leaves very little scope for use of any other techniques; it closes the door to them. Hence, it is possible that, in many instances, social action may be initiated with the collaborative or the bargaining strategies, and, ultimately move on to the confrontational/conflictual when there is no other alternative. However, it must be noted here that it is easier to mobilise people under the first two than the last. Hence, even as a preferred strategy, it may come only much later after people have experienced problem-solving around less threatening issues as well as with the less threatening techniques.

It is also possible that strategies would be based on whether the change agent seeks to affect change from within or, from without. Again, the options depend on what is being changed and the goals sought to be achieved, as well as the possible choice of the partners in the change effort.

There is also no consensus as to whether social action should always involve organising the beneficiaries, or whether to affect change through organising people with similar commitment e.g. in passing certain legislation or influencing a social policy. The former would imply a great deal of grass-roots organisational work and sustained effort of many to bring about the desired result. The latter may be accused of being a more "elitist" model, may involve experts or professionals and other "like-minded" persons who believe in the same cause. Even in the "elitist" model, Wickenden points out that, "in the one case they speak as authorities in a particular area of social organisation and activity: in the other, they speak as reporters and pleaders for a particular area of observed need." The difference lies in the fact that in some areas we have subject matter competence, whereas in others, we observe the need for change but need to utilise the expertise of others in the change effort e.g. lawyers, doctors, or urban planners.

Implications for Integration in the Curriculum

We have gone into some relevant issues related to social action because they are important to curricular choices and and emphases, to what the institution is willing to commit itself to. The choices are by no means easy.

Courses

In the first place, a specific subject can not be labelled as, "social action". Social action is a total way of thinking, feeling and acting. It cannot be relegated to one course. The institution must believe in it, to a large extent express it in its over-all philosophy or mission, and be willing to risk itself in the process both institutionally, and in the activities of its faculty and students outside the institution. The ideas inherent in social action can be aspects of the total curriculum. For instance, the courses on the "Problems of Development" and on "Political Economy" provide the opportunity for an analysis of the social structure, the location of decision-making, and the power and control over resources. Poverty is analysed in relation to such systematic analysis as the control over resources and decision-making leading to the issues arising from it in terms of the mobilisation and organisation of people for obtaining their just share of the goods and services of society, including the right to shelter and earning a livelihood. An analysis of the two social systems which most effect the poor (health and education), and alternative strategies for the delivery of these services, can be discussed within the parameters of these courses.

The courses related to human behaviour can highlight the role of conditioning in our ways of thinking, the psychologically created attitudes of fear of authority when numbers can make a difference, the effects of poverty on individual and group behaviour, and such other related concepts.

Many causes related to the family, women and children can be identified for social action, whereas we teach them only as social problems and the required services, or as the process of work with the individual and the family.

Courses in non-formal education, community work, and use of group theories in understanding the dynamics and the strategies of the mobilisation of people as a social force in the change effort, can bring out the broad strategies and the many techniques which are utilised in social action. In fact, it is difficult to sort out the strategies used in community work and in social action, and place them in watertight compartments. Courses in the history and philosophy of social work can identify mass movements and the methods of intervention of activists in order to identify trends and techniques. The course in social change places social action in the context of several other factors which bring, or have brought about change in world societies. There is no end to the possibilities of identifying social action in various aspects of the curriculum. To quote Paull, "No single course could produce social action proficiency, much less specialisation or expertise."

We must, therefore, make a search of our individual curricula to identify its reflection of our over-all goals, its configuration, what over-all messages it gives to the student, how evenly (or unevenly) it is presented by the teachers in the various subjects, and the total impact it can make.

Field Work

Field work is an important element in the curriculum. When field work is problem-oriented, and not method-oriented, the social action component becomes one of the essential strategies. For instance, in working on the problems of water or sanitation, the students may organise people and take them in a "morcha" to the ward office. A student in a Municipal School may organise parents to go to the Education Department because there is a chronic lack of adequate teachers in the particular school. What the student is learning is that it may become a necessary action in a given situation, but not in all situations. He learns to utilise it as an integral part of his work.

Another possibility is to identify the "cause" to which the institution is committed and build a special social action programme around it. Work in the community can be selected for its impact on the over-all objective of making people reflect on their problem, identify strategies for action, and initiate work around these activities.

Paull illustrates a course-cum-practicum in which his students joined social action groups in the community which were of special interest to the student. As course instructor, his role was as a consultant to the student about his own activities without in any way "interfering in the goals, organisation and the internal operations and problems of the project". This practicum was over and above the student's field work as it was allocated to hours taken from the course. Classes were conducted before the initiation and after the completion of the practicum. A journal or "log" was kept by the student in which he also integrated theoretical concepts. Readings were provided but they were not required. Such innovative styles can be tried out in field work also.

Research

Research can play a very powerful role in social action and it has been most under-utilised in this sphere. Research on the problems which affect the disadvantaged, and then conscientising them (the public as well as policy makers), can have considerable effects. Social work needs to highlight such research to a greater extent than the ordinary surveys of "social problems" which tend to neglect the interplay of powerful social forces çausing these problems.

Institutional Response to Social Action

We have been highlighting the role of the institution in creating the necessary social climate, the ethos, for undertaking social action. Students quickly recognise our own frailties and our lack of commitment. What is good for the students and the professional should also be good for the training institution. Unless we believe in the type of training we give, we cannot really train by simply introducing rather high sounding concepts in the curriculum. It not only gains no currency with the students, but actually can alienate them from their faculty.

Four years ago, our College faculty had some serious discussions about the impact of the profession on the major problems that afflict our society, as well as the role of the institutions for social work education with respect to the elimination of such problems. We were then not discussing the problems of what we term as a "residual group", but those which affect large numbers of our people; the poor who are, in fact, the backbone of this country, and labour to put us on the so-called "map of the world" with barely enough to feed, or cover their bodies, or, protect them from the vagaries of our weather. Exploitation of the poor, and creation of social systems which perpetuate their poverty, were being discussed as our major concerns. We reflected a great deal on the issues we raised and, at a subsequent meeting, We presented to the faculty, for their possible consideration, an institutional philosophy to guide us in our action programmes. It was agreed then that we focus our attention to those in the lowest economic groups—those living in urban slums and on the two systems that most affect their lives, education and health.

The Education System

At the time that this decision was taken, our College was already quite deeply involved in a programme to effect change in the problem of wastage and stagnation in education which perpetuated illiteracy. The poor in our city send their children to Municipal Schools where this phenomenon is observed. It was a deliberate decision taken in 1970, When we pulled out of the private schools for the lower middle class and the well-to-do. We entered the Municipal Schools rather naively anticipating the negative effects of poverty on the child's education, only to discover the whole national problem of wastage and stagnation in education and the need to develop effective strategies involving the school system, as well as the community, while attending to the needs of the individual child and his family. By 1972, we had changed our strategy, the turning point being a research project some students undertook which high-lighted the extent of the problem of dropouts.

In this project, we found that working from within the system, it was possible to learn about the intra-systematic problems, and through such analysis work on strategies related to change at various levels in the system. Both collaborative and bargaining strategies are utilised to bring about change at various levels—joining hands or to join issue as the case may be. The action system varies from being only a change agent system to joining with the teachers, or with the head teachers, or the Education Officer, or the community youth, or the parents as each issue requires a different strategy for work. Sometimes, this action system is our target system in lobbying for change. The goal is clearly to bring about change in which the system's response to education corresponds to the needs of the child and the community.

The Urban Slum

Similarly, we had been working in urban slums since 1956. In subsequent years, our involvement underwent a chequered history with a series of teachers of community work and their special predilections. Ultimately, in 1976-77, twenty years later, the faculty evaluated the College involvement in working with the urban poor living in the city's worst slums—the zopa-dpattis. Quoting from the Annual Report, 1977-78, which described the preparatory work in 1976-77, it was stated:

> The number of field placements made each year were reviewed, and the need to provide some exposure to work in communities to all students since our syllabus emphasises the integrated nature of social work practice. A survey of students' opinions provided important feed-back. After considerable deliberation, it was decided to move away from the "community centre" service delivery approach (where services to clients absorbed the major time and practice skills), to the process of people's involvement in development with justice. The objectives were to create awareness, promotion of action around pressing issues in the community and the development of a socially committed leadership...
>
> In the implementation of the plan this year, the type of tasks assigned to the students centred around the community, identification of action-oriented programmes around pressing issues, and the preparation of various, groups (e.g. youth, women, tenants) to deal with these issues.

In that year, we utilised existing placements in communities under the auspices of other organisations. However, we could not direct the processes in the requisite directions. Hence, in 1978-79, we selected a community which also had several other slums located adjacent to it. In line with the stated objectives, the first major issue dealt with was the problem of water in which a few tap owners, the more affluent group in the slum, exploited the rest. Through the organisation of women, and meeting the resistance created by the tap owners, who sought to pressurise by immediately cutting off access to the water, the community was ultimately able to obtain the water through the installation of water taps shared by groups of people. The issue of eviction has also been taken up. Expertise on this issue, and knowledge of relevant legislation is growing among the faculty, the social workers in the project, and the students involved. The work was strategically undertaken in a slum from which it could snowball to others as they were located in a cluster in the same geographical area — a zonal approach. In this case, some use of confrontational skills has become necessary at times although the bargaining and negotiation skills are used more extensively.

Involvement of Slum Youth

As the work progressed, this author voiced her own doubts to the faculty in community work as to whether this approach to a slum, or even a small group of slums, in which professional workers were catalytic agents could, in fact, lead to any impact since the problem of slums was so vast. She felt that it would be better to train young workers in the slums and develop an organisation embracing a network of slums. At this time a small group of students were looking for a challenge in their field work. (They were our own bachelor's degree students in the master's programme). With them, a methodology of intervention with youth in slums was developed. Existing youth groups were brought together from many slums of the city, especially where there were other organisations working, or where our own students had developed youth groups through the chain of Municipal schools located in slums. The attempt was to develop in them an awareness of the problem of slums and strategies to work on the problems. However, due to various factors such as differences among the group, and their needs, we could not keep these groups together.

Ultimately, we developed a 35-hour training programme for youth in slums. Several such programmes were held — some with youth deputed by organisations working in the slums and some where the organisation invited training for its entire youth group. Eventually, out of this activity, we have evolved a 9 month training programme for youth in slums. Our coverage and the scope for the involvement of slums on common issues affecting them, has greatly increased.

Non-Formal Education

Other programmes became supportive to this effort such as the establishment of the Non-Formal Education Cell in 1977, and the development of a non-formal education programme for adults through the NAEP, and also for children. Awareness and consciousness raising activity is being done through this activity as well as in working with secondary school children in the Municipal schools.

Social Service Syllabus in Secondary Schools

By 1979, we had established the Social Service Syllabus Cell to assist schools in Bombay which were trying to implement the social service syllabus of the Education Department, Government of Maharashtra. The work of the Cell includes the training of teachers and the preparation of educational materials which are ideal opportunities for the work of consciousness raising in children of the elite who become the target groups in the city's private schools.

Community Health and Rural Projects

In 1980, we commenced two community health programmes in the urban slums of the city. While health is the entry point, related issues are also undertaken. In 1980, we also commenced a rural placement, in a predominently adivasi area.

Linkages Between Projects

Hence, the faculty decision taken in 1977, to place priority of work with the poor in urban slums, and the two systems which affect them the most, has been realised. All activities are so conducted that there are inter-linkages. Thus, students in the community as well as in the Municipal schools are involved with NAEP through the College, or work on the Education Department scheme of non-formal education for dropouts below the age of 14 in the Municipal schools, while the students placed for field work in the community do the same in the slums. The Youth Training Programme is utilised to train slum youth for work in their slums as well as with the Municipal schools, where they are the extension arms in the community. Training of community health workers will be useful to slums served by Municipal schools as well as by communities where health may not necessarily be a priority or an entry point. Hence, our projects do not operate in isolation and attempts are made to utilise our scarce resources and develop expertise to the maximum.

The objective of all these action projects is to make some impact in the lives of the poor, and the major problems they face in dealing with the oppressive structures. Simultaneously, there is also faculty involvement at the level of the bureaucracy where there is need for change through collaboration, bargaining, or confrontational techniques. The total involvement of all the faculty, in the various aspects of the action programmes, is designed to give a message to the students of involvement and commitment. The class-room is the opportunity to discuss the live issues of the field and to relate them to the theoretical concepts in the literature. This has done a great deal to develop a collaborative approach between student and teacher, where the emphasis has been on a quest for knowledge in which each has an active role to play.

Seminars and Workshops

It was realised that all other activities undertaken in the College must also become supportive of the over-all objective of work in slums and with the system of education and health. In line with this decision, a series of seminars (one only in each year), have focused attention on these areas: Problems of Education of Children in Urban Slums, Non-Formal Education Strategies for Work in Urban Slums, Social Work Practice in the Field of Health, and Social Service Syllabus. These are a means for documentation and for bringing the outside public (professionals in our discipline and those in other disciplines), as well as administrators and bureaucrats, to focus on the issues.

Research Activities

The Research Unit of the College is now also moving into a similar direction to identify projects which would support this overall effort through action-research and documentation.

Implications

The above description is one institution's response to our social reality and the attempt to focus attention and work on that reality. We cannot claim any miracles, but we have the satisfaction that we are learning, and through experience fashioning actions in a sustained measure to produce change at least in the areas identified as our priorities.

An important issue that has now arisen is what the institution's response will be when, ultimately, pressure is brought to bear on it because the activities have reached a stage where they affect vested interests and threaten institutionalised structures. These issues would have to be separately answered by each institution in terms of the nature and problems of survival of highly institutionalised structures.

Summing Up

This paper has been presented in all humility for we do not claim to know a great deal about social action. All we can do is to present the dilemmas of a curriculum framer, and the experience of a person who has had to take considerable responsibility in formulating the philosophy (mission), and in sharing the responsibility for action strategies reflecting the mission. The team work of the faculty, their creativity and conviction that their involvement in the field can also make them teachers who speak from the book of experience, has unfolded the type and direction of work the College has undertaken. We agreed to take the responsibility to write this paper in the hope that through sharing we could learn more and experience further the satisfaction of having tried, even if we ultimately do not reach the objectives we set out to achieve.

References

Britto, G.A.A. "Toward A Typology of Social Action", Mimeographed (Ph. D. Seminar Paper, October 25, 1976).

Britto, G.A.A. "Some Principles of Social Action", Typed; Paper.

Else, John, "Social Actions: Lessons from the Recent Past and Prospects for the Near Future, "*Social Development Issues,* 3, No. 2 (Summer, 1979). pp. 24-37.

Keefe, Thomas. "Beyond Radicalism: An Historical Materialist Framework for the Social Policy Curriculum", *Journal of Education for Social Work,* 14, No. 2 (Spring, 1978), pp. 60-65.

Longres, John and Eileen McLeod, "Consciousness Raising and Social Work Practice, *Social Casework,* 61, No. 5, (May, 1980), pp. 267-276.

Specht, Harry. "Disruptive Tactics", *Social Work,* 14, No.. 2 (April, 1969).

Specht, Harry. "The Deprofessionalisation of Social Work", 17, No. 2 (March, 1972), pp. 3-15.

Thursz, Daniel. "The Arsenal of Social Action Strategies: Options for Social Workers", Social Work, 16, No. 1 (January, 1971), pp. 27-34.

Wineman, David and Adrienne James, "The Advocacy Challenge to Schools of Social Work", Social Work, 14, No. 2 (April, 1969), pp. 23-32.

Select Bibliography

Anderson, J.P., *'Social Work as a Profession'* in Social Work Year Book. National Association of Social Workers, New York, 1945.

Cahn, E.S. and Cahn, J.C.: "Citizen Participation" in Spiegel (ed.) Citizen Participation in Urban Development. Washington, D.C. NTL Instt. for Applied Behavioural Science, 1968, p. 223.

Cassidy, Harry M., *Social Security and Reconstruction in Canada,* Quoted by Friedlander, W.A. *op. cit.,* p. 4.

Clarke, Helen I., *Principles and Practice of Social Work,* Appleton Century Croft. Inc., New York, 1947, p. 16.

Cohen, Nathan, *Social Work in American Tradition.* New York: The Dryden Press, 1958, p. 3.

Cuber, John, and Harper, Robert, *Problems of American Society,* rev. (Henry Holt & Co., Inc., New York, 1951).

Datt, Ruddar, "Income Inequality and Consumption Pattern in India", Mainstream. May 4, 1974, p. 15.

Datta, Ruddar, "Nationalisation-Facts and Fancies", *Mainstream,* Vol. XVII, No. 30, March 24, 1979, p. 12.

De Marco, Joseph P. and Richmond, Samuel R. "Equality and Justice", *American Review,* Autumn 1977, p. 88.

Devine, Edward T., *Social Work,* Macmillan, New York, 1922, pp. 21-22.

Dunham, Arthur, *Community Welfare Organization* (Thomas Y. Crowell Company, New York, 1958).

Dwey, John: *Philosophy, Encyclopaedia of the Social Sciences,* Mac Millan, New York, 1935, p. 122.

Elliot, Studt, *et al.,* C-Unit: Search for Community *in* Prison. New York: Russell Sage Foundation, 1968.

Fenlason, Anne, *Essentials in Interviewing* (Harper & Brothers, New York, 1952).

Fink, Arthur; Wilson, Everett; and Conover, Merrill, *The Field of Social Work*, 3rd ed. (Henry Holt & Co., Inc., New York, 1955).

Frank, Lawrence K., "The Need for a New Political Theory", *Daedalus*, 96 (Summer 1967).

Friedlander, W.A., *Introduction of Social Welfare*, Prentice Hall, Inc. New York, 1955, p. 4.

Friedlander, W.A., Social Work Journal 1951, Vol XXXII, No. 1, p. 43.

Friedlander, Walter, ed., *Concepts and Methods of Social Work* (Prentice-Hall, Inc., Englewood Cliffs, N.J., 1958).

Ganguli, B.N.: Ideal Social Order, pp. 20-30 Quoted by Shankar Pathak. *Social Welfare*, Mc Millan Company, New Delhi, 1981, p. 108.

Goldstein, Howard, *Social Work Practice: A Unitary Approach*, University of South Carolina Press, New York, 1973.

Green T.F., "Schools and Communities: A Look Forward", Harward Educational Review, 39 (Spring 1969), pp. 221-252.

Hamilton, G., *Theory and Practice of Social Case Work* (second edition), Columbia University Press, New York, 1951, p. 27.

Hathway, N: *"Social Action or Inaction: The Challenge"* in Training for Social Work in the Department of Social Science, University of Toronto, 1914-1940, p. 33.

Hollis, Ernest, and Taylor, Alice, *Social Work Education in the United States* (Columbia University Press, New York, 1951).

Hook, Sidney, "The Philosophical Society, Yesterday, Today, Tomorrow —A Symposium. Mackenzie, F. (ed.). New York: Prentice Hall, 1937, p. 668.

Horowitz, Irwing Louis, *Professional Sociology*. Chicago: Aldine Press, 1968, p. 124.

Hoselitz, B. F., *Sociological Aspects of Economic Growth*. Bombay: Vakils, Feffer & Seimons, 1960, p. 14.

Howers, Swithum, "Social Work and Human Problem." *Social Case Work*, 35:190, May 1954.

James, William, Pragmatism. New Delhi: Eurasia Publishing House (P) Ltd., 1975, pp. 17-18.

Jones, quoted in Bisno, Herbert, *The Philosophy of Social Work.* Washington, D. C.: Public Affairs Press, 1952, p. 61.

Kasius, Cora, ed., *New Directions in Social Work* (Harper & Brother, New York, 1954).

Kher, B.G., Quoted in United Nations, *Training for Social Work; An International Survey,* 1947, p. 108.

Khinduka, S.K., *Social Work in India,* Sarvodaya Sahitya Samaj, Jaipur (India) 1962, p. 1.

Kidneigh, John C., "Administration of Social Agencies". *Social Work Year Book,* 1955, p. 76.

Klein, Philip, "The Social Theory of Professional Social Work" Barries, H. E., *et al.* (*ed.*). *Contemporary Social Theory.* New York; D. Applelon-Century Co., 1940, p. 758.

Kohs, S. C., *The Root of Social Work.* New York: Association Press, 1966.

Konopka, G., *Edward C. Lindeman and Social Work Philosophy.* The University of Minnesota Press, Minneapolis 1958, p. 83.

Konopka, G; and Edward C. Lindeman; *Social Work Philosophy.* The University of Minneasora Press, Minneapolis, 1958, p. 83.

Konopka, Gisela, *Eduard C. Lindeman and Social Work Philosophy.* Minneapolis: The University of Minnesota Press, 1958, p. 178.

Leonard, P.: *Social Work: Science or Mystique,* lecture given at study conference held under the auspices of the National Institute of Social Work, USA, 1969.

Miles, Arthur, *American Social Work Theory* (Harper & Brothers, New York, 1954).

Mirza R. Ahmad, *Samaj Karya—Darshan Avam Pranaliyan,* British Book Depot, Lucknow, 1969, p. 4.

Mises, Ludwing Von., *The Anti-Capitalistic Mentality.* Princeton: Van Nostrand, 1956, p. 20.

Moffett, J: *Concepts of Case Work Treatment*, 30. Routledge and Kegan Paul Ltd., London, 1968, p. 55.

Moorthy, M.V., *Social Work—Philosophy, Methods, and Fields,* Karnatak University, Dharwar, 1974, pp. 2-5.

Nanavati, M.C.: *Origin and Growth of Professional Social Work-Historical Aspects,* S. Dasgupta (ed.); Towards a Philosophy of Social Work, Popular Book Services, Delhi, 1967, p. 24.

Oza, A.N., "Our Economy: Sick or Healthy?", *The Illustrated Weekly of India,* February 25, 1979, p. 9.

Perlman, H. H., *Social Case Work*, Chicago University Press, Chicago, 1957, p. 67.

Pincus, Allen and Minaham, Anna, "A Model of Social Work Practice" Specht, Henry and Vickery, Anna *(ed.), Integrating Social Work Methods,* George Allen and Unwin, London, 1978, p. 78.

Pumphrey, M.W., *The Teaching of Values and Ethics in Social Work Education,* Vol. XIII, New York; CSWE, 1959, p. 40.

Ramamurti, P., "Our Economy: Sick or Healthy?", *The Illustrated Weekly of India*, February 25, 1979, p. 8.

Robinson, Virginia, *Changing Psychology in Social Work* (University of North Carolina Press, Chapel Hill, 1930).

Romanyshyn, J.M., and Romanyshyn, A.L., *Social Welfare, Charity to Justice,* Random House, New York, 1971, p. 3.

Romnyshyn, John. M. and Romanyshyn, Annie L., *Social Welfare: Charity to Justice,* Random House, New York, 1971, p. 356.

Ross A.D., "Philanthropy" *International Encyclopaedia of Social Sciences,* Macmillan Co., New York, 1968, p. 80.

Royce, Joseph R., *The Encapsulated Man.* Princeton: Van Nostrand, 1964.

Russell, James, ed., *National Policies for Education, Health and Social Services* (Doubleday & Company, Inc., New York, 1955).

Samler, Joseph, "Change in values: a goal in counseling", *Journal of Counseling Psychology,* 1960, pp. 32-39.

Sharma, M.D., *Dynamics of Social Work,* Jodhpur, (year not mentioned), p. 5.

Social Commission Economic and Social Council, United Nations: Training Social Work; An International Survey, United Nations, New York, 1958, Mimeo, pp. 18-20.

Solender, S., "Social Action" in *Social Work Year Book* 1957, pp. 517-518.

Sood, J. K., "Tax Laws Generate Black Money", *Pioneer*, April 14, 1979.

Srivastava, S.S., "Social Reforms and Social Sciences" Paper presented in a national *Seminar on Reforms and Change in Indian Society.* Institute of Social Sciences. Agra, 1958.

Stack Mourice, "The Meaning of Social Security" William Haber and Wilpur J.C. (ed.) *Reading in Social Security,* Prentice Hall, New York, 1948, p. 41.

Stein, Herman, and Cloward, Richard, *Social Perspectives on Behaviour* (The Free Press, Glencoe, III., 1958).

Stroup, H.H., *Social Work—An Introduction to the Field,* American Book Co., New York, 1960, pp. 1-2.

Szasz, Thomas S., " The Myth of Mental Illness", in Dinitz *et al. (eds.), Deviance.* New York: Oxford University Press, 1969, p. 429.

Tilbury, D.E.F., *Case Work in Context, op. cit.* p. 85.

Towle, Charlotte, *Common Human Needs,* American Association of Social Workers, New York, 1952, p. 9.

Trecker, H.B., *Social Group Work—Principles and Practices,* Association Press, New York, 1955, p. 5.

U.N. Department of Social Affairs: *Training for Social Work, an International Survey, United Nations,* New York, 1950.

Varlett, Harrier M., *The Common Vase of Social Work Practice,* National Association of Social Workers, New York, 1970, p. 104.

White, Leonard D., "Meaning of Principles", *The Frontiers of Public Administration,* University of Chicago Press, Chicago, 1936, p. 21.

Wickenden, Elizabeth, *Social Welfare in a Charging World* U.S.

Dept. of Health, Education and Welfare, Washington, D.C. 1965, p. VII.

Willlamson, E. G., "Value Orientations in Counseling", *Personnel and Guidance Journal,* 1958, pp. 520-28.

Witmer, Helen I., Quoted by Modan, G.R., *Indian Social Problems,* Allied Publishers, Bombay, 1973, p. 15.

Yongdahl, B.E., "Social Work as Profession" *Social Work Year Book,* Russell Sage Foundation, New York, 1954, p. 506.

Index

❑❑❑